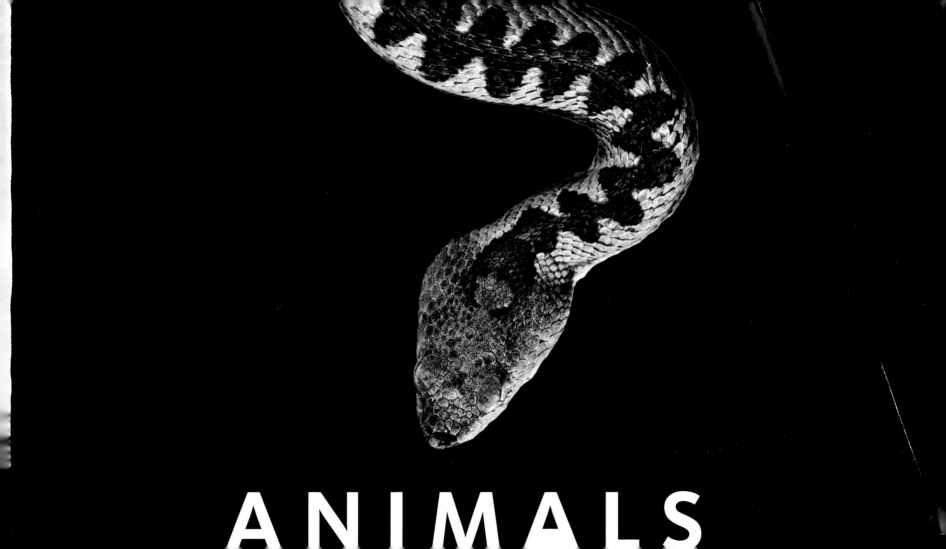

ANIMALS

ANIM

IALS

■SCHOLASTIC

Art director: Bryn Walls

Managing editor: Miranda Smith

Designer: Tory Gordon-Harris

Consultant: Dr. Kim Dennis Bryan, Associate Lecturer
with the Open University and Fellow of the
Zoological Society of London

Copyright © 2019 by Scholastic Inc.

All rights reserved. Published by Scholastic Inc.,
Publishers since 1920. SCHOLASTIC and associated
logos are trademarks and/or registered trademarks
of Scholastic Inc.

The publisher does not have any control over and does
not assume any responsibility for author or third-party
websites or their content.

No part of this publication may be reproduced,
stored in a retrieval system, or transmitted in
any form or by any means, electronic, mechanical,
photocopying, recording, or otherwise,
without written permission of the publisher.
For information regarding permission, write to
Scholastic Inc., Attention: Permissions Department,
557 Broadway, New York, NY 10012.

ISBN 978-1-338-36005-9

10 9 8 7 6 5 4 3 2 1   19 20 21 22 23

Printed in China 62
First edition, October 2019

Mud crab (*Scylla serata*)

CONTENTS

FOREWORD

We share a planet with the most amazing animals. Some are so small or secretive we hardly see them. Others are so large and magnificent that we can only marvel. The different ways that animal bodies have adapted for life in water, in the air, and on land are staggering—from wings to stings, jaws to claws, tails to hair. Just as remarkable is how animals have adapted for survival and reproduction.

Animals flourish in the darkest depths of the oceans, the freezing air of the highest peaks, and the furnace-like heat of a sun-blasted day in the desert. Humans have come to dominate the planet, but we cannot live in this range of diverse habitats as well as animals do. Our activities impact delicate ecosystems, endangering tens of thousands of animal species.

This book takes you on a journey to every corner of the world to see what lives there and how it survives. We are still learning about the rich variety of animals on Earth today and in the past, and thousands of new animal species are being discovered each year. There is so much more to find out about our planet's incredible creatures, how they keep our planet healthy and productive, and what we can do to protect them.

Hoffmann's two-toed sloth (*Choloepus hoffmanni*) lives in the rain forests of Central and South America. It is camouflaged green by algae growing on its fur. In turn the algae obtain water and shelter from their host.

Habitats rich in biodiversity
From forests, rivers, and wetlands to rain forests, grasslands, and coral reefs, most of the world is teeming with animal life. The more diverse the habitat, the larger the number of species it supports. The rain forests are hotspots for wildlife on land as are the coral reefs in the ocean.

ANIMAL LIFE

Antarctic
midge

Antarctic
landscape

Animals are remarkable creatures that share a pattern of life: they grow, most reproduce, and then they die—sometimes in a grisly way in the jaws of another creature, sometimes as soon as they have cleared a way for the next generation. How they do this is just as fascinating and varied as the millions of different ways they look and their different behaviors.

Life in the extreme

It is tough surviving on Antarctica, the coldest continent on Earth. The Antarctic midge (*Belgica antarctica*), is the only animal that can live there all year round. This true insect takes two years to mature, and survives freezing winter temperatures, dehydration, and low oxygen levels for two bleak winters—most of its life. When it emerges as an adult, it has no wings, a slender black body, and only lives for around a week.

ANIMAL BUILDING BLOCKS

Every living thing is made of tiny building blocks called cells. Some animals are little more that a group of cells that act together as one organism, while others, like us, are made of billions of cells that form tissues and organs. Over millions of years, animals have increased in complexity, having a head that contains most of the sense organs, and developing limbs that give better mobility and lungs to breathe air. Animals that have a backbone to support their body are known as vertebrates. Animals that do not have a backbone are said to be invertebrates—instead of an internal skeleton they have a soft body like a squid, or a hard outer exoskeleton like a crab. Most animals are cold-blooded—they need the sun or hot rocks to warm up their bodies and give them energy. Birds and mammals are warm-blooded and can control temperature internally.

STAYING ALIVE

Animals have developed muscles for movement and senses to help them hunt or escape being eaten. They cannot make their own food, so they have to eat or obtain nutrients from elsewhere. Where food is seasonal, animals cache it, move to a different place, or die. If animals eat plants they are herbivores. Those that eat other animals are carnivores. Those that eat either

Finding and
eating plants

Catching
meat to
eat

Sourcing food

Animals find food in many diverse ways. Some forage for plants and fruits, some actively hunt or stalk prey, some subdue their prey with venomous bites or toxic stings, and others scavenge on dead animals.

plants or animals are omnivores. In their habitat, animals form part of a food chain that starts with plant producers, passing through a number of different animal consumers and ending with a top predator. Some animals are parasitic or feed on organic matter, but also fit into the food chain, creating a food web in a habitat. Organisms that use the sun to make food are eaten by herbivores or omnivores, and they in turn are eaten by carnivores. Animals at all levels may become sick and die, and are eaten by scavengers and detritus feeders.

Low profile

Look carefully! This Henkel's leaf-tailed gecko is so amazingly camouflaged that you would have to be an exceptionally sharp-eyed predator to spot it.

CLASSIFYING ANIMALS

The science of classification is called taxonomy. In the 18th century, Swedish scientist Carolus Linnaeus used a two-part Latin name to describe a species instead of the longer Latin description of the time. The first part of the name denotes the genus that the animal belongs to, while the second gives its species.

Kingdoms are broken into different levels. First is phylum: living things built to the same underlying plan (in the case of Animalia e.g. the Chordata phylum, which contains vertebrates). The next level is class: animals that share key features (e.g., Mammalia, animals that feed their young on milk). The level following is order: animals

THE SIX KINGDOMS

As more and more species were identified, it became increasingly difficult to group them. So taxonomists have established six kingdoms that are used today to describe all life forms: animals (includes all vertebrate and invertebrate life forms); plants (multi-celled plants that make food from sunlight); fungi (e.g. molds and mushrooms); protists (such as amoebas and algae); bacteria (microscopic organisms made of just one cell); Archaea (bacteria that can survive in places no other organism can).

● Invertebrate species
● Vertebrate species

Invertebrates

No less than 97 percent of all animal species on Earth are invertebrates. It is not known exactly how many species there are in total.

Invertebrates

Invertebrates are incredibly varied in structure and form, feeding methods, and respiratory and reproductive systems. They range from tardigrades (water bears) to annelids (e.g. earthworms), echinoderms (e.g. starfish), and mollusks (e.g. snails and squid). They are all multicellular, lack a backbone, and are cold-blooded. Many grow by molting or changing form through metamorphosis.

Wasp

Leopard slug

Medicinal leech

Earthworm

Cat flea

Rotifer

Daphnia

Rose chafer

Sea urchin

Strawberry hermit crab

Hydra

Blue pansy butterfly

Jewel beetle

Seven-spotted ladybug

European praying mantis

Sponge

Forest ant

Coral

Jellyfish

Spurge hawkmoth caterpillar

Wasp Spider

African giant black millipede

Fish

Fish live in water, which can be rivers or lakes, or the salty seas, but not all can cope with both. They are vertebrates and most have scales and use fins when swimming. Instead of lungs, they breathe through gills. There are at least 31,000 different species.

Black grouper

Atlantic herring

Jewel cichlid

Titan triggerfish

Yellow tang

Warty frog fish

Black-spotted moray eel

Two-barred rabbitfish

Yellow multi-banded pipefish

Tasselled wobbegong

Simplest animal

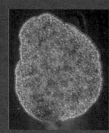

Tridoplax adhaerens has the simplest structure of all the multi-celled animals. It is a marine invertebrate found in tropical waters worldwide.

that have a similar body shape or features (e.g. Carnivora, meat-eating mammals with teeth modified to cut through hide and flesh). The next level is family: animals with more similarities (e.g. the cats Felidae, with well-developed claws). The following level is genus: animals that are closely related but do not breed together (e.g. *Felis* are small cats that have eyes with pupils that contract to a vertical slit in bright light). The final level is species: a single or small group of animals that will breed together (e.g. *Felis lynx*).

Kingdom Animalia
Phylum Chordata
Class Mammalia
Order Rodentia
Family Muridae
Genus Mus
Species *Mus musculus*

Taxonomy and clades

Taxonomists looking at the different levels of the kingdoms (above) also generate cladograms (right). This has brought some traditional groupings into question, for example that crocodiles are more closely related to birds than to other reptile groups.

Turtles · Lizards · Snakes · Birds · Non-avian dinosaurs · Crocodiles

Reptiles and birds clade

Common ancestor

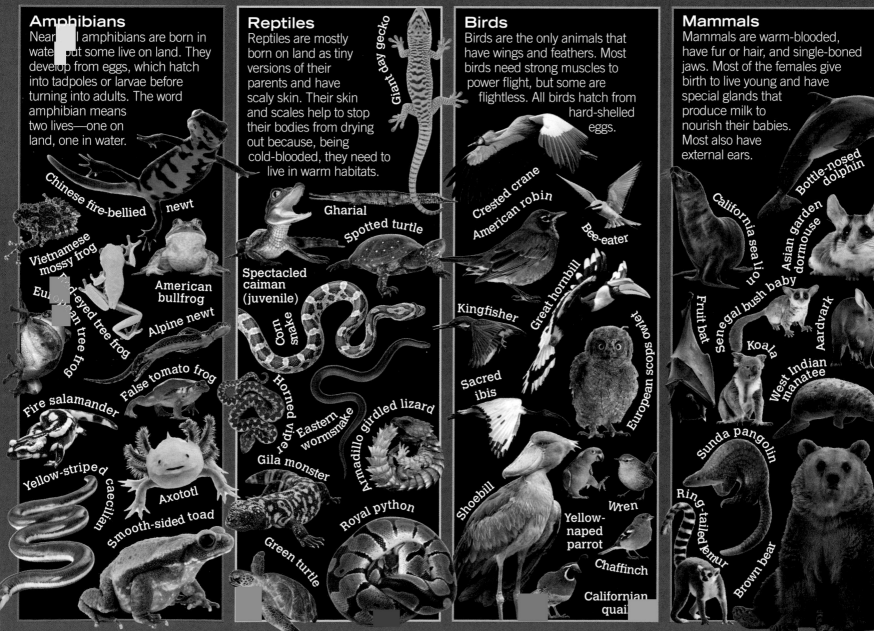

Amphibians

Nearly all amphibians are born in water but some live on land. They develop from eggs, which hatch into tadpoles or larvae before turning into adults. The word amphibian means two lives—one on land, one in water.

- Chinese fire-bellied newt
- Vietnamese mossy frog
- Red-eyed tree frog
- European tree frog
- American bullfrog
- Alpine newt
- Fire salamander
- False tomato frog
- Yellow-striped caecilian
- Axototl
- Smooth-sided toad

Reptiles

Reptiles are mostly born on land as tiny versions of their parents and have scaly skin. Their skin and scales help to stop their bodies from drying out because, being cold-blooded, they need to live in warm habitats.

- Giant day gecko
- Gharial
- Spotted turtle
- Spectacled caiman (juvenile)
- Corn snake
- Horned viper
- Eastern wormsnake
- Gila monster
- Armadillo girdled lizard
- Royal python
- Green turtle

Birds

Birds are the only animals that have wings and feathers. Most birds need strong muscles to power flight, but some are flightless. All birds hatch from hard-shelled eggs.

- Crested crane
- American robin
- Bee-eater
- Great hornbill
- Kingfisher
- European scops owlet
- Sacred ibis
- Shoebill
- Wren
- Yellow-naped parrot
- Chaffinch
- Californian quail

Mammals

Mammals are warm-blooded, have fur or hair, and single-boned jaws. Most of the females give birth to live young and have special glands that produce milk to nourish their babies. Most also have external ears.

- Bottle-nosed dolphin
- California sea lion
- Asian garden dormouse
- Senegal bush baby
- Fruit bat
- Koala
- Aardvark
- West Indian manatee
- Sunda pangolin
- Ring-tailed lemur
- Brown bear

DANGEROUS PLANET

Earth's ecosystems are communities of plants and animals, interacting with each other and their physical environment. Rapid environmental change caused by humans has had a devastating effect as the flora and fauna cannot cope and there is nowhere left to go.

Gone but not forgotten
The flightless dodo (*Raphus cucullatus*) lived on the volcanic island of Mauritius in the Indian Ocean. Last seen in the 1660s, it became extinct because of hunting and the destruction of its habitat.

NOWHERE TO GO
As human population and consumption grow, millions of acres of tropical forest are cut down every year for logging and farming. Some estimates suggest that about half the world's tropical forests have already been cleared. Pollution from factories, farms, and mountains of human waste has altered landscapes and poisoned the air, soil, and waterways. We are pouring greenhouse gases into the air, including carbon dioxide (CO_2), which is released when fossil fuels such as coal and oil are burned. The Earth is getting warmer, and this climate change is leading to devastating wildfires and rising sea levels, the bleaching of coral, and the pollution and acidification of seawater.

Endangered black spider monkey

Conservation success
In the 1970s, on the island of Rodrigues in the western Indian Ocean, the population of the endangered Rodrigues fruit bat (*Pteropus rodricensis*) dwindled to around 70–100. Increased forest cover and protection has been provided and the species has now recovered to more than 25,000.

THREATS OF EXTINCTION
In 1964, the International Union for Conservation of Nature (IUCN) created its first Red List of Threatened Species. This classifies species according to the risk of extinction. Today, it states that more than 26,500 species are threatened with extinction, including 40 percent of all amphibians, 33 percent of corals, 25 percent of mammals, and 14 percent of birds. Orangutans, gorillas, and plains zebras are among the species listed, while more than half of the world's raptors are falling in number.

MAKE AN IMPACT
Despite their ability to adapt, animals need help to survive. You can make a real difference by using energy more efficiently in the home, reducing water waste, and buying and recycling eco-friendly products. You can make your backyard animal friendly, avoiding the use of herbicides and pesticides that may damage small mammals and insects. Or you could get together with others to adopt an animal from a wildlife conservation organization, donate money, volunteer your time—zoos and other wildlife organizations have programs for this— or campaign against illegal wildlife trafficking and to protect endangered species and their habitats.

Fish swim with and swallow plastics in the sea

Sea mammals get caught in fishing nets

Peril at sea
Plastic waste wraps around animals, and if eaten, blocks digestion. Dumped in the ocean, plastics alter the chemistry of fish, affecting every animal in their food chain, including humans.

A valley in the Amazon basin stripped of its trees

Threats to the Amazon biome
The Amazon River of South America flows through the largest rain forest and river basin on the planet. One in ten of all known plant and animal species lives here, with many more still to be identified. The World Wide Fund for nature (WWF) estimates that 27% of this biome will be without trees by 2030 if deforestation for wood, fuel, and farming is not stopped. The black spider monkey (*Ateles fusciceps*) is only one of the species now critically endangered by habitat loss.

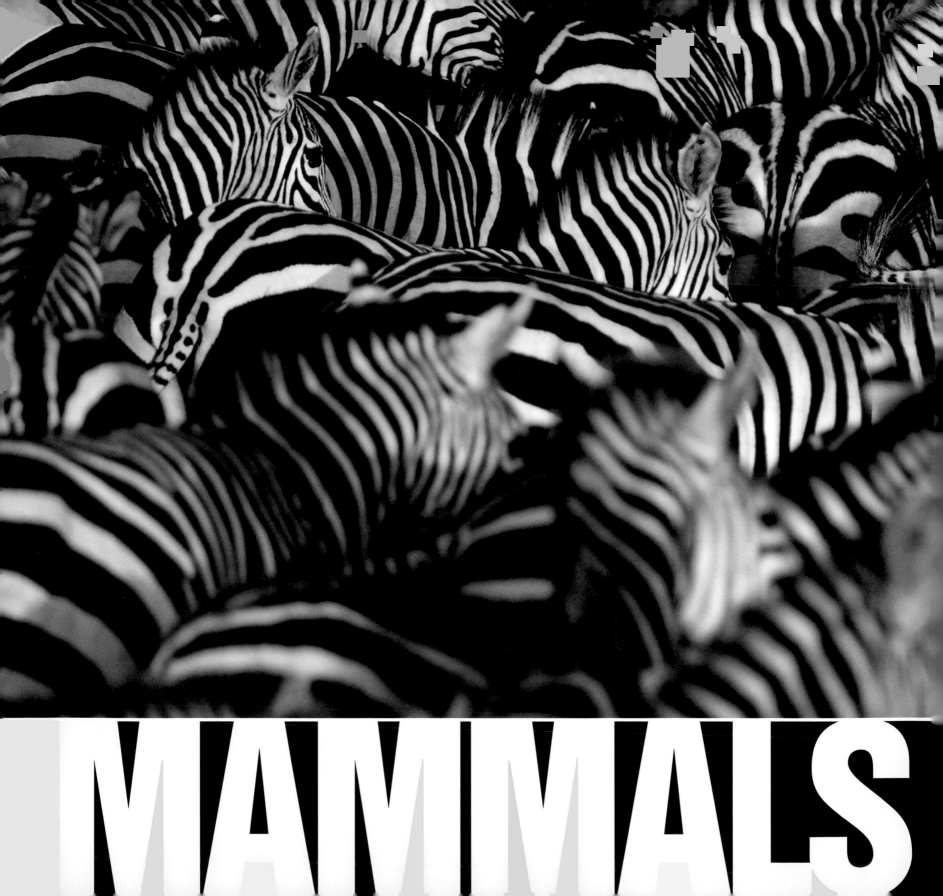

MAMMALS

MAMMALS

There are more than 5,400 types of mammal and they are all shapes and sizes, from tiny bats to massive whales—and that includes us! All mammals are vertebrates and breathe air. They are warm-blooded with a body temperature that is regulated internally, independent of their surroundings. They are named for the mammary glands with which the females feed their young.

Capybara

Senegal bush baby

Brown bear

Fruit bat

Sunda pangolin

Bottlenose dolphin

Short-beaked echidna

California sea lion

Asian garden dormouse

Blue wildebeest

Greater mouse-eared bat

Lesser grison

Elephant shrew

West Indian manatee

White rhinoceros

Aardvark

Mandrill

Koala

TYPES OF MAMMALS

Mammals can be divided into three groups depending on how they give birth and care for their young. Most are placental, meaning their young are small versions of adults, although they need a lot of care over time and may be born blind. The second group are marsupials, which carry their young in a pouch or skinfold, for example kangaroos and opossums. The smallest group are monotremes, animals that lay soft-shelled eggs. These include the platypus and the long-nosed spiny anteater (echidna).

ADAPTABLE ANIMALS

Over time, mammals have adapted really well to different habitats, some living underground and others on land, while still more swim the oceans and a few fly through the air. They have fur or hair to help maintain a steady temperature, although some—dolphins and whales—lose that after birth. Mammals also shiver to warm up and some sweat to cool down. This helps them to survive in the extreme cold of the Arctic (polar bears and Arctic foxes), or hot deserts (camels and coyotes), or the steamy tropics (elephants and chimpanzees). Mammals are tetrapods— most have four limbs that they can move around on, while humans are among those that are bipedal, walking on two legs. Flying mammals such as bats have skin between their limbs to form wings, while swimmers such as seals and walruses have flippers.

Pine marten

MONOTREMES

EGG-LAYING MAMMALS

Monotremes are the only mammals that lay eggs. There are only five species—the duck-billed platypus and four species of echidna—and they live in Australia and New Guinea. The adults have beak-like mouths but no teeth and they feed their young on milk, although they do not have teats. The milk is excreted by mammary glands and scattered over the mother's skin.

SHORT-BEAKED ECHIDNA

TACHYGLOSSUS ACULEATUS

The only species of echidna in Australia, this animal also lives in Tasmania and the lowlands of New Guinea. The female lays a single egg. When it hatches, the baby, a "puggle," stays in her pouch until it develops spines. Then it is kept safe in a burrow.

Thorny problem
The echidna is also called the "spiny anteater"—its long, sticky tongue is used to search for insects such as ants or termites under bark. Its spines are actually hollow hairs that protect it from predators.

PLATYPUS

ORNITHORHYNCHUS ANATINUS

The platypus is a very strange animal. It has webbed feet for swimming, yet it digs burrows on land, its webbed feet retracting to expose nails. The female nurses her young for four months. The male has poisonous spurs on its hind legs, possibly to defend the burrow.

Strong swimmer
The platypus spends most of its time in the freshwater of rivers, streams, billabongs, and estuaries. It steers with its beaver-like tail to hunt for insects, shellfish, and worms.

MARSUPIALS

POUCHED MAMMALS

Marsupials are mammals that raise their young inside a pouch, a fold, or a flap of various sizes. The young are born live but are not fully developed, so they reach or remain in the marsupiam, or pouch, where they are nursed on the mother's milk and remain safely until their bodies are fully formed. There are around 330 species of marsupials in the world, two-thirds of them in Australia or New Guinea, and the rest in the Americas.

Growing strong
A kangaroo joey will fasten itself onto one of the teats in its mother's pouch to feed. At six months, it is large enough to feed outside.

COMMON WOMBAT

VOMBATUS URSINUS

Tiny and defenseless
A female wombat gives birth to a single joey the size of a jelly bean. The young are weaned when they reach ten months.

Also known as the bare-nosed or coarse-haired wombat, this is one of the world's largest burrowing animals. It lives in the coastal regions of southeastern Australia and Tasmania. It is nocturnal, feeding on roots, grasses, herbs, and bark. Getting water from its food, it can live for years without drinking. It may spend up to 16 hours a day asleep in the burrow.

VIRGINIA OPOSSUM

DIDELPHIS VIRGINIANA

This is the only marsupial in North America and is about the size of a large pet cat. It lives in trees and hunts at night, eating anything it can find. When threatened, it reacts by "playing possum," or pretending to be dead.

Multiple births
The female gives birth to 8 or 9 babies, but may have up to 25. Hairless at first, the young are so small that 20 could fit onto a teaspoon.

RED KANGAROO
MACROPUS RUFUS

This is the largest marsupial of all and the largest of the six species of kangaroo—the red, the eastern gray, the western gray and three species of wallaroo, a smaller and stockier animal. All kangaroos have two legs, and they move not by walking, but by hopping or bouncing. They are all herbivores that forage in the cooler parts of the day. Groups or mobs can number from ten to several hundred when there is plenty of food and water.

A tough life
The red kangaroo has adapted to living in hot and dry conditions where the rainfall is less than 20 in (500 mm) a year. It ranges widely and can survive on water from the plants it eats. The female carries the young in her pouch and is able to nurse joeys of different ages at the same time.

Red and smelly
The red kangaroo's name comes from the color of its fur. The males also secrete a strong-smelling red powder from glands onto their necks and chest to attract females and warn off other males.

Scientific name: *Macropus rufus*

Common names: plains kangaroo

Group name: mob

Size: up to 6.9 ft (2.1 m) height; up to 5 ft (1.5 m) head and body length

Weight: up to 200 lbs (91 kg)

Diet: herbivore

Lifespan in wild: up to 23 years

Location: semi-arid and arid regions of Australia, Tasmania

Versatile tail
Measuring up to 3.3 ft (1 m) long, the tail balances when hopping and serves as a fifth leg for balance.

Hind legs
These are so strong that the kangaroo can leap the length of two average-sized cars in one bound.

On the alert
Red kangaroos have excellent vision and hearing. When one spots danger it warns the others by thumping the ground.

INSECT EATERS

FORAGING INSECTIVORES

Many mammals eat insects, but some stick to munching just these tiny creatures, while others eat them as a main course in a mixed diet. Animals such as aardvarks, pangolins, and anteaters actively hunt for termites and ants, while underground mammals such as moles and shrews eat them if they happen upon them. Armadillos hunt for insects and other invertebrates such as grubs, worms, and moth larvae, while hedgehogs supplement their insect food with pretty much anything, including baby mice, frogs, fish, worms, small snakes, eggs, and fallen fruit.

Food in bulk
Raiding termite (above) or ant nests is a way to find plenty of food in one place. Insectivores usually only help themselves to some food from each nest, then move on, allowing the nests to be replenished for the next time.

GIANT ANTEATER

MYRMECOPHAGA TRIDACTYLA

The giant anteater is the largest of the three species of anteaters—the others are the southern tamandua (*Tamandua tetradactyla*) and the northern tamandua (*Tamandua mexicana*). The giant anteater needs a large area for its survival so ranges the open grasslands and rain forests of Central and South America. It lives mainly on a diet of ants and termites, finding the nests with a sense of smell that is 40 times more powerful than that of a human.

Scientific name:
Myrmecophaga tridactyla

Size: up to 7 ft (2.1 m) from tip of snout to tip of tail

Weight: up to 140 lbs (63.5 kg)

Diet: insectivore

Lifespan in wild: 14 years

Location: Central and South America

Speedy feeder
The giant anteater sweeps up vast quantities of insects from ant and termite nests with its specialized tongue. It tears a hole in the nest with its sharp claws and flicks its tongue in and out at up to 160 times a minute.

Clinging on
Once a year, the female has a single baby, born with a full coat of hair. For its first year, the baby rides on the mother's back as she visits up to 200 nests a day searching for food.

Under attack
Giant anteaters have few predators. And they put up a good fight with their sharp claws if attacked by a predator, such as a jaguar (left) or puma.

A **giant anteater** can eat up to **35,000 ants** and **termites** in a single **day**.

Fighting back
If threatened, the anteater will rear up on its hind legs, using its tail for balance.

Fearsome hunter
An anteater has a very long ultra-sticky tongue that starts at the breastbone and is covered in backward-facing spines. It does not have teeth, so it swallows its insect prey whole.

Sharp claws
The feet are curled up when the animal walks so that the claws stay sharp for defense or to dig for food.

Long face
The long nose houses a stretchy, sticky tongue that is even longer—up to 2 ft (60 cm) in length.

AARDVARK

ORYCTEROPUS AFER

Also called the "antbear" or "earth pig," the aardvark lives in sub-Saharan Africa. Like the anteater, it uses claws to break into nests and its tongue to lick up ants and termites. It also eats other insects, such as the pupae of scarab beetles. It is nocturnal, eating up to 50,000 insects in a single night.

Self-protection
When it is delving for food, an aardvaak can seal up its nostrils to keep out earth, dust, or insects. Its thick skin protects it from insect bites.

DWARF ARMADILLO

ZAEDYUS PICHIY

Also known as the pichi, this mammal burrows down to make shallow dens in the sandy soil of open ground in Patagonia. It is mainly nocturnal, foraging for insects, worms, and small animals, as well as roots and seed pods.

Armored coat
The skin of an armadillo develops into bony plates that form a lightweight shell. This acts as armor to protect the animal from a predator's bite, but it is flexible enough to allow the animal to hunt and burrow.

Food in bulk
This hedgehog has a varied diet. It hunts for frogs, snails, eggs, scorpions, and small birds, but also eats roots, seeds, and fungi.

FOUR-TOED HEDGEHOG

ATELERIX ALBIVENTRIS

Unlike other hedgehogs, this one only has four toes on each of its back feet. It lives in central and east African forests and savannas, and when threatened by predators, curls up into a prickly ball. It is resistant to snake venom.

PYGMY SHREW

SOREX MINUTUS

This tiny European animal has a big appetite. It has to eat around 125 percent of its body weight in flies, beetles, woodlice, and spiders every day in order to survive. This shrew is active by day and night, hunting all the while and only stopping to sleep for a few minutes at a time.

Taking advantage
Unlike other shrews, pygmies do not dig for prey. Instead, they use runways through grasses and burrows that have been made by other small mammals.

Body covered in keratin scales

Defensive ball

Armor-plated
The word "pangolin" comes from the Malay word *penggulung*, which means "one that rolls up." When the animal is threatened, it curls itself into a ball that predators cannot penetrate.

GROUND PANGOLIN

SMUTSIA TEMMINCKII

This is one of four species of pangolin that live in Africa. Four more species live in Asia. Pangolins are covered in scales made of keratin, the same substance as human finger- and toenails. They do not have teeth so swallow their food whole. They also swallow stones to help grind up the food in their stomachs.

EUROPEAN MOLE

TALPA EUROPAEA

Spending most of its time underground, the mole has very poor eyesight, but it has excellent senses of smell and touch. It digs a network of tunnels and pushes up the soil into molehills on the surface. It patrols its tunnels regularly, catching and eating any earthworms or larvae of beetles and flies that fall in.

Huge paws and sharp claws to dig

Earthworm meal

Food in the larder
The mole's saliva paralyzes its prey, so it can store living food for later. Special "larders" have been found with more than 1,000 worms.

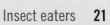

COLUGOS AND TREE SHREWS

GLIDERS AND CLIMBERS

These mammals live in southeast Asia, but are very different. Colugos are nocturnal and the largest gliding mammals in the world. Tree shrews are active by day and fascinate scientists because they look like fossils of Earth's earliest mammals.

SUNDA COLUGO

GALEOPTERUS VARIEGATUS

There are only two species of colugo, also known as flying lemurs. Although they are not lemurs, they are closely related to the primates. This colugo is found in southeast Asia, while *C. volans* lives in the Philippines. They eat leaves, shoots, and sap.

Climbing with a series of hops

Taking flight
When a flying lemur spreads its limbs, a membrane of skin turns its body into a parachute. It can soar from tree to tree, at distances of up to 330 ft (100 m).

Mother gliding with baby clinging to body

COMMON TREE SHREW

TUPAIA GLIS

This small mammal climbs with its long, sharp claws, but also forages for food on the ground for earthworms, insects, spiders, fruit, leaves, and an occasional mouse. These shrews are unique as parents in that they construct two separate nests. Their young stay in one nest while they sleep in the other.

Is that a shrew?
This tree shrew looks very like a squirrel with its long, bushy tail, but it has a longer face and no whiskers.

Early evening flight
In Gunung Mulu National Park on the island of Borneo, a colony of up to 3.5 million wrinkled-lipped bats leaves Deer Cave to hunt for food.

BATS

MASTERS OF THE NIGHT SKY

Some mammals can glide, but bats actually fly just like birds, flapping thin-skin wings that stretch across their fingers. They spend the day asleep, hanging upside down in trees or from the roofs of caves. At night, they fly out in search of food, most "seeing" by echolocation—sending out high-pitched squeaks and listening for the echoes that bounce back. They hunt for fruit, flowers, or insects, although some species feed on blood.

All in a name
The character of Dracula was based on a Romanian prince, Vlad Dracul, who is said to have had a taste for blood.

Film favorite
Many movies have reinforced the bad name that mythology and fiction—particularly Bram Stoker's 1897 novel *Dracula*—have given these winged animals.

VAMPIRE BAT

DESMODUS ROTUNDUS

These notorious leaf-nosed bats live in Mexico, and Central and South America. Groups of 100–1,000 live together, sleeping in caves during the day and emerging to drink blood from animals at night. They sleep hanging upside down from the roof of a cave, but approach victims from the ground, striking with razor-sharp teeth.

INDIAN FLYING FOX

PTEROPUS GIGANTEUS

The Indian flying fox is mainly nocturnal, but unlike other bats, it does not echolocate, instead using sight and smell to find the fruits, flowers, nectar, and pollen that it eats. However, all flying foxes play a vital role—nearly 300 plant species worldwide rely on them to disperse their seeds. After the bats eat, the seeds stay in the gut for several hours, which allows the bat to move to a different area before excreting them.

Gripping claws
Long, curved claws on the toes allow the bat to hang upside down with no effort.

Scientific name: *Pteropus giganteus*

Common name: greater Indian fruit bat

Size: up to 8.7 ins (22 cms) body length

Weight: up to 3.5 lbs (1.6 kg)

Diet: fruit, flowers

Lifespan in wild: 15 years

Location: southeast Asia

Daytime roosting
Flying foxes roost together in very large colonies, called camps, of at least 1,000 bats. During the day, they can be seen hanging from the branches of rain forest trees.

Aerial childcare
Baby flying foxes are born feet first so they can grab onto the mother. They continue to hold on very effectively as they travel everywhere with her.

Wing membrane
Supported by four very elongated fingers, this is wrapped around the body when the bat roosts.

Sharp eyesight
The bat's eyes are equipped for both day and night vision.

Pecking order
Dominant males can be found roosting upside down in the best spots, near the top of the tree in sunshine, or sheltering under branches if it is too hot or there is heavy rain.

BROWN LONG-EARED BAT

PLECOTUS AURITUS

A small Eurasian mammal, this brown long-eared bat is a slow flier but able to maneuver easily in the air. It even hovers as it hunts for insects to eat. It often roosts in roof spaces in older buildings.

Large ears
This bat's ears are nearly as long as its body and it uses them to listen for the rustling sounds of insects. It curls the ears back like ram's horns or tucks them under its wings when it is at rest.

Hunting on the wing
Natterer's bat hunts for insects that it takes in midair, often over water.

NATTERER'S BAT

MYOTIS NATTERERI

This European bat with a pink face feeds on crane flies, midges, and other small insects. The species hibernates in small rock crevices and mines, lying on their backs or sides, or even on their heads.

ORANGE NECTAR BAT

LONCHOPHYLLA ROBUSTA

This is one of the most common long-tongued bats in the rain forests of the Amazon basin in South America. It feeds on nectar as well as beetles and moths.

Sweet stuff
This bat is using its long, grooved tongue to feed on the nectar of the flowers of the golden trumpet vine.

Nighttime drinker

A pallid bat (*Antrozous pallidus*) stretches out its wings and swoops over a pond in southern Arizona to scoop up water. This species is voracious, able to eat half of its own body weight in one night. It lives in rocky mountain areas in the southwestern United States, Cuba, and Mexico, where it hunts on the ground for cicadas, praying mantises, long-horned beetles, lizards, and rodents. It is said to be resistant to the venom of the scorpions it eats. It carries its prey away to eat it far from the threat of predators such as racoons, coyotes, and snakes.

PROSIMIANS AND MONKEYS

LIFE IN THE TREES

These two primate groups are sociable, living together, usually in trees. Both groups like to groom each other's fur, but prosimians such as lemurs are less developed and cannot comb fur with their fingers, so they use their teeth. The monkey group further divides into two. They all have tails, but the New World monkeys (those that live in the Americas and Oceania) use their tails to hold and grasp things. The Old World monkeys (Africa, Asia, and Europe) cannot use their tails like this, and they look slightly different, with narrower noses that have downward-pointing nostrils.

LESSER BUSH BABY
GALAGO MOHOLI

One of the world's smallest primates, the lesser bush baby, or galago, makes a loud noise that sounds just like a baby crying! All bush babies live in African forests, where they leap from branch to branch hunting for flying insects at night. They have eyes that are so large they cannot move them in their sockets, so they have to turn their heads to spot prey.

Flexible ears
Batlike ears allow this prosimian to track insects in the dark, catching them in flight. It folds back its ears to protect them in thorny trees.

RING-TAILED LEMUR
LEMUR CATTA

Like all other lemurs, this prosimian lives only on Madagascar and some other small islands off the east coast of Africa. Lemurs live together in groups called troops, made up of up to 30 animals, with a dominant female. Their tails are longer than their bodies.

On the ground
Most other lemurs stay in the trees, but ring-tailed lemurs spend more than one-third of the time foraging for food on the ground. As well as fruit and leaves, they eat flowers, bark, earth, small insects, and spiders' webs.

Strong grip
When they sleep, slow lorises curl up into a tight ball clinging onto a branch. Their strong fingers and feet help them hang on.

SLOW LORIS
NYCTICEBUS PYGMAEUS

This slow-moving nocturnal prosimian from southeast Asia has a toxic bite—it licks a gland on its arm before sinking its teeth into a predator. It has one of the longest tongues of all the primates, which it uses to sip nectar. It also eats insects and spiders.

AYE-AYE
DAUBENTONIA MADAGASCARIENSIS

With sensitive hearing and ears that rotate independently, this prosimian is an efficient hunter. It taps bark with its long middle finger until it hears grubs moving about. Then it rips off the bark with its teeth and pulls food out.

Meat eater
The aye-aye is the world's largest nocturnal primate. It lives in the Madagascan rain forest, sleeping during the day in a nest built of leaves and twigs at the top of a large tree.

COMMON MARMOSET

CALLITHRIX JACCHUS

These small New World monkeys have sharp lower teeth that they use to make holes in gum trees to feed on the liquid gum. They also hunt for fruits, flowers, and nectar, as well as small animals such as lizards and spiders in their forest habitat.

White ear tufts
Native to Brazil, the monkey's distinctive white tufts only appear as they get older. If it is scared or threatened it flattens the tufts against its head.

Tail grip
These gray woolly monkeys have very strong tails, and can often be seen hanging from them while they reach out for the fruits that they like to eat.

GRAY WOOLLY MONKEY

LAGOTHRIX CANA

This monkey lives at high altitudes of up to 8,200 ft (2,500 m) above sea level in the cloud forests of Brazil and Peru. Gray woolly monkeys spend almost all of their time in the trees and are superb climbers. They travel in troops of up to 50 individuals.

VERVET MONKEY

CHLOROCEBUS PYGERYTHRUS

Vervet monkeys live in woodland near water in east Africa. These plant-eating monkeys are known for their black faces, framed by their silver-gray fur. They move on all fours, both on the ground and in the trees, and descend from trees headfirst. They can also swim.

Troop living
Vervets live in groups of up to 50 monkeys, mainly mothers and babies. They spend several hours a day grooming each other.

MANDRILL

MANDRILLUS SPHINX

The powerful male mandrill is the largest of all the monkeys, and the heaviest. It travels through African rain forests for long distances on the ground, climbing a different tree each night to sleep. The mandrill eats seeds, nuts, and fruits, but also takes small animals.

Scientific name: *Mandrillus sphinx*

Size: males up to 2.7 ft (1.1 m) long

Weight: up to 73 lbs (33 kg)

Diet: omnivore

Lifespan in wild: up to 20 years

Location: tropical rain forests of central western Africa

Colorful front

Colorful rear

Bright attraction
The alpha male has a brightly colored red-and-blue face and a rear to match. This is to impress the females when it is time to mate.

Cheek pouches
These are used as larders to store food to eat later.

Stumpy tail
The powerful body ends in a short tail, which is raised all the time.

Fierce protector
The female mandrill takes great care of her babies. She refuses to mate again until the young are old enough to fend for themselves. She and her young find food in the trees.

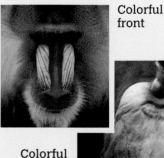

Strong defenses
The large male mandrill defends his territory fiecely and is able to fend off attacks by predators such as the leopard or crowned eagle. He paces back and forth, and bares his fearsome teeth.

APES

Apes are smart—they can use tools, build shelters, and communicate with others. They differ from monkeys because they have shorter and broader noses, larger brains, and no tail. Apes have fingernails instead of claws, hair rather than fur, and they walk on their knuckles. There are two families: the great apes—gorillas, chimpanzees, bonobos, and orangutans; and the lesser apes, the gibbons.

Handy digits
Like humans, apes have opposable thumbs—thumbs that can touch the other four digits. And apes also have four fingers. However, apes have longer curved fingers that give a grasp perfect for swinging through trees.

Facial expressions
The bare face is very mobile, and plays a vital role in the communication with other chimps.

CHIMPANZEE
PAN TROGLODYTES

On July 14, 1960, Jane Goodall arrived at the Gombe Stream Chimpanzee Reserve in Tanzania. She wanted to study these forest animals that everybody thought were vegetarian. She was the first person to observe chimps hunting and eating colobus monkeys, and the first to see chimps use tools. Her work is now world famous.

Thick coat
Its body is covered in long black or brown hair and it has a short white beard.

In appearance
Chimps have thickset bodies with short legs and long arms that reach below their knees. Their face, ears, fingers, and toes are bare.

Using tools
Jane Goodall saw two chimps she called David Greybeard and Goliath stripping leaves off sticks. They pushed the sticks into termite mounds and pulled out termites to eat.

Scientific name: *Pan troglodytes*

Size: up to 5.5 ft (1.7 m)

Weight: up to 155 lbs (70 kg)

Diet: omnivore

Lifespan in wild: up to about 50 years

Location: Africa

Chimpanzees and **bonobos** share **98.8%** of their **DNA** with **humans**.

Social system
Chimpanzees live together in very large groups. They also form temporary groups of 5–8 animals that last a short time, then re-form or join the main group again.

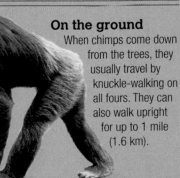

On the ground
When chimps come down from the trees, they usually travel by knuckle-walking on all fours. They can also walk upright for up to 1 mile (1.6 km).

Deft digits
The nimble fingers can be used to groom other chimps to remove parasites, dirt, and dead skin.

Expert swingers
Lar gibbons are famous for the way they use brachiation (swinging from arm to arm) to move with ease through the rain forest. They also move very fast on the ground.

LAR GIBBON
HYLOBATES LAR

Lar gibbons live in the tropical forests of southeast Asia in small family groups. They are almost white at birth and do not reach their true color, ranging from black through brown to cream, until they are around three years old. They eat fruit, leaves, and buds, as well as young birds and their eggs.

BONOBO
PAN PANISCUS

Unlike their close relatives, the chimpanzees, the bonobos have dominant females. They are also the only great apes that do not kill their own kind. Bonobos use calls and squeals to communicate to others in their group where, for example, tasty fruit, vegetation, insects, and eggs can be found.

Endangered animals
These peaceful apes are under threat in their rain forest habitat in the Democratic Republic of the Congo. Poachers, disease, and deforestation are the biggest problems.

WESTERN GORILLA
GORILLA GORILLA

There are two species of gorilla—the western (*G. gorilla*) and the eastern (*G. beringei*). The western gorilla lives deep in the rain forests of west central Africa. It is a quiet animal and does not attack unless it is threatened, but males fight over females. Gorillas are intelligent animals and the largest primates. They live on the ground, although females and their babies nest in trees at night. Both the western and eastern gorilla populations are suffering from hunting and destruction of habitat, and they are now critically endangered.

Family group

Female and baby

Dominant silverback

All in the family
These apes live together in family groups of up to 20. They move slowly through the forest foraging for fruit, leaves, and stems of herbs and vines. They make day nests for resting and night nests for sleeping by tucking vegetation around themselves either on the ground or in the trees.

Follow the leader
Each group of western gorillas is led by a large male. When this young male matures he will weigh around 400 lbs (180 kg) and have an armspan of 8 ft (2.4 m). Like all other apes, each of these gorillas has unique fingerprints.

BORNEAN ORANGUTAN
PONGO PYGMAEUS

This extraordinary animal is the second-largest great ape after the gorilla (*see p. 29*). It eats and sleeps mainly in the treetops of jungle canopy on the island of Borneo in southeast Asia. Orangutans are being hunted and poached, and their habitat destroyed by logging and palm oil plantations. Conservationists are warning that they could be extinct in ten years. A century ago, there were more than 230,000 orangutans in the wild. Today, it is estimated there are only 104,700 in Borneo and 13,840 on Sumatra.

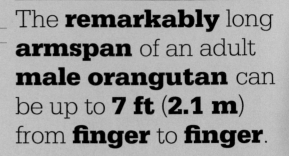

The **remarkably** long **armspan** of an adult **male orangutan** can be up to **7 ft (2.1 m)** from **finger** to **finger**.

Scientific name: *Pongo pygmaeus*

Common names: n/a

Size: male up to 4.6 ft (1.4 m) height; female up to 3.9 ft (1.2 m)

Weight: male up to 220 lbs (100 kg); female up to 110 lbs (50 kg)

Diet: mostly herbivore, with some insects

Lifespan in wild: up to 45 years

Location: Borneo

Big cheeks
The adult males are either "flanged" or "unflanged." Flanged males are larger with fleshy cheek pads, or flanges, on either side of their faces, and a large throat sac to make sounds that attract females.

Small differences
The Bornean orangutan has a broader face and a shorter beard than the Sumatran orangutan (Pongo abelii).

Life in the trees
The word "orangutan" means "man of the wild forest" in Malay, and is the perfect description of these apes. Orangutans have strong hands and handlike feet that they use to swing from branch to branch in their rain forest habitat. At night they build nests from bent branches high up in the canopy.

Long limbs for moving around

Baby orangutan in treetop nest

Distinctive hair
Long, shaggy, reddish-orange hair covers the dark skin of the orangutan's body.

Upper body strength
The arms are longer than the legs and the shoulders wider than the hips.

Well-camouflaged color
The dense canopy reflects green in the dappled sunlight and absorbs red-orange light. This makes the orangutan virtually invisible.

Using tools
Branches make handy sticks to poke around for food on the forest floor and the leaves make great umbrellas (above) and can be placed across the mouth to modify calls. Some orangutans use sticks to measure the depth of a stream, to pry open fruit, or to probe for honey.

Family life
Orangutans are the slowest breeding of all the primates. The females give birth to one baby, on average only every eight years, although sometimes they have twins. The young stays with its mother for up to eight years—the longest of any animal—and for half that time rides around on her when she is foraging for durians and other fruit, flowers, honey, bark, leaves, and insects. Orangutans are solitary, but a mother and her children can form a small group.

Killer whales

Orcas are superb hunters and at Punta Norte in Patagonia they show just how good they are. Between February and April every year, sea lion pups play in the surf, preparing to go to sea. The orcas use echolocation to target the prey, then wait for the right wave. They travel with the wave right up onto the beach, snatch a pup, then wait for the next waves to take them back to deep water.

HUNTING STRATEGIES

It is a battlefield out there, and some creatures have developed amazing ways of getting ahead of their rivals and outwitting prey to snap up a vital meal. Some team up as a group, while others work alone with specialist weapons such as nets or lures that fool victims into straying that tiny bit too close. Some whales even hunt using air bubbles, while a species of shrimp stuns its prey with shockwaves.

Black heron (*Egretta ardesiaca*)

Shade fishing
Herons are patient fishers—they can stand motionless waiting for their fish prey to swim near. The black heron uses its wings to form a cloak so that it can see into the water without reflections. The fish may also think that the shade is simply a safe spot to hide.

Luring prey
Camouflaged against a riverbed, the alligator snapping turtle (*Macrochelys temminckii*) lies in wait for its prey. Its mouth is wide open and inside, a pink wormlike lure wiggles. The fish it likes to eat swim straight in and snap!

Sharp-edged beak to tear flesh

Net-casting
There is a family of spiders that has developed a unique way of catching prey. The spider makes a silk frame and fills it with with elastic silk. Then it hangs headfirst from a thread of silk and waits. When an insect such as a beetle passes underneath, the spider stretches out the net and pushes it down quickly over the prey. The entangled victim is paralyzed, wrapped, and eaten.

Ogre-faced spider (genus *Deinopis*)

Modest snapping shrimp (*Synalpheus modestus*)

Stunning prey
Snapping shrimp snap shut one oversize front claw to create a shockwave that stuns prey. The claw may grow up to half the length of their body. The sound is louder than a rifle shot, so the shrimp have earned the name "pistol."

Plunge diving
This is a unique method of foraging for fish prey that only certain water birds use. Among them, only one family, the *Sulidae* (gannets and boobies), do this at high speed. The northern gannet (*Morus bassanus*) dives from heights of around 100 ft (30 m) and hits the water at up to 60 mph (100 km/h). In the water, the birds can reach depths of around 65 ft (20 m).

Northern gannets and high-speed diving

"Flying" underwater to catch prey

Group effort
Hunting is teamwork for a lion pride. Most lions hunt after dark as they are less likely to be spotted. However, if there is adequate cover, the pride will hunt prey such as zebras or wildebeests in daylight. Lionesses drive the prey toward other members of the pride hiding in tall grass. The lionesses then attack the prey from the sides or the rear. The pride then eats together and so do not need to guard the kill.

Lioness (*Panthera leo*)

Attack on a wildebeest

A pistol shrimp's **shockwave** moves at **100 ft (30 m)** a second.

RODENTS

MOST NUMEROUS OF THE MAMMALS

Nearly half of all mammals are rodents. How are they so successful? First, there are rodents everywhere except Antarctica, and they cope well in many different environments—gophers burrow underground, "flying" squirrels live in the trees of forests, jerboas survive in the heat of the desert, and pig-sized capybara spend half their life in water. Rodents also have a short breeding cycle—female mice can have as many as 15 litters a year with an average of 7 babies each time, and the babies are able to have their own babies only six weeks later.

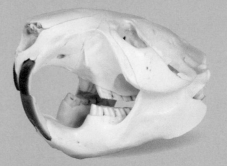

Never-ending gnawing
Rodents eat almost anything! They need to munch nearly all the time because the two long incisors in the front of each jaw never stop growing.

CAPYBARA

HYDROCHOERUS HYDROCHAERIS

Also called the water hog, this is the largest rodent, at up to 4 ft (1.2 m) long and weighing 145 lbs (66 kg). It lives along the banks of South American lakes and rivers, needing the water to keep cool.

Daily life
The capybara grazes on water plants and grasses, up to 8 lbs (3.6 kg) a day. It has webbed feet and can stay up to five minutes underwater when hiding from predators.

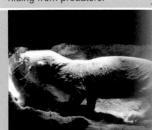

Well adapted
The mole rat's eyes are tiny and it finds its way without sight. Its lips are just behind its front teeth, keeping dirt out of its mouth when digging.

NAKED MOLE RAT

HETEROCEPHALUS GLABER

These African rodents have pink, hairless, wrinkled bodies. They live entirely underground, chewing on roots and tubers in the tunnels that they build. They live in colonies of up to 300 animals.

CRESTED PORCUPINE

HYSTRIX CRISTATA

The North African crested porcupine is the largest of the species of porcupine and one of the largest rodents. It lives in hilly, rocky areas, sleeping in caves or hollows during the day and foraging at night for food such as bark, roots, fruits, berries, and carrion. All porcupines have long, sharp quills that they use as a defense. Their young are known as "porcupettes."

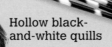

Hollow black-and-white quills

Sharp quills
These have tiny barbs on the ends that stick painfully into an attacker.

Warning sign
If the porcupine is threatened, it shakes quills near its tail, making a rattling noise. Then it charges backward into the predator.

Determined defense

Scientific name: *Hystrix cristata*

Common names: n/a

Group name: prickle

Size: up to 3 ft (1 m) long

Weight: up to 65 lbs (30 kg)

Diet: herbivore

Lifespan in wild: up to 20 years

Location: sub-Saharan and North Africa; Italy

Furred underbelly
By contrast to its prickly back, the porcupine has a vulnerable, soft underbelly.

All in the name
This porcupine raises the quills along its head and back into a crest. The fearsome quills are around 10 ins (35 cm) long and deter predators such as lions and hyenas.

AMERICAN BEAVER
CASTOR CANADENSIS

Beavers are extraordinary builders. They use their sharp teeth to cut down trees to dam streams and create lakes in which they will be safe from predators such as wolves and bears. Then they build large lodges with underwater entrances in which they raise their young, or "kits."

Felling a tree with teeth

Versatile rodent
Beavers are slow on land but swim well using webbed feet and their tail as a rudder. If they spot a predator, they slap the water with their large, flat tails to raise the alarm.

Building a dam

Dual purpose
Some dams are over 1,640 ft (500 m) long. The beavers use the wood, branches, and leaves in their building, but they also eat the wood of many of the trees, as well as pondweed and water lilies.

HOUSE MOUSE
MUS MUSCULUS

This is probably the best known of the 41 species of mice in the genus *Mus*. The house mouse is nocturnal with poor eyesight, but it has excellent hearing and smell, and uses its whiskers to feel surfaces as it moves. It is also good at jumping, climbing, and swimming.

Home territory
Every winter, mice invade homes looking for food and shelter. They can squeeze through any tiny crack.

Predator warning
Prairie dogs communicate very efficiently with warning barks. These vary in frequency and pitch to give different types of description.

PRAIRIE DOG
CYNOMYS LUDOVICIANUS

These black-tailed prairie dogs live in burrows on the great plains of North America. They are very social rodents, living in large colonies that are made up of small familes called coteries. They feed on grasses, roots, and seeds.

RABBITS AND RELATIVES
POPULAR PREY FOOD

These plant-eating mammals live in open country, from grassland to mountain slope, and escape danger by bolting for the nearest hole. They are closely related to rodents but have unique features, including four upper incisors instead of a rodent's two.

EUROPEAN RABBIT
ORYCTOLAGUS CUNICULUS

Also known as a coney, this rabbit is native to southern Europe but was introduced to many countries, including Australia, where it is considered a pest. The does dig burrows called warrens in which up to 30 rabbits live.

Thorny problem
Rabbits are important prey species and are hunted by a wide variety of predators. But they are very successful breeders—a pair can produce up to 40 young in a single year.

Snow living
It is tough living through the Arctic winter, and the hares have to dig down through the snow to find plants, mosses, and lichens to eat.

AMERICAN PIKA
OCHOTONA PRINCEPS

Despite its short ears, this is a close relative of rabbits and hares. It spends its day foraging for food and can often be seen sunning itself on rocks.

ARCTIC HARE
LEPUS ARCTICUS

The thick coat of the Arctic hare is white in winter and blue-gray in summer. This means it can blend in better in its habitat.

Easy prey
This rodent lives on mountain slopes in among the rocks. These provide plenty of places for it to hide from eagles, coyotes, foxes, and bobcats.

DOLPHINS AND WHALES

LIVING IN WATER

Cetaceans are whales, dolphins, and porpoises and include the largest animals on the planet. They are mammals that have adapted to live in water and their name comes from the ancient Greek for "sea monster." Front legs have became fins and layers of blubber stop the cold getting in. Cetaceans swim by arching their backs and moving their tails up and down. They have to rise to the surface to breathe air, but can survive for long periods underwater.

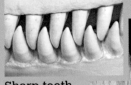

Sharp teeth for tearing

Filtering baleen

Teeth or no teeth
Dolphins, porpoises, and some whales use teeth to tackle fish prey. Many whales have baleen plates instead of teeth. Their food is filtered through the baleen's comblike strands.

ORCA

ORCINUS ORCA

This is the largest member of the dolphin family and one of the most intelligent. Orcas are top predators found in every ocean and can swim fast, at up to 28 mph (45 km/h). Depending on where they live, the orca families have developed different hunting strategies and diets, as well as individual sounds to communicate with each other.

Family groups
Pods, or families, of these toothed whales usually number up to 40, but communities containing several pods can number 100. Offspring stay with their mothers for life.

Tail-slapping
This is used to talk to other members of a pod.

Echolocating prey
Like all other dolphins, orcas use echolocation to hunt. They bounce high-pitched clicks off prey to accurately figure out its location.

Melon
This focuses the sounds produced by the orca into a beam of sound waves that travel through the water.

Scientific name:	*Orcinus orca*
Common names:	killer whale
Group name:	pod
Size:	males up to 32 ft (9.8 m) long; females up to 28 ft (8.5 m)
Weight:	males up to 10 tons; females up to 6 tons
Diet:	fish, sea birds, turtles
Lifespan in wild:	up to 60 years
Location:	oceans worldwide

Traveling together
Orcas often travel and hunt together effectively in a pack, communicating with each other to find shoals of fish, or tackle large prey such as sea lions (see p.32) and walruses, and if the pod is large enough, even sperm whales. They can breach, jumping right out of the water, although whether they do this to breathe in air or just for fun remains a mystery.

BELUGA WHALE
DELPHINAPTERUS LEUCAS

This small whale lives in the Arctic, where its white skin is camouflaged against the ice. It spends much of its time in water that can reach freezing point. Belugas are very social, and their pods can be very large. They are called the "canaries of the sea" because of the range of sounds they produce.

Easy moves
Unlike other whales, the neck bones of the beluga are not fused together. This means that it can move its head easily in all directions. It can also swim right under the ice because it does not have a dorsal fin.

AMAZON RIVER DOLPHIN
INIA GEOFFRENSIS

Some species of dolphin live in fresh water and this is the largest. Also known as the boto, it is found in the Amazon and Orinoco Rivers in South America. It is difficult to know exactly how many botos there are because they are difficult to count in the murky river waters, but they are under threat from hydroelectric plants and irrigation practices.

Spy-hopping
Orcas, other dolphins, and some whales spy-hop, bobbing out of the water to scan their surroundings for prey or danger. They have to kick hard with their tail flukes to hold the rest of the body upright. Some orcas can do this for minutes at a time.

SPERM WHALE
PHYSETER MACROCEPHALUS

This remarkable 55-ton toothed whale dives after giant squid in the ocean, reaching depths of over a mile (2 km). It has a single nostril, or blowhole, on the side of its head, which produces a plume of vapor as it breathes out at the surface.

Dolphin features
When young, this river dolphin is gray, slowly turning pink as it ages, particularly the males. Its long beak, lined with up to 29 pairs of teeth, probes in the mud of the riverbed for fish and crustaceans.

Weak eyes in murky water

Long, thin beak

Head room
A sperm whale hunts for its prey using echolocation—the bulbous front of its large head contains an oily substance called spermaceti, which channels beams of sound. The whale controls its buoyancy by changing the temperature and therefore the density of the spermaceti.

HARBOR PORPOISE
PHOCOENA PHOCOENA

Harbor porpoises are usually solitary, but sometimes herd fish such as herring or whiting in small pods of around five animals. Often seen in bays and estuaries in northern Atlantic and Pacific waters, harbor porpoises sometimes swim up rivers.

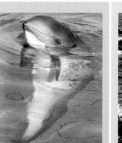

Nickname
This cetacean was once called the "puffing pig" because of the puffing sound it makes when it surfaces and breathes.

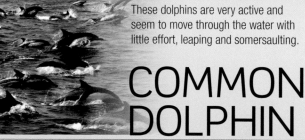

Effortless movement
These dolphins are very active and seem to move through the water with little effort, leaping and somersaulting.

COMMON DOLPHIN
DELPHINUS DELPHIS

Common dolphins live in very large pods of several hundreds or even thousands. They chase schools of fish and have up to 60 pairs of teeth to grab fish and squid, before swallowing them whole.

Whale spotting

Blue whales cruise through all the world's oceans and migrate long distances. They can be spotted as they surface when they "blow," the spray from their blowhole rising 30 ft (9 m) into the air.

HUMPBACK WHALE

MEGAPTERA NOVAEANGLIAE

Humpbacks are extraordinary in many different ways. They breach more than any other baleen whale, they slap the water with their tails and flukes, they migrate long distances, they blow bubble nets to catch fish, and all humpbacks in the same area sing the same songs.

Aerodynamic

The humpback has very long flippers—up to 16 ft (5 m)—with bumps called tubercles on their front edges. These help the whale to be very agile, both in the water and out of it as it breaches.

New life

A female humpback pushes her newborn calf up to the surface so that it can take its first breath of air. The calf is around a third of the length of its mother and will stay near her for a year.

Southern migration

Southern right whales give birth off the coasts of South America, South Africa, and Australia. Then they head south to feeding grounds in Antarctic waters.

Distinctive growths

The lumps on these whales are colonies of barnacles, whale lice called cyamids, and parasitic worms.

SOUTHERN RIGHT WHALE

EUBALAENA AUSTRALIS

Right whales were thought to be the "right" whales to hunt because they swim slowly and float when they die. Between 1805 and 1844 alone, 45,000 right whales were killed by whalers. Hunting continued until in 1935 it was agreed that they should be officially protected. Today, there are around 12,000 southern right whales.

BLUE WHALE
BALAENOPTERA MUSCULUS

The blue whale is the largest animal that has ever lived. It is up to 105 ft (32 m) long and can weigh as much as 150 tons, which is as much as the heaviest dinosaurs. Its tongue alone is as heavy as a bull elephant. Yet this largest of whales lives on a diet of the tiniest creatures, a single adult blue whale swallowing a filtered four tons of shrimp-like krill a day.

Big appetite
The blue whale and its relatives, which include the gray whale, are known as rorquals. These whales have deep grooves running down their throats. When they want to feed, the grooves open out to let their mouths expand.

GRAY WHALE
ESCHRICHTIUS ROBUSTUS

Famous for its long migrations, the gray whale travels from the Arctic to breed off the coast of Mexico, 6,200 miles (10,000 km) away. The heads of gray whales are often encrusted with the whale barnacle *Cryptolepas rhachianecti*. The barnacles attach when they are larvae and stay until they die, feeding as the whale travels.

ID marks
When barnacles die and fall off, they leave white circles. These scars are different on each whale and help scientists identify particular individuals.

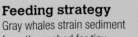

Feeding strategy
Gray whales strain sediment from the seabed for tiny creatures called amphipods. They grab a mouthful and head for the surface, trailing mud and sand behind them.

MINKE WHALE
BALAENOPTERA ACUTOROSTRATA

The minke is the smallest rorqual at up to 35 ft (10.7 m) long, and is a solitary whale that can stay underwater for up to 20 minutes. These whales are found in all the oceans, even the Arctic. They are inquisitive, sometimes approaching boats and spy-hopping to see what is going on.

Lunge feeding
Minkes practice an unusual way of feeding. They lunge feed, charging at prey at full speed from below. Scientists have recorded whales lunging up to 24 times during a single dive.

BOWHEAD WHALE
BALAENA MYSTICETUS

This whale spends most of its time in the cold waters of the Arctic, and is capable of breaking through sea ice using its large skull. Scientists have established the rate at which the bowhead eye lens ages and estimate that these whales may live as long as 200 years, making them possibly the longest-living mammals on the planet.

Soviet tribute

V-shaped blow

Heads first
This whale has an enormous head with a big arched upper jaw. It also has the longest baleen, up to 16.5 ft (5 m), of any whale.

DOGS AND RELATIVES

CARNIVOROUS MAMMALS

Many of us have owned a pet dog, so we know they like company and most are not fussy eaters. More than 30 species of dog live in the wild where these traits are terrific advantages. These adaptable carnivores (meat eaters) are brilliantly equipped for hunting. They can spot prey by sound, scent, and sight, and most can follow it for many miles on their long legs, and finish it off with bone-cracking and flesh-ripping teeth. Dog species often live in groups called packs, and use sounds and body language to ensure every member knows their place in a strict pecking order.

Anatomy of a carnivore
As this fox skull demonstrates, meat-eating carnivores have teeth for tearing and skulls formed to bite with great force.

AFRICAN WILD DOG

LYCAON PICTUS

Although this colorful dog is small and lightly built, when it hunts in a pack, it can kill animals much larger than itself, including wildebeests. African wild dogs are the second-most endangered carnivore in Africa (after the Ethiopian wolf)—there are less than 6,500 left, mainly in game reserves and national parks.

Hunting packs
Hunting at dawn and dusk, these are intelligent cooperative hunters that have a success rate of almost 80 percent when they are chasing and bringing down exhausted prey.

Scientific name: *Lycaon pictus*

Common names: painted hunting dog, painted wolf

Group name: pack

Size: up to 2.6 ft (80 cm) height at shoulder

Weight: up to 70 lbs (32 kg)

Diet: carnivore

Lifespan in wild: up to 11 years

Location: eastern and southern Africa

Mother and pups

On the move
The hunting dog is a nomad, traveling around a very large territory and only staying in an area long enough to have pups. Its long legs carry it along at speeds of up to 44 mph (70 km/h) and it has the most powerful bite for body size of any animal in the world.

Family ties
A pack of up to 25 dogs has an alpha male and female. They are usually the only pair that breeds, but the whole pack looks after the pups, which number up to 16 at a time. Both males and females babysit the young.

9-week-old pups

BUSH DOG
SPEOTHOS VENATICUS

This rare carnivore lives in the forests and on the savannas of Central and South America. It is semiaquatic and has webbed feet for swimming. Bush dogs live in packs of up to 12, and they hunt together to catch rodents, birds, and snakes.

Hunting in a pack
Bush dogs hunt in daylight, together taking down large rodents such as agouti and paca. As they run through thick forest, they make high-pitched squeaks to keep in touch with each other.

Fast predator
A coyote can run at speeds of up to 40 mph (65 km/h). It uses its excellent senses of smell, sight, and hearing to track down prey such as small mammals and rodents. It also eats fish and fruits.

COYOTE
CANIS LATRANS

The coyote is found throughout North America and is a mythical animal for many Native American tribes. It has adapted well to different habitats, and at night, it can be heard howling to communicate with other coyotes or to defend its territory.

RED FOX
VULPES VULPES

Foxes hunt by stealth, ambushing or silently moving toward prey before pouncing, and the red fox, the largest of all foxes, is no exception. It is a solitary nocturnal hunter that is very efficient at catching small prey, but will eat earthworms, birds, eggs, fruit, and vegetables. The dog and vixen raise up to ten cubs each year in underground dens.

City slicker
At night, the red fox is a familiar sight on the streets of cities and towns in the northern hemisphere. It is adaptable, changing its diet where necessary, and using sheds and other places in urban gardens for a den.

Folklore hero
A trickster fox is the central character in a number of folklore tales from medieval Europe. Reynard the Fox is a wily creature who lies, cheats, and exploits animals he comes across, using his cunning to escape.

Well adapted
The red fox's large, sensitive ears are alert to the slightest movement of a mouse or vole, and it can pinpoint the exact position even under snow. Red foxes cache food—they bury it, then dig it up later when they are hungry.

MANED WOLF
CHRYSOCYON BRACHYURUS

This South American animal looks like a long-legged red fox, and it is called a wolf, but it is neither. It is a separate species, a wild dog that is the only member of the genus *Chrysocyon*.

Long-legged predator
The maned wolf is the largest canid in South America, standing around 3 ft (90 cm) at the shoulder. It hunts in the grasslands for small animals, and also eats fruits.

Short and stumpy
This nocturnal fox feeds on rodents, other small animals, and plants. Its fur keeps it warm at night when desert temperatures plummet.

FENNEC FOX
VULPES ZERDA

This is the smallest member of the fox family, although its ears are enormous! It lives in the deserts of North Africa, and the sensitive ears help it to hunt and also dissipate heat to keep it cool.

Eating machine
The jaws of the gray wolf have twice the crushing power of a domestic dog the same size, and an adult can eat up to 20 lbs (9 kg) of meat in a day but then go 14 days without food. As well as large prey, gray wolves hunt smaller animals such as hares, rodents, birds, and fish.

GRAY WOLF
CANIS LUPUS

The spine-chilling sound of a wolf's howl is a reminder that this is a dangerous hunter that can call up partners to hunt you down, which this large wild member of the dog family is well equipped to do. Gray wolves may howl in unison as a rallying call. They work in packs, showing a scary amount of skill in trapping and bringing down prey that is far bigger than themselves—caribou, moose, bison, and deer are not safe from these stalkers.

Black

Brown

White not albino

Color casts
Despite their name, the family of wolves vary greatly in color, from white to brown to grizzled gray or black. This gives them with good camouflage in their forest habitat and through all the seasons.

Scientific name: *Canis lupus*

Common name: timber wolf

Group name: pack

Size: up to 2.6 ft (80 cm) height at the shoulder

Weight: up to 175 lbs (80 kg)

Diet: carnivore

Lifespan in wild: up to 12 years

Location: North America, Europe, and Asia

Pecking order
There is a strict order of seniority in a pack, and junior wolves have to give way to larger, older animals. They put their tails between their legs and often lower their bodies onto the ground while pawing at the higher-ranking wolf.

Pack life
Gray wolves live in well-organized families where only the alpha male and female breed, but the whole group looks after the young. They travel in packs that consist of the dominant pair, their pups, and older offspring. The pack leaders track the prey, establish dens, and mark out the pack's territory.

Norse wolf monster Fenrir

"Little Red Riding Hood" fairy tale

Sharp hearing
The ears move from side to side to pick up the direction of any sounds from prey.

Thick layers of fur
There are two layers of fur, guard hairs to keep dry over short fur for warmth.

Tail with a message
A scent gland on the back of the tail is used to mark territory.

Sensitive nose
Its 200 million smelling cells mean the wolf can smell 100 times better than a human.

Wolves in stories
For centuries wolves have had bad publicity. These misunderstood animals are the stuff of myths and legends, and from werewolves in horror films to wolves in children's stories, have inspired fear.

Twins Romulus and Remus raised by a caring she-wolf

Adaptation
The gray wolf is known as the timber wolf in North America, and the white wolf in the Arctic. It adapts well to live in a variety of habitats, from tundra and mountain areas, to grasslands, forests, woodlands, and deserts.

BEARS

JAWS, PAWS, AND CLAWS

With their heavy bodies and powerful jaws, the bear family includes Earth's largest land carnivores. They have adapted to many habitats from the freezing Arctic to tropical forests. Bears spend most of their time alone, using mainly their acute sense of smell to sniff for food, rivals, and mates, and they have no predators.

Large, sharp claws
Grizzly bear pawprints show partial or full nail prints with the tips measuring up to 4 in (10 cm) in length.

Climbing skills
Black bears are excellent climbers, their short, nonretractable claws giving them a good hold on trees. Even very young cubs can climb and will zip up the nearest tree trunk if threatened.

AMERICAN BLACK BEAR

URSUS AMERICANUS

This small bear is widespread in North America, and often raids campsites in national parks for food. Their usual diet is grasses, roots, berries, and insects, but they also take fish and mammals. Females give birth to two or three cubs in winter, and they stay with their mother for two years.

GIANT PANDA

AILUROPODA MELANOLEUCA

There is some dispute among scientists about whether the panda is a relative of the red panda and raccoon, or whether it is an unusual kind of bear. It lives high up in the mountains of central China and spends its day eating, sometimes for up to 12 hours! There are only around 1,800 pandas in the wild.

A true giant
The male giant panda may be up to 6 ft (1.8 m) long, and weigh over 300 lbs. (135 kg). Pandas can easily stand up on their back legs, and are good swimmers and climbers.

Vegetarian bear
The giant panda lives in bamboo forests and feeds almost entirely on bamboo shoots. It eats sitting down, holding them in its front paws.

SUN BEAR

HELARCTOS MALAYANUS

Roaming the tropical forests of southeast Asia is the smallest member of the bear family, only about 5 ft (1.5 m) long. At dusk it forages both on the ground and in the trees, looking for berries, roots, and fruits, as well as small animals and insects. Sun bears are threatened by habitat destruction.

Well equipped
This bear really does love honey! Its 10-inch- (25-cm-) long tongue is used to reach honey in bees' nests and to pull termites out of their mounds. Its nose leads it to the food, and it uses curved claws to climb up to the nests or tear open the mounds.

POLAR BEAR

URSUS MARITIMUS

This is the largest bear, with males up to 10 ft (3 m) long and 1,765 lbs. (800 kg) in weight, twice the size of the females. Its fur is translucent, so appears white because it reflects light—the skin is actually black. A polar bear can smell its seal prey on the ice at a distance of many miles!

Icy births
Once every three years, female polar bears dig dens in snowdrifts or on the sea ice. One or two cubs are born in midwinter in the den, and the family emerges in spring.

BROWN BEAR
URSUS ARCTOS

This impressive animal hunts and fishes in forests and mountains, although much of its diet consists of berries, fruit, roots, and leaves. It can eat upward of 90 lbs. (41 kg) of food a day. The bears make dens for overwintering in rock crevices and caves, or dig into hillsides or under trees. Females give birth to two to four cubs, which stay with their mothers for at least a year.

Scientific name: *Ursus arctos*

Group name: sloth, sleuth

Size: up to 9 ft (2.7 m) long

Weight: up to 1,210 lbs. (550 kg)

Diet: omnivore

Lifespan in wild: up to 25 years

Location: northwestern North America, Europe, and Asia

In winter, **brown bears** go into a **deep sleep** called **torpor**, from which they **wake up** easily.

Good eyesight
Despite myths to the contrary, bears can see well at a distance and have excellent night vision.

Concave nose
The bear has a keen sense of smell and acute hearing.

Shoulder hump
Brown bears can be recognized by their strong shoulder muscles in the distinctive large "hump."

Standing tall
When a brown bear stands on its hind legs it can reach a terrifying and apparently threatening height of 10 ft (3 m). However, it does this out of curiosity because it can see more from this angle.

An easy catch
These bears love to eat fish. They are a familiar sight in parts of North America when thousands of salmon travel upstream to their spawning grounds. The brown bears stand in the rivers and catch leaping salmon in their open mouths or with their paws.

Grizzly bear
(*Ursus arctos horribilis*)

Kodiak bear
(*Ursus arctos middendorffi*)

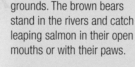

Top predator
This is a powerful animal with a large home range. It usually moves slowly but can run at more than 35 mph (56 km/h) over a 2-mile (3-km) distance. It may compete with other carnivores such as wolves or mountain lions for food.

Subspecies
There are two common types of brown bear in North America. The grizzly is found all over the continent, while the Kodiak bear lives in Alaska. Other subspecies live in Europe and Asia.

Sharp claws
The toes of the front paws have longer claws than the back paws because the front paws are used for digging.

Sea bear on a frozen ocean

When a polar bear emerges from her winter den, she is thin and very hungry so she traverses the cold Arctic expanse looking for ringed and bearded seals as they come up for air or to rest on the ice. A layer of blubber up to 4.3 ins (11 cm) thick keeps the polar bear warm both on the Arctic ice floes and in the cold seas, where her slightly webbed front paws do "doggy paddle" to propel her through the water. In the future, these magnificent creatures may become a rare sight—the Earth is warming and their icy territories are shrinking.

RACCOONS AND RELATIVES

OMNIVORE OPPORTUNISTS

These animals all live in the Americas apart from the red panda, and with the exception of the coati, are active at night, using sight and smell to find food. Their tails have light and dark rings, they are good climbers, and when on the ground, walk on the soles of their feet like bears.

Black mask
This helps the raccoon see more clearly by reducing glare.

Masked raiders
Raccoons look like bandits with their mask-like black strip across their faces. And they act like raiders in urban areas as they dive into dumpsters for an easy meal.

Dextrous hands
Toes are very flexible and good at pulling things apart and holding them down.

Bushy tail
The thick, furry tail can be up to 16 ins (40 cm) long—half the length of the whole body.

RACCOON

PROCYON LOTOR

This nocturnal, solitary animal mostly lives near water where its reflexes and quick wits help it to catch crayfish, frogs, and other aquatic prey. It is an excellent swimmer, although its fur is not waterproof so it does not swim for long. It is omnivorous, so it also eats fruits, nuts, berries, insects, rodents, and eggs.

Raccoon kits (babies) in a tree hollow

Urban raccoon raiding bin

Adaptable animal
The nimble long-fingered paws that raccoons use on trash cans developed to help them climb the trees that are their homes in the natural world. They are good climbers and can travel quickly down a tree face first.

SOUTH AMERICAN COATI

NASUA NASUA

Coatis are active by day, searching with their long noses for fruits, seeds, and small animals on forest floors. They have strong claws to dig out food, and like to eat tarantulas, rolling the spiders around first to get rid of the irritating hairs.

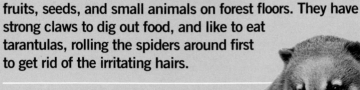

Day to day life
Male coatis tend to be solitary, but the females and their young travel in groups of up to 30 animals. They climb well, jumping from branch to branch, and sleep, mate, nest, and give birth in trees.

RED PANDA

AILURUS FULGENS

Red pandas live in the mountain forests of southern Asia and China, sometimes in areas up to 13,000 ft (4,000 m) high. It is well adapted to the cold, and when asleep, wraps its long striped tail around its body to keep warm. This is an endangered species, with less than 10,000 left in the wild.

All in a day's work
This skillful acrobat spends most of its life in trees, although it comes down to the forest floor to find bamboo shoots and roots, as well as the small animals that it eats.

MUSTELIDS
FAST AND FURIOUS

Most mustelids are long-bodied with short legs. They eat mainly meat, searching for prey in burrows, trees, and crevices, apart from the aquatic types that fish underwater. They use scent to hunt, mark territory, communicate, and deter attackers. This group is ferocious, well practiced at killing prey and chasing off rivals—you do not mess with a mustelid!

AMERICAN BADGER
TAXIDEA TAXUS

This solitary animal lives on the plains and prairies of Canada, Mexico, and the western US. It digs prey such as ground squirrels, rats, and gophers out of the ground with its sharp claws.

Self-defense
The badger has thick, loose fur that gives it time to turn and bite an attacking predator. If it is cornered, it will make loud noises and release an unpleasant musky smell.

SEA OTTER
ENHYDRA LUTRIS

Unlike most sea mammals, otters do not have blubber to keep warm. They have the thickest fur of any mammal, and this traps a layer of air so their skin never gets wet.

All at sea
This otter lives in the sea in coastal beds of giant kelp. To eat clams, it floats on its back and smashes a clam with a rock.

LEAST WEASEL
MUSTELA NIVALIS

The smallest mustelid, the weasel is also the smallest carnivore. It only measures 13 in (33 cm) including tail, and weighs 9 oz (250 g).

Camouflaged hunter
The least weasel is brown and white. In northern areas, its coat turns white in winter. It is small enough to chase its mice prey into their burrows.

Life in the trees
Pine martens rest and breed in the trees, making dens in tree holes usually created by other animals such as squirrels and birds.

Predator and prey
The pine marten is a typical mustelid with its long, thin, fast-moving body ideal for scampering after prey. In turn, it is sometimes preyed on by the golden eagle and red fox.

Well adapted
In winter, wolverines become scavengers, feeding on dead animals. They travel great distances to find food, and may move more than 18 miles (30 km) in one night.

WOLVERINE
GULO GULO

Wolverines are the largest land mustelids. They live in the northern forests of Europe and North America, and are formidable hunters of caribou, moose, and reindeer.

PINE MARTEN
MARTES MARTES

This shy, cat-sized member of the family is found throughout Europe, and as its name suggests, lives mainly in woodland, usually in pine trees. It is mostly nocturnal, hunting voles, rabbits, squirrels, and birds, but also searching for honey, berries, fungi, and nuts. During the summer mating season, pine martens make shrill, catlike calls.

Warm coat
The thick fur grows longer and silkier during winter months.

Sharp ears
These are small and rounded but highly sensitive.

Whiskered nose
The pointed muzzle has whiskers that "feel" for prey in the dark.

WILD CATS
SOFT-FOOTED PREDATORS

The house cat's wild relatives can be split into two groups. Small cats can purr but not roar, crouch to eat, and rest with paws tucked in. Big cats have different throats to allow them to roar (apart from snow and clouded leopards), eat lying down, and rest with their paws out in front. All are stealthy hunters, and have keen senses and quick reflexes. They live in a wide variety of habitats from the desert to the sub-Arctic.

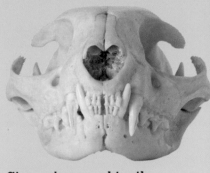

Strong jaws and teeth
Cats are carnivorous, although they also eat grass or other plants to aid digestion. They have flexible wrists with strong, retractable claws to grip prey that they kill with powerful bites, and slice the meat with sharp teeth.

Adept swimmer

Fishing techniques
The fishing cat waits at the water's edge and uses its paw to flip the fish out of the water. Sometimes it dives in and catches fish with its teeth.

Hunter at water's edge

SERVAL
LEPTAILURUS SERVAL

Servals are found on central African savannas where there are streams—they like to leap and play in the water. Females make dens in thick vegetation where they give birth to up to three kittens that double in size in two weeks.

Nimble hunter
This cat is adept at listening for small prey in scrub undergrowth. Its remarkable large ears are so sensitive that it can hear mole rats tunneling underground.

Body camouflage
The serval's orange fur is covered with stripes and rows of dark spots that vary from animal to animal. Long necks and legs give them height in long grass.

FISHING CAT
PRIONAILURUS VIVERRINUS

There are not many cats that like water, but this one not only loves a swim, but has partly webbed feet and a taste for fish. Its main habitats are marshes, swamps, and mangroves in India and southeast Asia, where its diet also includes crabs, frogs, snakes, rodents, and young deer.

OCELOT
LEOPARDUS PARDALIS

This uniquely patterned wildcat of the Americas is about twice the size of a domestic cat. Its name comes from the Aztec word *tlalocelot* or "field tiger." Ocelots are sometimes preyed on by pumas, jaguars, and anacondas.

Keen senses
Ocelots are nocturnal, using their excellent eyesight and hearing to hunt rodents, birds, monkeys, tortoises, sloths, and snakes.

Living life in the extremes
Thick fur between the paws protects this small cat's feet from the scorching sand in deserts where temperatures can soar to 135°F (57°C).

SAND CAT
FELIS MARGARITA

This is the only true desert cat, native to deserts in Africa and Asia. It is nocturnal, spending its days in burrows in sand dunes. At night, in temperatures as low as 23°F (−5°C), it travels a long way to find jerboas, reptiles, and insects to eat.

CARACAL

CARACAL CARACAL

The caracal lives on rocky hills and grasslands in Africa, India, and southwestern Asia. It hunts rodents, antelope, and gazelles, and even takes low-flying birds right out of the air.

Smart appearance
Also called the desert lynx, the red-gold caracal has faded orange spots on its cream-colored belly. Its legs are long, with the back legs taller and very muscular.

EUROPEAN WILDCAT

FELIS SILVESTRIS

A domestic tabby cat look-alike, this cat is about one-third larger and is found in forests all over Europe as well as parts of Asia. It is solitary and most active in daylight, hunting prey such as small birds, frogs, insects, rabbits, and hares at speeds of up to 30 mph (50 km/h).

Oversized tabby
This wildcat has a broad head, a flat face, and long legs. Its striped coat is long and thick for cold weather, and its tail is marked with dark rings and a black tip.

EURASIAN LYNX

LYNX LYNX

The lynx has a short tail and tufted ears, but you might find it difficult to spot because it is secretive, adept at hiding in the dense forests of the northern hemisphere. It has disappeared from parts of western Europe but is being reintroduced into some countries. In many myths around the world, the lynx sees what others cannot and reveals hidden truths.

Scientific name: *Lynx lynx*

Common names: common lynx, European lynx, Siberian lynx, Mongolian lynx

Size: up to 5 ft (1.5 m) long including tail

Weight: up to 62 lbs. (28 kg)

Diet: carnivore

Lifespan in wild: up to 17 years

Location: Europe, central Asia, Siberia and east Asia

Hunting ace
This nocturnal hunter and strict carnivore chokes or suffocates its prey, even animals larger than itself such as roe and red deer.

Cool cat
Its long legs and the snowshoe-like webbed paws with their thick fur make this cat an efficient predator. They give the cat greater control on snowy terrain.

Tufted ears
Some scientists think the black hairs on the ears help to improve the lynx's hearing; others think they act like whiskers to detect things above the head.

Sharp eyesight
A lynx can spot a mouse rustling in the undergrowth at a distance of 250 ft (75 m).

Bushy ruff
The thick coat forms a distinctive ruff around the neck, framing its face.

Family life
Lynx are solitary creatures except when they are with females and their offspring. Even when the cubs are old enough, they may travel and hunt with their mother for several months.

COUGAR

PUMA CONCOLOR

Also known as the mountain lion and puma, among many other names, the cougar is found in the Americas from the Canadian Yukon all the way down to the southern Andes in Patagonia. Seldom seen in the rocky canyons or dense forests that are its habitat, this is a powerful animal, with an ability to leap vertically 15 ft (4.6 m) into the air.

Warning sign
This road sign in Arizona warns that cougars may be crossing the road. Some signs are put up as warnings because, although attacks are rare, some cougars try to find an easy target.

NEXT 2 MILES

Living spaces
Cougars live in a variety of habitats where they have no predators. They hunt large and small prey that include deer, elk, bighorn sheep, and rodents.

Mountain lairs

Dense forests

Strong and sleek
This large cat cannot roar—it is only able to purr. The color of cougars vary from light brown to gray, and a large male may weigh up to 220 lbs. (100 kg) and stand around 2.3 ft (0.7 m) at the shoulders.

Water cat
Jaguars live mainly in forests and swamps. They often hunt otters and turtles along the banks of rivers and are excellent swimmers. They scoop fish out of the water with their paws and sometimes lash their tails in the water, which mimics the sound and movement of falling fruit and attracts the fish to the bank.

JAGUAR

PANTHERA ONCA

This heavily built cat's tan or orange coat is covered in large black patterns called "rosettes" that are shaped like roses with spots at their centers. The jaguar is a loner with strong jaws and sharp teeth. It is the largest cat in Central and South America, with adult males reaching more than 6 ft (1.9 m) in length and weighing up to 250 lbs. (113 kg).

CHEETAH

ACINONYX JUBATUS

Cheetahs rely on speed to catch prey such as warthogs, springboks, and antelopes on the African plains. They are the only cats that can turn in midair while they are sprinting, and they bring down animals by knocking them over and grabbing their throats to suffocate them.

Targeting prey
Cheetahs often live and hunt together in family groups. They stand on raised areas, such as termite mounds (left) and fallen logs, to search for prey, then stalk it using the long grasses as camouflage.

Beat that!
Cheetahs can run faster than any other animal on land, reaching a speed of 60 mph (95 km/h) in only 3.3 seconds. The fastest person on Earth, Usain Bolt, achieved 27.8 mph (44.72 km/h) on August 16, 2009.

SNOW LEOPARD
PANTHERA UNCIA

This hardy cat lives in the high, rocky mountains of central Asia, mainly above a height of 10,000 ft (3,000 m). It preys on Himalayan blue sheep and mountain ibex, as well as marmots, hares, pikas, and birds. Their spotted coats change from white in winter to yellow-gray in summer.

Surviving the big freeze
Snow leopards live in harsh conditions. Thick hair protects them from the cold, wide paws act as snowshoes, and long tails wrap around them at night to keep them warm.

LEOPARD
PANTHERA PARDUS

Home range
This leopard has a large territory and will not tolerate other leopards intruding unless it is to mate. Like other cats, it marks its territory with urine.

Found in all kinds of habitats both in Africa and in central and southern Asia, this cat is very adaptable. It is a strong climber and will haul dead prey heavier than itself up into trees to protect it from scavengers.

Melanic (dark-colored) form

Normal coloration

LION
PANTHERA LEO

Signature mane
The male's mane indicates age—the darker the mane, the older the lion is.

The second-largest cat after the tiger (*see pp. 54–55*), this magnificent beast is one of the few cats that hunts in groups. A typical pride numbers around 15 animals, with two or three adult males, and females and their cubs. The females do most of the hunting across the grasslands of sub-Saharan Africa, but the whole pride benefits from a kill.

Family life
Although male lions protect the females and cubs in their pride, a younger male lion may challenge for leadership. If he wins, he will kill all the cubs that are not his own.

Family group

Pride leader roaring

Heavyweight
The male may weigh up to 500 lbs. (227 kg).

Light of foot
A lion's heels do not touch the ground as it walks.

Seeing off rivals
Until they reach two years of age, lions cannot roar. An adult male's roar is deeper than the female's and is one of the loudest calls of any animal. It is a warning to other males and can be heard 5 miles (8 km) away.

There are **only 3,890 wild tigers left**—numbers have **dropped 95%** since **the start** of the **20th century**.

TIGER
PANTHERA TIGRIS

The tiger is the largest and most powerful of all the cat family. It is a ferocious stalk-and-ambush predator, able to approach unsuspecting prey in almost total silence before pouncing. Tigers hunt mainly at dusk and dawn, and can take prey larger than themselves, such as water buffalo, rhino, and small elephants. These endangered animals are solitary and have a large territory, marking their domain, as well as raking trees with their claws and roaring to deter rival males.

Scientific name: *Panthera tigris*

Size: up to 9.5 ft (2.9 m) long, including tail

Weight: up to 660 lbs. (300 kg)

Diet: carnivore

Lifespan in wild: up to 20 years

Location: southern and southeast Asia, eastern Siberia

White genes
Rare white tigers with blue eyes (usually cross-eyed) are a color variation of the Bengal tiger, *Panthera tigris tigris*. They are only born when both parents carry a particular gene, calculated to occur in only one in every 10,000 births.

Strong head
The big skull gives the head a broad, rounded shape and houses powerful jaws.

Mouth of a killer
A tiger has the longest canines of any cat, and a tongue covered with hard papillae, to scrape flesh off the bones of prey.

Muscular power
A short, thick neck and powerful shoulders lend weight to the dense bones of the front legs to bring down large prey.

Revered cat
Through history, the tiger has held a special place in Asian myth, folklore, and belief systems. In China, the tiger is the symbol of courage and inner strength; in Korea, the animal wards off evil spirits; and in India, the Hindu warrior goddess Durga rides a tiger into battle.

Chinese temple plaque

Curved claws
Long, retractable claws in the toes of the large, padded feet are ideal for holding down wriggling prey.

Strength of a top predator
Tigers grip prey with their sharp front claws, but kill with their mouths, by strangulation or a bite to the throat. Young tigers learn how to stalk and kill prey from their mothers. They become independent hunters at the age of two.

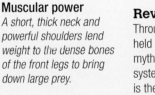

Korean tiger pagoda

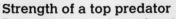

Fur identification
This tiger's fur is covered in dark, vertical stripes and no two tigers have the same pattern. The different subspecies vary in size and coat color. The Sumatran is the smallest with the darkest fur, while the Siberian is the largest with the palest fur.

CIVETS AND RELATIVES

SLENDER-BODIED PREDATORS

Civets, mongooses, and meerkats belong to the same cat-like family, and are fast, quick-witted carnivores ready for a fight. Civets are the most secretive, emerging at night, and they use powerful scents to warn off rivals. Mongooses make more fuss, taunting snakes to tire them out before sinking in sharp teeth for the kill—they seem to be resistant to snake venom. Meerkats are the most sociable of the three, living in groups and keeping watch for each other.

BANDED MONGOOSE

MUNGOS MUNGO

A small carnivore, the banded mongoose lives in the forests and on the grasslands of central and eastern Africa. These mongooses live in packs of up to 40 adults and pups, and they are nomadic, moving from place to place every few days.

It's in the name
Named for the dark bands across its back, the banded mongoose likes to eat beetles and termites. It will also use an old termite mound as a home.

Sought-after scent
The African civet marks its territory with a musk that it secretes from glands near its tail. This musk. or civetone, has been used in perfumes for centuries.

AFRICAN CIVET

CIVETTICTIS CIVETTA

This gray-and-black masked animal is the largest civet in Africa. It lives on savannas and in forests near water, and swims well. It is nocturnal and an omnivore, with a diet that includes lizards, rodents, insects, reptiles, fruits, and other plants.

MEERKAT

SURICATA SURICATTA

These squirrel-sized animals are vulnerable to attacks from predators and other meerkat groups, or mobs. They dig burrows for their own mob to shelter in, and feed during the day, using a wide range of calls to communicate with each other.

Scientific name: *Suricata suricalla*	**Weight:** up to 2.2 lbs. (1 kg)
Group name: mob	**Diet:** omnivore
Size: up to 21 ins (54 cm) length from head to tip of tail	**Lifespan in wild:** up to 14 years
	Location: deserts and grasslands of Africa

Keen lookout
While the mob is foraging for food, one meerkat acts as sentry, standing on its hind legs and watching for predators such as eagles, snakes, or jackals.

Good appetites
These omnivores will eat almost anything, including insects, spiders, and scorpions. They also search out eggs, fruit, and plants.

Family life
Young meerkats are never left on their own in the burrow. There are always "babysitters" left behind to look after them..

Furry portrait
The binturong's catlike face is framed by whiskers that are 8 ins (20 cm) long, It is one of the few mammals that has a prehensile tail, which it uses in the trees like a fifth leg.

BINTURONG
ARCTICTIS BINTURONG

This native of the tropical rain forests of south and southeast Asia is also known as the bearcat. It lives high up in the forest canopy and mostly eats fruit such as the strangler fig. It marks its territory with a scent that smells to humans like popcorn.

COMMON GENET
GENETTA GENETTA

The common genet is a slender, catlike carnivore with a dark line that runs from its shoulders to its tail. It lives in woodlands in Europe, Africa, and the Middle East. A solitary animal, it spends its days in rock or tree crevices that protect it from predators such as leopards, servals, and honey badgers.

Long tail held horizontal to ground

Sharp eyes and ears to find prey

Nocturnal predator
Still under threat from large owls, this is a night hunter, eating any small animals that it can catch. It usually lives in areas where there are lots of its favorite prey, the wood mouse.

HYENAS
LAUGHING KILLERS

Hyenas often scavenge for dead meat on their own—they have powerful jaws to crush up the bones and are able to digest what others leave. However, they also gang up to overpower big prey such as wildebeests and zebras, communicating with loud laugh-like calls. They look a bit like dogs, but are more closely related to mongooses.

AARDWOLF
PROTELES CRISTATA

An unusual member of this family, the aardwolf has weak jaws, small peg-like teeth, and feeds mainly on termites. It lives in southern and eastern Africa, and its name means "earth-wolf" in Afrikaans. If it is threatened, the hairs of a long, dark-colored stripe along its back rise.

Finding prey
The aardwolf's acute hearing helps it find its termite food. It feeds after dark, digging up insects from the ground and out of termite mounds, lapping them up with its sticky tongue.

Odd sight
Identified by its sloping back and ungainly walk, this hyena has one of the strongest bites of all the animals and a very keen sense of smell.

SPOTTED HYENA
CROCUTA CROCUTA

The largest and most powerful of the four species of hyenas, packs of these animals up to 80 strong successfully hunt large prey such as zebras and wildebeests across the open plains of Africa. An adult hyena can tear off and swallow up to 40 lbs (18 kg) of meat in one sitting, and a pack can eat an entire zebra in only 25 minutes.

Muscling in
Hyenas are great scavengers, well known for eating the leftovers of other animals. They are also capable of stealing prey off predators much larger than themselves, including lions.

Supersonic sound system

When okapis, the only living relatives of giraffes (*see p. 73*), want to communicate with mates or their young, they sometimes stretch their necks, throw their heads back, and emit calls that are infrasonic. These very low-frequency sounds cannot be heard by humans, but more importantly, they cannot be heard by predators.

EXTREME ANIMALS

We watch movies to marvel at superheroes with amazing powers, but some animals have tricks that would make a comic book crusader jealous. There are creatures that can "see" in the dark, and animals that live in boiling water at depths in the oceans where the pressure would crush our skulls. Others can last days without water and months without food.

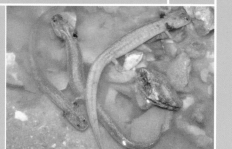

Grotto salamander larvae

In the dark
As larvae, grotto salamanders live in streams near caverns and can see. When they lose their orange gills and metamorphose into adults, they move deep inside the caves. There, in complete darkness, their eyelids fuse partially or completely shut as they no longer need sight.

Northern gannet

Safe sleep
During long, hot summers, the African bullfrog burrows deep into the soil. There, it cloaks itself in a watertight cocoon made of dead skin layers. This stops any body fluids from evaporating, and the frog goes into estivation, a type of hibernation, until the rains come.

African bullfrog

Hard knocks
Gannets hit the surface of the water at incredible speeds of up to 62 mph (100 km/h). This would kill most creatures, but gannets have no nostril holes, and there are built-in airbags under their skin that inflate to absorb the impact.

Diving gannets

Liquid blood
Inside the blood of Antarctic icefish are proteins and sugars that act as antifreeze. They suppress the growth of ice crystals as the fish swim in the freezing waters of the Southern Ocean.

Antarctic icefish larva

The **weta** has **its ears** on the **knees** of its **front legs**.

Heat from the center of the Earth
In the depths of the ocean, some extraordinary animals survive superheated water flowing out of cracks in the planet's surface and intense pressure. The "black smokers" are home to animal survivors such as the Yeti crab.

Crabs and marine snails around a black smoker

Common garter snakes

Mating tactics
Common garter snakes often hibernate in the thousands, piled on top of each another to keep safe and warm. When they emerge in spring, the males come out first. Some males are able to make themselves smell like females and can lure the other males away. This allows them to be the first to mate.

Giant weta

Zombie insect
Eighty percent of the mountain stone weta of New Zealand literally freezes solid when the temperature drops below 41°F (5°C). It does not breathe, its heart stops, and there is no brain activity. It is able to survive repeated freeze and thaw.

SEALS AND RELATIVES

FLIPPER-FOOTED MAMMALS

Seals, walruses, and sea lions form a group called pinnipeds, "fin-footed," because of their front and rear flippers that power smooth torpedo-like bodies. They live mostly in the water, moving—some more easily than others—onto the land to rest and breed. Long, sensitive whiskers sense the slightest movement beneath the waves to "see" prey such as fish and squid far away. There are two types of seal: "eared" with ear flaps, and the more streamlined "true" without ear flaps.

Ear flaps
These are visible as little flaps of skin on the sides of the head.

Hindquarters
A layer of blubber, or fat, insulates the sea lion's body.

Deep divers
When diving, the sea lions close their ears and nostrils. They can reach a depth of 900 ft (274 m) and stay underwater for 11 minutes.

CALIFORNIA SEA LION

ZALOPHUS CALIFORNIANUS

This eared seal is sleek and lithe. It is also faster than any other sea lion or seal, reaching speeds in the water of 30 mph (48 km/h) and moving faster than a human when running on land.

Scientific name: *Zalophus californianus*	**Lifespan in wild:** 20 years
Size: up to 7 ft (2 m) long	**Location:** western North America
Weight: 880 lbs (400 kg)	
Diet: fish and cephalopods	

Living together
These social seals live on rocky coasts and feed on fish and squid. They often jump out of the water and sometimes "surf" the waves.

Moving on land
On land, the front flippers are strong enough to hold the heavy body off the ground. The back flippers turn forward to act as feet.

LEOPARD SEAL

HYDRURGA LEPTONYX

This true seal lives up to its name—it is a ferocious predator of the Southern Ocean. Its favorite food is penguin—it waits in the water near colonies and grabs its prey as the penguins enter the water.

Top predator
Leopard seals hunt in the water and haul their long, slender bodies out on the ice to rest. As well as penguins, they use their powerful jaws and long teeth to eat fish and other seals.

Prey and preyed on
Monk seals feed on cephalopods, crustaceans, and fish. They in turn are preyed on by tiger sharks, and gray and white-tipped reef sharks.

MONK SEAL

NEOMONACHUS SCHAUINSLANDI

This is the most endangered marine mammal and is found on uninhabited Hawaiian islands. When on land, these seals haul themselves out on sand, corals, and volcanic rocks.

SOUTHERN ELEPHANT SEAL
MIROUNGA LEONINA

The largest of all the seals, these animals inhabit the cold waters near Antarctica, fishing mainly for squid. They breed on land, and the pups are nursed there for about three weeks, before the mothers return to the sea. The pups follow them around 10 weeks later.

Nose can be inflated to roar

Heavyweight match
At up to four tons in weight, the male southern elephant seal can weigh four times more than the female. They use this weight to batlle other males for a mate.

Females crowd together

WALRUS
ODOBENUS ROSMARUS

A native of the Arctic Circle, the walrus is famed for its large, downward-pointing tusks, which may be up to 3 ft (1 m) long. It uses the tusks to haul itself out of the water, to break breathing holes in the ice, to find food, and as a defense against predatory orcas or polar bears.

Resting on the ice

Muscling in
Herds of walruses congregate in large numbers on the pack ice. They dive deep and use their whiskers to find food such as mollusks and clams.

Bobbing in the water

MANATEES AND DUGONGS
GIANT HERBIVORES OF THE SEA

These "sea cows" do not have thick insulating blubber like seals—their large bodies are mostly made up of the stomach and intestines needed to deal with the vast piles of plants that they munch. These sirenians were mistaken for mermaids by early sailors, including Christopher Columbus in 1492.

WEST INDIAN MANATEE
TRICHECHUS MANATUS

A manatee is a bit like an aquatic elephant, and indeed they are related. This huge, slow beast feeds on plants as it roams the warm coastal seas, sometimes swimming into freshwater rivers but never coming ashore. Its teeth grow all the time from the back, easing forward to push out the front ones worn down by sea plants.

Graceful swimmer
The manatee has a rounded, paddle-like tail that it moves in an up-and-down motion as it moves easily through the water.

DUGONG
DUGONG DUGON

The dugong lives in the salt water of mangroves and bays in shallow coastal waters from east Africa to Australia. It has a flat muzzle and a mouth with a muscular upper lip. These are angled down because that helps this bottom-feeding specialist to graze on sea grasses.

Tale of a tail
The dugong's tail is more whale-like than the manatee's. It sometimes stands on its tail to support its head above the water, when it surfaces to breathe.

A successful conservation story

The Svalbard Islands are in the Arctic Ocean, halfway between Norway and the North Pole. Much of this area is covered in ice all year round and there is no daylight from October to March, but this Arctic wilderness is home to colonies of walruses. Here, for three centuries, this animal was hunted for its blubber and ivory tusks almost to extinction. It was not until 1952, when there were only 100 left around the Svarlbard Islands, that it was made a protected species. Today there are around 2,000 in this area.

HYRAXES

ELEPHANT COUSINS

The hyrax is closely related to the elephant. It has similar toes and skull as well as broad, plant-munching teeth accompanied by long, pointed incisors that are like tusks. Hyraxes live in groups in dry habitats. Some feed in a circle, each looking out and ready to give the danger signal—they communicate well with a mix of grunts, growls, whistles, and shrieks.

ROCK HYRAX

PROCAVIA CAPENSIS

Also called the rock badger and rock rabbit, this small furry mammal is a native of Africa and the Middle East. It lives in groups of up to 50 animals, and they huddle together for warmth at night.

Agile animal
The rock hyrax can climb nimbly up and down rocks because of the excellent grip from moist, rubbery pads on its feet. It feeds during the day on grass and the leaves of shrubs.

SOUTHERN TREE HYRAX

DENDROHYRAX ARBOREUS

This nocturnal hyrax lives in the forests in eastern and southern Africa. It spends most of its time in the trees and is quite clumsy on the ground, having some difficulty walking. It has a distinctive blood-curdling call to announce its territory.

Hearty appetite
This herbivore eats leaves, shoots, and twigs, as well as fruits and seeds. It can eat one-third of its body weight in a single day.

ELEPHANTS

GIANT PACHYDERMS

Elephants are remarkable animals for more reasons than their huge size: they are intelligent with good memories (handy for finding food and recognizing friends); communicate with touch, taste, and smell; and are highly sociable. There are two main types: large-eared African and small-eared Asian.

Toenails not hooves
On an elephant's foot, separated toes have been replaced by a single pad with large nails. The nails grow continuously.

Civil duties
Asian elephants are trained for forestry and farm work, as well as for tourist rides. They also often appear in ceremonial parades, like this one in Thailand.

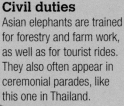

ASIAN ELEPHANT

ELEPHAS MAXIMUS

This animal is smaller than the African elephant and has compact, rounded ears. Most females and some males have small tusks known as tushes, that are often inside the mouth. Asian elephants live in forests where many plants rely on them for seed dispersal—the seeds they eat in one part of the forest come out in dung in another.

Second largest
Asian elephants weigh up to 5.5 tons and measure up to 10 ft (3 m) at the shoulder. They are gray, but may have pink or white coloring on their ears, trunk, head, or neck.

AFRICAN FOREST ELEPHANT

LOXODONTA CYCLOTIS

These elusive elephants live in the dense rain forests of west and central Africa. They are smaller than the African elephant and have pink tusks that are nearly straight. Their tusks make them a target for poachers—it is thought that 10 percent of them are killed every year. They are also under threat from habitat loss.

Tight units
African forest elephants have been observed in small groups consisting of a mother and her dependent offspring.

AFRICAN ELEPHANT

LOXODONTA AFRICANA

African elephants are the world's largest land animals. They need to eat vast amounts of greenery to stay alive, so they have huge stomachs and long intestines to store and digest food, and pillar-like legs to stay upright. Their trunks are long noses with sensitive tips, flexible and strong enough to fell trees or hold leaves. The tusks are long incisor teeth for display, defense, and digging up food; and the ears listen, but also flap air onto the body and cool the blood.

Scientific name: *Loxodonta Africana*

Common names: savanna elephant

Group name: herd

Size: up to 13 ft (4 m) height; from shoulder to toe

Weight: up to 7 tons

Diet: herbivore

Lifespan in wild: up to 70 years

Location: Africa

Elephants are **left-** or **right-tusked**, favoring **one tusk** over **the other**.

Under threat
Lions are the only predators powerful enough to kill an elephant, but they tend to go after younger animals and calves. These lionesses are no match for a charging bull elephant.

Wrinkles
Heavy folds of skin trap moisture to keep the animal cooler for longer.

Sun screen
Although they look tough, elephants have sensitive skin. To avoid sunburn, they cover themselves with mud after taking a bath.

Keeping cool
On the open savanna, this elephant is exposed to the hot sun. Heavy folds of skin all over the elephant's body trap moisture and keep the animal cooler for longer.

Big ears
A large surface area helps to radiate heat away from the body.

Multitasking
The trunk is used to smell, breath, suck up water, hold objects, and caress young.

Family life
Elephants have strong family bonds. The herd is made up of mothers and their young, sisters, and female cousins, led by a matriarch. The males leave the herd when they are around 14 years old. The elephants communicate with each other with low frequency sounds.

HOOVED ANIMALS

ODD- AND EVEN-TOED UNGULATES

Hooves are a keratin covering that allows an animal to walk on its toes, giving good grip and helping it run faster. Those with an even number of toes are called "cloven-hooved" and mostly chew the cud, munching their plant food several times to get maximum energy from it. Among these are cows, camels and deer, while non-cud chewers include the pig and hippo families. The other group has an uneven number of toes—one to five—and includes horses, rhinos, and tapirs.

At first sight
This animal has a deer-like body. Both males and females have the backward-curving horns with forward-pointing prongs that they are named for. The males have a black mark that runs from their eyes down the snout.

AMERICAN BISON

BISON BISON

This massive, thick-coated animal spends its day chewing the cud—munching grasses and sedges more than once to get more energy from them—or giving itself a dust bath by rolling around on the ground. It is the largest land animal in North America, with males standing up to 6.5 ft (2 m) tall at the shoulder and weighing up to 1 ton.

Native Americans hunting bison

Free-roaming bison today

Under threat
There were once around 30 million wild bison on North American plains, hunted by Native Americans. In the 19th century, they were hunted to near extinction by European settlers. Today, there are around 500,000.

PRONGHORN ANTELOPE

ANTILOCAPRA AMERICANA

Despite its species name translating as "American goat-antelope," this animal is neither a goat nor an antelope—it is the only surviving member of its family. Like other even-toed animals, they chew the cud, eat grass, sagebrush, and other prairie plants.

MALAYAN TAPIR

ACROCODIA INDICA

This odd-toed animal is the largest of five species of tapir. It lives near water in the rain forests of Southeast Asia, and feeds after dark. Its young have white stripes and spots.

Appearances
The tapir has a piglike body and a snout that it uses to feel for food.

Hard life
Vicuña live in small herds on barren mountain slopes where they graze on grass and other plants.

VICUÑA

VICUGNA VICUGNA

The smallest member of the camel family (*see p. 72*), but apparently a much more dainty animal, the vicuña is equally as tough. It lives in the high Andes of South America, surviving harsh conditions.

MOUNTAIN GOAT
OREAMNOS AMERICANUS

This member of the antelope family is known for its mountaineering agility. They live high up in the Rocky Mountains of North America, where their long, snow-white coats protect them from freezing winds and provide camouflage in winter.

Herd life
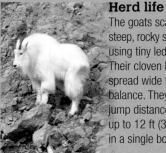
The goats scale steep, rocky surfaces using tiny ledges. Their cloven hooves spread wide for balance. They can jump distances of up to 12 ft (3.7 m) in a single bound.

Japanese tale

Boars often play a role in myths and legends. Here, a Samurai warrior confronts a Buddhist god riding on the back of a wild boar.

Protective layers
Boars have two coats—a soft undercoat and a bristly upper coat.

Dangerous tusks
Two pairs of short tusks are used to fight enemies if they are attacked.

Safety stripes

The piglets have stripes running the length of their backs. Their camouflage helps protect them from predators such as coyotes and bobcats.

Scientific name: *Sus scrofa*

Common names: Russian boar, wild boar, razorback

Size: up to 3 ft (1 m) at the shoulder; up to 5 ft (1.5 m) body length

Weight: up to 705 lbs (320 kg)

Diet: omnivore

Lifespan in wild: up to 13 years

Location: Europe, Asia, North Africa

Even-toed
This ungulate has cloven hooves like deer and domestic pigs.

Sensing danger
Wild boars have poor eyesight but a great sense of smell, which helps them find food and, together with acute hearing, spot danger from predators such as leopards, lynx, wolves, tigers, and bears.

EURASIAN BOAR
SUS SCROFA

This animal is the ancestor of our domestic pig. It is mainly nocturnal and forages with its snout on the forest floor for plants, fruits, nuts, and roots, but also eats eggs, carrion, small rodents, and worms. Most males are solitary, but the females and young live in small groups called "sounders."

PLAINS ZEBRA
EQUUS QUAGGA

Every zebra has a pattern of black-and-white stripes that is individual. Also known as the common zebra or quagga, plains zebras live on open grasslands in Africa. They depend on speeds of up to 35 mph (56 km/h) to escape from predators such as lions and cheetahs.

Identification
This is the most abundant of three species. It is easy to identify because it has a striped underbelly.

Herd life
These herbivores live in family groups that join up to form very large herds that travel together.

ONE-HORNED RHINOCEROS
RHINOCEROS UNICORNIS

This solitary grazer lives on the floodplains and in the grassy swamps of northern India and southern Nepal. It feeds on leaves, branches, and fruits and sinks into the water to eat aquatic plants. Males sometimes fight to the death over territory.

Gray grazer
The thick gray skin hangs in heavy folds like armor plating. It is hairless and there is flexible skin between the folds.

"Grass" grazer
The white rhino lives on the grasslands and savannas of Africa, and is able to eat plants that are toxic to other animals. It moves along with its wide mouth to the ground vacuuming up the grass very fast.

WHITE RHINOCEROS
CERATOTHERIUM SIMUM

The African white rhinoceros or square-lipped rhinoceros is the second-largest land mammal after the elephant. The name rhinoceros means "nose horn," and its horns are made from keratin, the stuff inside our fingernails and hair. The horns are handy for warning off other animals, breaking branches to get at leaves, and digging for roots. When not munching greenery, the rhino often wallows in mud. This helps it stay cool and provides a covering shield against the sun and insect bites.

Protecting the species
Tourists are drawn by the millions every year to see these wonderful animals in the wild. Safaris give people a better understanding of the rhinos and bring to their attention the importance of conservation.

18th-century Chinese rhino-horn cup

White rhino

Scientific name:
Ceratotherium simum

Other name: square-lipped rhinoceros

Group name: crash

Size: up to 6 ft (1.8 m) at the shoulders

Weight: up to 4 tons

Diet: herbivore

Lifespan in wild: up to 50 years

Location: northeastern and southern Africa

Red-billed oxpeckers

Dung beetle rolling feces away

Cleaning partnerships
Other animals play mutually beneficial roles in this rhino's life. Red-billed oxpeckers feed on the ticks that irritate it, and dung beetles clear away and eat its feces.

Threats to the species
The poaching of rhino horn to sell has done much damage to numbers. The horns are made into jewelry, figurines, and other items. In parts of Asia, powdered rhino horn is believed to have magical healing properties.

Powerful neck
The neck muscles are very strong because it bends its head to the ground to eat.

Clean-shaven
White rhinos have hair only on their ears, tail tips, and eyelashes.

Large horn
The front horn on a female is longer and can reach a length of 60 in (150 cm).

Origin of name
The term "white" probably comes from the Afrikaans word for "wide," a description of the mouth and upper lip.

Bringing up baby
When a calf is born it already weighs 90–130 lbs (40–60 kg). It is able to stand up and walk unsteadily within minutes of the birth. It stays with its mother for up to three years.

Threat response
If a rhinoceros is threatened, it will charge, which is terrifying because it weighs up to four tons and has a massive horn on its head. The white rhino is known for its placid and sociable nature, but it is still able to do a lot of damage if it attacks.

DEER

HOOFED RUMINANTS

Deer include elk, caribou, and moose. They live in herds that graze on grasses, plants, and shrubs. On constant alert for predators, they sprint away on their long legs at the slightest sign of danger. They jump well and are good swimmers, so they are getaway experts. Male deer, together with female caribou, are the only mammals that grow antlers each year—no pair is the same. The young are fawns or calves, the female is a doe, while the male is a buck that may grow to a stag.

Smallest deer
The southern and northern pudu are the smallest deer in the world. The southern has a shoulder height of only 15 ins. (38 cm)

SOUTHERN PUDU

PUDA PUDA

Small herds of pudus forage night and day for fruit, buds, ferns, vines, and tree foliage, often standing on their hind legs to reach the plants. The southern pudu lives in the dense forests of south Chile and southwest Argentina and are under threat from hunting and destruction of habitat. It is thought there are less than 10,000 of these deer left.

Family unit
The one or two calves each year stay with their mother, and need protection from wolves in winter.

MOOSE

ALCES ALCES

The name moose comes from the Algonquian word *moosh*, which means "stripper and eater of bark." These ruminants, with four parts to their stomachs, eat the buds, leaves, and twigs of shrubs and trees. They are great swimmers and dive after plants such as water lilies in lakes, staying underwater for up to a minute.

Scientific name:	*Alces alces*
Group name:	herd
Size:	up to 7 ft (2 m) tall at the shoulder
Weight:	up to 1,870 lbs (850 kg)
Diet:	herbivore
Lifespan in wild:	up to 25 years
Location:	North America, northern Europe, Asia

Distinctive looks
Moose have a big muzzle and a dangling pendant of fur under their throat called a bell. They are enormous beasts with long legs, and the males have wide antlers that they shed every winter and quickly grow again in spring.

REEVES' MUNTJAC

MUNTIACUS REEVESI

This deer, also known as the Chinese muntjac, is called the "barking deer" because it makes a loud, continuous, barking sound when it is alarmed. It lives in forests in eastern Asia, feeding at night when it is safe from attack.

Small forest deer
The muntjac is small and stocky. It is a red-brown color in summer and gray-brown in winter.

Stag duels
Red deer stags have shaggy manes and antlers up to 5 ft (1.5 m) long. In autumn, they roar a challenge at other bucks to win a mate. They lock antlers, pushing and twisting to throw a rival off balance.

RED DEER

CERVUS ELAPHUS

One of the largest and most widespread species, red deer are found across much of Europe and western Asia, as well as parts of North Africa. They live in male or female herds, joining together to mate. The fawns have white spots for camouflage.

Woodland animal

White-tailed deer have adapted to live in a wide variety of American woodland habitats, from cold Canadian forests to the steamy rain forests of Central and South America.

WHITE-TAILED DEER

ODOCOILEUS VIRGINIANUS

This ruminant's diets depends on its habitat. It regurgitates plant matter, rechews it, and swallows it again. Like other deer, the does leave their fawns hidden in undergrowth for hours while they feed.

REINDEER

RANGIFER TARANDUS

Reindeer, or caribou, dig for lichen, moss, and fungi during the long cold winters of northern Europe, Siberia, and North America. In the wild, vast herds of some 500,000 animals migrate between tundra and forest over distances of more than 3,000 miles (5,000 km) in search of food.

Reindeer herding

For centuries, nomadic reindeer herders such as the Sámi of Norway have relied on reindeer for meat and fur. They also use them to pull sleighs and sledges.

Reindeer transportation

Herd life

HIPPOPOTAMUSES

RIVER HORSES

These barrel-bodied beasts defend their territory fiercely, using their vast bulk and fearsome canine teeth to ward off threats. They cannot really swim, although they can stay several minutes underwater. Underneath those water-level eyes and nostrils, they stand on or push themselves along the bottom of rivers.

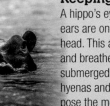

At home in the water

The hippo's ears and nose close when it is underwater. Its closest living relatives are the whales and dolphins (*see pp. 36–39*).

PYGMY HIPPOPOTAMUS

CHOEROPSIS LIBERIENSIS

This rare hippo lives in African rain forests and is a small version of the hippopotamus. It is the stuff of legends—one tells of it finding its way in the forest by carrying a diamond in its mouth to light the way.

Scientific name:
Hippopotamus amphibius

Group names: bloat, herd, pod, dale, crash

Size: up to 16.5 ft (5 m) long

Weight: up to 5 tons

Diet: herbivore

Lifespan in wild: up to 40 years

Location: eastern Africa

Big mouth

A hippo has a large "gape"—it can open its mouth up to 4 ft (1.2 m) wide! At the front are its fighting tusks that can inflict terrible wounds.

Male hippo calls

Territorial-guarding calls of up to 115 decibels are as loud as a rock concert.

Keeping watch

A hippo's eyes, nose, and ears are on top of the head. This allows it to see and breathe but remain submerged. Big cats, hyenas and crocodiles pose the most danger.

Skin shield

Hippos sweat an oily red liquid that shields their sensitive skin from the sun.

HIPPOPOTAMUS

HIPPOPOTAMUS AMPHIBIUS

Its name means "river horse," and this animal protects its skin from the hot African sun by staying in rivers and lakes for most of the day, emerging at night to munch grasses and fallen fruit. Hippos live in groups of up to 30, led by a dominant male.

CAMELS

HUMPED MAMMALS

This family is split among three continents. Camels live in Africa and Asia, and there are two types: the dromedary (one hump) and the Bactrian (two humps). Their cousins, the vicuña (*see p. 66*), llama, alpaca, and guanoco, live in South America. Camelids all have long necks, a cleft upper lip, padded two-toed feet, and a three-chambered stomach.

One-humped

Camels' humps do not contain water. They store fat that the camel uses if food is scarce. If it does that, the hump gets limp and droops. When the camel next feeds, the hump becomes upright again.

Road warning about Australia's feral population

Beast of burden

Dromedaries are capable of carrying goods through the desert for enormous distances in temperatures that can reach 120°F (49°C). They close their nostrils to keep out sand.

Salt train in Ethiopia

DROMEDARY

CAMELUS DROMEDARIUS

Dromedaries, also known as Arabian camels, are no longer found in the wild, although there are feral camels in Australia. Domesticated more than 4,000 years ago to carry people and their goods, these "ships of the desert" were used to expand trade routes across the Arabian Peninsula.

BACTRIAN

CAMELUS BACTRIANUS

There are still a few hundred wild Bactrians, but most of these camels are domesticated. The wild camels live in the deserts of central Asia, where summer temperatures reach more than 100°F (38°C) and in winter drop as low as –20°F (–29°C). They live in herds of up to 30 animals, with a dominant male.

Place in history

Throughout history, Bactrian camels have held a special place in Tibetan myth and legend. This is a painting on part of a ceremonial Tibetan banner depicting the camel and its load.

Scientific name: *Camelus Bactrianus*

Group name: herd

Size: up to 7 ft (2 m) tall at the hump

Weight: up to 1,325 lbs (600 kg)

Diet: herbivore

Lifespan in wild: up to 50 years

Location: central and east Asia

Changeable fur

Its coat is thicker and heavier on head, neck, hump, forelegs, and tail. In summer, the coat is dark-colored. In spring, fur peels away in long patches.

Two-humped

The humps store up to 80 lbs. (36 kg) of fat until it is needed.

Steppe camel

This Bactrian is in its cream-colored winter coat. It is specially adapted to eating snow and ice in the cold desert winters, looking for food in the daytime, and sleeping in the open at night.

OKAPI AND GIRAFFES
LONG-NECKED MAMMALS

A giraffe's long, thin legs and extended, flexible neck make it the tallest mammal on the planet. Giraffes live in herds, seeking out tasty leaves, buds, and fruits beyond the reach of other animals. This contrasts with their relatives the okapi, which are shorter for life in the lower branches of their rain forest habitat. Okapi are solitary and very hard to spot.

Browsing leaves with its long tongue

"Forest giraffe"

OKAPI
OKAPIA JOHNSTONI

In 1901, the British explorer Harry Johnston sent two pieces of zebra-like skin to London to be analyzed. Before then, the okapi was not known to anyone outside central Africa. It remains elusive to this day as it lives alone in dense rain forest and its stripes break up its outline, making it hard to see.

Giraffe cousin
The okapi has a long neck and a black tongue that is long enough to lick its eyes. Its body and legs look like those of a horse.

Spotty legged
Unlike other giraffe species that have a faded color on their lower legs, the southern giraffe has spots all over its limbs, although they become smaller nearer the feet.

SOUTHERN GIRAFFE
GIRAFFA GIRAFFA

The southern giraffe lives on the savannas and in the forests of southern Africa. They are predated on by leopards and suffer coordinated attacks by packs of hyenas and wild dogs. If they dip their necks to drink, they may be taken by crocodiles.

High feeder
Only the elephant can reach into the tops of the tree as high as this giraffe can.

RETICULATED GIRAFFE
GIRAFFA RETICULATA

All giraffes have only seven neck vertebrae, just like you, yet their necks are 6 ft (1.8 m) long—half their height! They are needed to reach leaves at the top of their favorite acacia trees. Thick saliva protects their tongues from the thorns.

Longest neck
The neck is lowered to drink or when the giraffe sleeps standing up.

Legs spread to drink

Necking during courtship

Social animal
This social giraffe usually lives in herds of up to 30 animals. It eats 75 lbs. (34 kg) of leaves a day, and splays its legs to drink.

Scientific name:	*Giraffa reticulata*
Group name:	herd
Size:	up to 18 ft (5.5 m) tall
Weight:	up to 2 tons
Diet:	herbivore
Lifespan in wild:	up to 25 years
Location:	Somalia and Kenya, Africa

Identification
This giraffe's coat has large five-sided spots outlined by bright white lines. The eight other subspecies of giraffe have different coat patterns.

BIRDS

BIRDS

Birds do so much more than just fly. They glide, dive, hover, zoom lightning-fast between the tangled branches of a tree, but stop in a moment. No plane can match this. There are more than 10,700 species and they live in every imaginable place, from cities to oceans, and wheatfields and forests, to frozen tundra.

Sacred ibis

Kingfisher

Scarlet macaw

Scarlet-breasted roller

Snowy owl

Giant storm petrel

Chinese egret

Hooded vulture

Black woodpecker

Eurasian eagle owl

Shoebill

American robin

European scops owlet

Rockhopper penguin

Chaffinch

Turkey vulture

Blue-tailed bee-eater

Crested crane

Broad-billed hummingbird

Great hornbill

Wreathed hornbill

Mute swan

Rock dove

Wren

Superb starling

Yellow-naped Amazon parrot

HIGH FLIERS

Bird's wings are curved from front to back. Air flowing over the top travels faster than air flowing underneath. This creates "lift" and is also how airplanes stay up. A bird that floats high on warm thermal currents has long, broad wings to catch the air like a hang glider, while a smaller speedster has narrower, tapering wings for sprints, like a jet fighter. On the wings, every feather is slightly curved to help generate lift. Feathers are made of keratin. Each has a central shaft (rachis) with strands (barbs) radiating from it that have hooked barbules that hold the feathers together. Birds preen their feathers to keep them smooth and glossy, and to press the barbs close together to reduce air resistance. Flapping the wings on powerful chest muscles allows birds to go faster and change height very quickly—great for hunting and escaping.

BONES AND BEAKS

Birds can twist and turn in midair partly because their bodies are so light. Unlike humans, their bones are hollow like a straw, but strengthened by struts that hold them together. Birds cannot use their wings to pick up anything. Some use their feet but all of them use their beak to grab food and rip it up into small pieces, as they have no teeth. Some beaks, such as that of the toucan, look big but inside they are like a honeycomb, strong and light like the bones.

Californian quail

FLIGHTLESS BIRDS
LIFE ON THE GROUND

Flying takes up lots of energy and requires strong, powerful wings. Some birds adapted to life on the ground and became flightless. This happened on some oceanic islands where there were few predators and they found plenty of food on the ground or in water. These birds have become large and heavy, with thick, strong legs or flippers.

Keeping warm
A dense double layer of feathers and large fat reserves conserve body heat.

EMPEROR PENGUIN
APTENODYTES FORSTERI

The largest of 18 penguin species, this bird lives in one of the harshest environments on Earth—Antarctica and the freezing waters around that continent. Winter temperatures on the open ice can fall below –40°F (–40°C), yet the emperor penguin has adapted to be able to breed and raise young in these conditions.

Scientific name:
Aptenodytes forsteri

Common names: n/a

Group name: colony, waddle, rookery, penguinery

Size: up to 4.3 ft (1.3 m) in height

Weight: up to 88 lbs (40 kg)

Diet: fish, squid, and krill

Lifespan in wild: up to 20 years

Location: Antarctica and Southern Ocean

Marching in line
As winter approaches, emperors waddle to their breeding ground. The males huddle for warmth, incubating the eggs on their feet. The females head for the sea to find food that they bring back to feed the newly hatched chicks.

Survival
The emperor penguin recycles its own body heat. Its blood is pre-cooled on the way to its feet, wings, and bill, and warmed on the way back to the heart.

Raising young
The chick feeds on fish that is regurgitated by its mother.

HUMBOLDT PENGUIN
SPHENISCUS HUMBOLDTI

These banded penguins are found along the coasts of Chile and Peru in South America. They take their name from the chilly Humboldt current that flows there.

On land and at sea
Humboldt penguins are excellent swimmers as well as climbers, jumping over the rocks they live on and using their flippers to balance. They have spots on their bellies that are unique, like fingerprints.

OSTRICH
STRUTHIO CAMELUS

This is the largest bird of all and the fastest creature on two legs. It is the only bird with two toes, which, together with powerful legs and flexible knees, contribute to its running speed. Ostriches mainly eat seeds and fruit, but also snap up insects and plants.

Hatching out
Ostrich eggs are the largest on Earth at up to 8 ins (20 cm) long. When the eggs hatch, the male takes charge of up to 12 chicks.

Getting out of trouble
The 9-ft- (2.8-m-) tall ostrich can run at speeds of up to 45 mph (70 km/h) on the African plains to avoid predators such as cheetahs or hyenas. It can also kick out its feet, using its sharp claws as weapons.

NORTH ISLAND BROWN KIWI
APTERYX MANTELLI

A forager for worms, larvae, spiders, and weta by night, this kiwi rests in a burrow or hollow log by day. It lives in New Zealand's forests and lays the second-largest egg for its body size of any bird. A water-resistant hairlike coat covers its body.

Sensitive nose
When searching for food, the kiwi walks along slowly, tapping the ground with its long bill. When it finds prey such as small invertebrates and larvae, it probes for them in the leaf litter.

TAKAHE
PORPHYRIO HOCHSTETTERI

The takehe of New Zealand was thought to have become extinct in the 1800s, but was rediscovered in the Murchison Mountains of South Island in 1948. It is the largest rail in the world, and is protected. The birds live in pairs or family groups.

Long-legged waterbird
This freshwater bird grows to around 2 ft (0.6 m) long and feed on seeds that it strips from grasses, holding the tussocks down with its flexible feet.

SOUTHERN CASSOWARRY
CASUARIUS CASUARIUS

These 6.5-ft- (2-m-) tall, solitary birds live in the rain forests of Papua New Guinea and northern Australia. They are important for the survival of the rain forests because they help spread seeds in their dung. They use dagger-shaped claws to scratch and fight other birds.

Large casque on top of head

Sharp claws for fighting

Distinctive plumage
The adult bird is brightly colored, with a vivid blue neck and long, drooping red wattles. The bony casque on top of its head is spongy inside, possibly acting as a hearing aid to pick up vibrating noises from other cassowaries, or maybe protecting the bird's head from the rain forest thickets.

INACCESSIBLE ISLAND RAIL
ATLANTISIA ROGERSI

Around 8,400 of the world's smallest flightless birds are only found on the 6 sq. miles (16 sq. km) of Inaccessible Island in the south Atlantic Ocean.

Inaccessible bird
The rail shelters and breeds in tunnels on the island. It eats worms, beetles, moths, other insects and insect larvae, as well as berries and seeds.

DIVERS, GREBES, AND PETRELS

WATERY ACROBATS

Divers and grebes have webbed feet on legs set far back on the body so they can dive below the surface of rivers and lakes. Their petrel relatives soar across the seas and use their wings to swim underwater. They are all superbly adapted to watery worlds.

GREAT CRESTED GREBE

PODICEPS CRISTATUS

This diving freshwater bird with its ornate head plumes is found in lakes and reservoirs across Europe and Asia. It feeds on small fish and invertebrates.

Elaborate moves
The courtship dance of the great crested grebe is a beautiful display of head bobbing and coordinated moves that lasts for several hours.

WANDERING ALBATROSS

DIOMEDEA EXULANS

This efficient flier glides over the oceans with hardly a beat of its wings. It spends six or more years airborne and can travel 10,000 miles (16,000 km) in a single journey. It has the largest wingspan at 11.8 ft (3.6 m).

Narrow, long wings

Mating for life

Family life
Albatrosses come to land to breed. Both parents incubate the single egg that is laid in a mound of grasses and moss, and the chicks do not fly until they are a year old.

SOOTY SHEARWATER

ARDENNA GRISEA

These common seabirds breed in huge colonies, nesting in burrows on rocky islands off Australia and South America.

Long migration
After summer breeding in the southern hemisphere, this bird migrates to the far north of the Atlantic and Pacific oceans to feed on fish, squid, and crustaceans.

PELICANS AND RELATIVES

HUNTERS OF FISH

These birds all hunt fish, but use different methods. Most of them live at sea, spending much of their time on the wing. Pelicans, darters, and cormorants are also found on lakes inland. They are all strong fliers, but many find it difficult to move about on land. Pelicans, cormorants, gannets (*see pp. 82–83*), and frigate birds are the only birds with webbing between all four toes, making them super-swimmers.

Booby with egg

Easy to spot
This bird is named for its feet, which become a brighter blue when the males are courting. They use a high-stepping strut to show off the feet.

Male courting

Bird colony
These birds nest on land. They lay the eggs on bare rocks and keep the eggs and young warm with their feet.

BLUE-FOOTED BOOBY

SULA NEBOUXI

The blue-footed booby catches its fish prey by plunge-diving. They search for shoals of fish off the western coasts of Central and South America, often in large groups of up to 200 birds.

GREAT CORMORANT
PHALACROCORAX CARBO

Great cormorants are a familiar sight on rocky shorelines standing with their wings spread out wide to dry. These birds are found by rivers and near coasts in the northern Atlantic, Africa, Eurasia, and Australasia.

Underwater chase
Cormorants pursue their prey underwater, pushing themselves along with their feet and staying submerged for up to a minute.

DALMATIAN PELICAN
PELECANUS CRISPUS

Found in shallow lakes across Eurasia, this bird is the largest in the pelican family, with a wingspan of more than 11 ft (3.4 m).

Distinctive features
The pelican has curly feathers on its head and gray legs. In the breeding season, its bill and the skin pouch are bright red.

BROWN PELICAN
PELECANUS OCCIDENTALIS

These pelicans of the Americas fly low over coastal waves in line, all flapping or gliding at the same time. When they spot a shoal of fish, they dive into the water together, surfacing with food in their bills. They then drain water out of their pouches and swallow the fish whole.

Non-breeding adult

Living together
Brown pelicans nest in colonies in trees or on rocky ground, and the young can fly around 12 weeks after they hatch. In flight, like the other pelicans, brown pelicans fold their long necks back on their bodies.

Dark-headed immature bird

FRIGATE BIRD
FREGATA MAGNIFICENS

This pirate of the air steals food from other birds! It harasses its target until it regurgitates its catch, then snatches the food in midair. The frigatebird is not waterproof so it glides for days at a time and rarely lands on water.

Identification
This young bird soars effortlessly on its long wings, using its forked tail to steer. Juvenile frigatebirds have white heads and breasts; adult males are mostly black.

Fish-eating tool
The bird grabs prey from the water with its hooked beak.

Throat pouch
This is inflated during the breeding season, to attract females.

Scientific name: *Fregata magnificens*

Common names: pirate, frigate pelican

Group name: fleet, flotilla

Size: up to 45 ins (114 cm) long; wingspan of up to 96 ins (244 cm)

Weight: up to 4.2 lbs (1.9 kg)

Diet: fish, jellyfish, hatchling turtles, crustaceans, eggs

Lifespan in wild: up to 20 years

Location: coastlines of the eastern Pacific and Atlantic oceans

Bright display
The male perches with its red throat pouch inflated like a balloon and calls to females flying overhead. The females choose mates and then build nests.

ORIENTAL DARTER
ANHINGA MELANOGASTER

Darters, or snakebirds, live in lakes and swamps in southern and southeast Asia. They often swim with only their neck and head visible. They impale fish underwater, before flicking them into the air and swallowing them whole.

Rapid force
This cormorant-like species has a very long neck, which can be flexed and "darted" forward to stab fish. The birds often gather in flocks of up to 100 birds, but will stab at other birds when nesting.

Plunge-diving gannets

These gannets are diving for mackerel, hitting the water at up to 60 mph (100 km/h). This plunge-diving by "companies" of the largest seabirds in the North Atlantic does not harm the birds because their head shape reduces the drag, and they contract their muscles to straighten their S-shaped necks before impact. Once underwater they "fly" along, using their wings to propel themselves toward their prey. They often swallow the fish before they resurface. This prevents other seabirds such as great skuas from stealing the food.

HERONS AND RELATIVES
WATER WADERS

These birds mostly feed in shallow waters, and have long legs for wading and extended necks to search for food. Herons' necks are in an S-shape that works like a spring to launch a dagger-like beak. Flamingo beaks curve down, and stork beaks are pointed for stabbing.

Filtered food
To feed, flamingos sweep their bills through the water, filtering out crustaceans, mollusks, plankton, crabs, fish, and larvae.

GREATER FLAMINGO
PHOENICOPTERUS ROSEUS

This African species is the largest and most widespread of the family. Flamingos are the only birds that filter-feed, dipping their beaks upside down and pumping the water through slits in the beak and tongue.

In a crowd
The greater flamingo feeds in shallow lakes, in flocks that sometimes number more than one million.

Lake Natron, Tanzania

Lake Nakuru, Kenya

Colorful feathers
Carotenoid pigments in the algae and the crustaceans the bird eats turn its feathers pink.

Scientific name:
Phoenicopterus roseus

Group name: flamboyance, stand

Size: up to 5 ft (1.5 m) height; up to 5.5 ft (1.7 m) wingspan

Weight: up to 9 lbs (4 kg)

Diet: invertebrates, fish, worms, insects, plankton

Lifespan in wild: up to 50 years

Location: Africa, Middle East, India, southern Europe, Asia, Central America, Caribbean

Pink legs
The long legs and web feet stir up tiny fish and larvae from the lake bed.

GRAY HERON
ARDEA CINEREA

A tall bird, the gray heron can be found across Europe, Africa, and Asia. The male and female build a nest high in a tree where the eggs are safe from predators, and then share the care of the chicks.

Hunting heron
Herons catch their prey by stealth, standing stock-still in the water until a fish or frog gets close. Then they flick out their S-shaped necks and stab the animals with their long, daggerlike beaks.

Heron with fish prey

Long-legged hunter

MARABOU STORK
LEPTOPTILOS CRUMENIFER

This stork acts just like a vulture. It soars over the African grasslands looking for dead animals to scavenge. It has wings that are only slightly smaller than those of the condor.

Land bird
On the ground, the stork stands with its body hunched and its fleshy pink pouch hanging from its neck. Marabous build large nests in the treetops.

SCARLET IBIS
EUDOCIMUS RUBER

The scarlet ibis lives and breeds in very large colonies in the swamps and shallow bays of northern South America. It is the national bird of Trinidad and Tobago.

Bright color
Like flamingos, the red color of the bird's feathers comes from the carotenoids in the crustaceans it eats.

Long beak acts as probe

Mating display

WATERFOWL

EQUIPPED FOR WATER

Waterfowl are brilliantly adapted to live in and near water. They have long necks; wide, webbed feet; flat beaks; and oily, waterproof feathers sitting over soft down that keeps their skin extra warm. Their legs are ideal for both walking and swimming, and they have short, powerful wings that are perfect for quick takeoffs and to keep them in the air—these birds are top fliers.

MANDARIN DUCK

AIX GALERICULATA

This beautiful duck is a native of China and Japan. The drake's amazing plumage in the mating season has made it a favorite in oriental art. Mandarins live in rivers and lakes in forests, and nest in holes up to 30 ft (9 m) up in trees. Clutch sizes vary from nine to twelve white, oval eggs.

Diet
In the summer, the duck feeds on frogs, mollusks, small snakes, water plants, worms, and fish. In winter, it eats mainly rice and other grains.

Contrasting pair
As with many birds, there is a big difference in coloration between the male and female mandarin. The male has a bright red beak and orange wing feathers, while the female is a dull brown.

BLACK SWAN

CYGNUS ATRATUS

The black swan is the state bird of western Australia, although it has been introduced to many other countries. It pairs for life and is sociable, living in large flocks that may be thousands strong.

All-black bird
This large waterbird searches for algae and weeds to eat by plunging its head underwater in shallow wetlands. It is all black except for broad white wingtips, which can be seen in flight.

SNOW GOOSE

ANSER CAERULESCENS

This goose breeds in the Arctic tundra of Siberia, Greenland, and North America. In spring, flocks migrate in large numbers south to warmer areas.

V-shaped flight

White variant

Color forms
Snow geese have two different color forms. Most are white all over, apart from black wingtips (left), but some are are white-headed with a blue-gray body.

MALLARD

ANAS PLATYRHYNCHOS

The mallard duck is probably the world's most common duck. It dabbles for insects, seeds, and aquatic plants on the surface of ponds, rivers, and lakes worldwide, sometimes tipping up on end to reach them underwater.

Coloration
The bold plumage colors of green head and curly tail belong to the males of this species. The females are mostly brown with an orange bill.

Stocky bird
The eider's wedge-shaped bill is used to forage for mollusks and crabs on rocky coasts. The males are black and white, while the females are brown.

EIDER DUCK

SOMATERIA MOLLISSIMA

These sea ducks need good plumage because they breed farther north than other birds. Eiders nest on the ground, lining their nests with "eider down," which we used to fill pillows and quilts.

COMMON MERGANSER

MERGUS MERGANSER

The common merganser, or goosander, is a large fish-eating duck found in lakes and rivers across Europe, Asia, and North America. It may nest in holes in trees.

Care of young
Females look after their young for several weeks after hatching, often carrying chicks on their backs.

BIRDS OF PREY

KILLERS OF THE SKIES

Birds of prey are also called raptors from the Greek word meaning "to seize," because they grab smaller animals, sometimes in midair, then rip them into pieces small enough to swallow. Raptors fly and glide on wide wings, seeking prey with eyes so big that there is no room for muscles—raptors have to turn their heads to look around. Then they dive and grab with strong feet, using knife-sharp talons to finish the job.

Broad wings
With a giant wingspan of 7.2 ft (2.2 m), these huge powerful wings are folded into the sides of the body when the bird dives on prey.

GOLDEN EAGLE

AQUILA CHRYSAETOS

The most widely found eagle, this bird soars high on air currents above open moorland and mountains, using its excellent eyesight to spot prey. Golden eagles are swift fliers, diving at up to 200 mph (320 km/h).

Scientific name: *Aquila chrysaetos*

Common names: American gold eagle

Group names: convocation, congregation

Size: up to 3.3 ft (1 m) length; up to 7.5 ft (2.3 m) wingspan

Weight: up to 15 lbs (7 kg)

Diet: birds, mammals, carrion

Lifespan in wild: up to 25 years

Location: Europe, northern Africa, Asia, North America

Nest-building
Eagle pairs build large nests, or eyries, out of sticks on cliffs or trees, or on tall, built structures such as towers. They add to the nests each year, and some are huge—one was a record 20 ft (6 m) tall and 8.5 ft (2.3 m) wide.

Sharp talons
These are the golden eagle's real weapons—it uses its hooked beak to eat when it has made a kill.

Good appetite
Golden eagles hunt for birds and mammals such as rabbits and marmots. They will take larger mammals such as deer or lambs, and eat carrion when they find it.

MONKEY-EATING EAGLE

PITHECOPHAGA JEFFERYI

The Philippine monkey-eating eagle is named for its favorite food, and it particularly likes macaques. It is one of the world's largest and most powerful birds of prey.

Fierce hunter
This raptor is more than 3 ft (1 m) tall and has a headdress of spiky feathers. As well as monkeys, it preys on rodents, bats, wild pigs, and monitor lizards.

SNAIL KITE

ROSTRHAMUS SOCIABILIS

Also known as the Everglades kite, this bird of prey feeds almost entirely on one kind of freshwater snail—the apple snail. It hunts by gliding slowly and low down over marshes and reed beds.

One of a kind
The kite perches, holding the snail shell with one foot. The long curved beak is ideal for prizing the snail out of its shell. When this treat is not available, the kite will eat small turtles, rodents, or crabs.

Snail kite with apple snail

With snail prey on a fence

OSPREY
PANDION HALIAETUS

This fish hawk is found on lakes, rivers, and coastlines worldwide. It hovers over water before plunging in feetfirst to snatch up fish in its talons. It flies away, carrying the fish headfirst in both feet. Ospreys will also eat small mammals, birds, or reptiles.

High nesting site
The osprey's nest is impressively large. Pairs nest close to freshwater lakes, putting together a bulky pile of sticks that they line with other found materials. They may build on this for many years.

HEN HARRIER
CIRCUS CYANEUS

Keen-eyed hunter
Harriers hunt by flying low forward and backward over an area of ground. They are searching for small mammals such as mice, or small birds such as meadow pipits.

Hen harriers live in open areas such as farmland, heathland, and river valleys in North America, Europe, and northern Asia. The males are famous for their courtship "sky dancing."

NORTHERN GOSHAWK
ACCIPITER GENTILIS

Shades of gray
Short, broad wings and a long tail give this gray-colored hawk great agility in the air.

This is a large hawk found across North America, and northern Europe and Asia. It is a fierce hunter that targets prey with its piercing orange eyes, homing in on wood pigeons, gamebirds, and rabbits with lightning speed. It will even attack people if they get too close to its nesting site.

RED KITE
MILVUS MILVUS

Easy to spot in the sky because of its forked tail and fingerlike wingtips, the red kite is one of the most beautiful birds of prey. It mates for life and pairs make their nests of sticks lined with sheep's wool high up in the fork of a tree.

Red kite in flight

Great hunter
The kite soars high above farmland using its sharp eyesight to search out mammals including voles and mice, and carrion such as sheep carcasses.

Up to 100 birds in one roost

AFRICAN FISH EAGLE
HALIAEETUS VOCIFER

As its name suggests, this raptor feeds mainly on fish, but will also prey on flamingos and other water birds. Found throughout Africa south of the Sahara, its call is referred to as "the voice of Africa."

In for the kill
The bird of prey sits high in vegetation by the side of a river, by a lake, or along the coast. When it sees movement in the water, it swoops down, carrying the fish back to its perch to eat.

Elegant bird
The red kite is a rare, medium-sized bird of prey with a wingspan of up to 80 ins (200 cm). It is found in woodlands and valleys throughout Europe and northwest Africa.

COMMON BUZZARD

BUTEO BUTEO

You often hear this bird's mewling call before you spot it circling in thermals near hills and cliffs throughout Europe, Asia, and parts of Africa.

Easy to spot
The bird often holds its broad, rounded wings in a v-shape when gliding or soaring. Buzzards vary in color, but they all have dark wingtips and a barred tail.

PEREGRINE FALCON

FALCO PEREGRINUS

With a diving speed of about 186 mph (300 km/h) the peregrine is the world's fastest bird. It attacks birds such as pigeons in midair, slashing them with its talons, then following them to the ground.

Peregrine "stooping" with folded wings

Aerial predator
This large falcon has dark, slate-gray plumage with white below, and black bars. It is found above sea cliffs or perched on tall buildings in cities.

Slender-bodied bird

SECRETARY BIRD

SAGITTARIUS SERPENTARIUS

Looking more like a crane than a bird of prey, this unusual bird has long legs and an extraordinary crest of feathers on its head. The latter look like the quill pens that human secretaries used in the 19th century. The bird is native to Africa south of the Sahara Desert.

Scientific name:
Sagittarius serpentarius

Common names: n/a

Size: up to 4.5 ft (1.3 m) height; up to 6.8 ft (2.1 m) wingspan

Weight: up to 9.5 lbs (4.3 kg)

Diet: snakes, frogs, lizards, rodents

Lifespan in wild: up to 15 years

Location: Africa south of the Sahara

Ground hunter
The secretary bird spends much of its time on the ground, searching for frogs, lizards, rodents, and snakes. It will often stamp its prey to death, then swallow it whole. When it attacks venomous snakes, it flaps its wings to distract the prey. It nests high in trees, usually thorny acacias.

Tough fighters
Secretary birds will fight each other to establish territory, during courtship, or to defend a nest. They also fight with each other and other birds over prey.

Headdress
The crest of long feathers are raised when the bird is excited.

Strong wings
The large, broad wings help this bird to soar in thermals.

Partially feathered
The long legs are only covered with feathers halfway down, so the bird looks like it is wearing short trousers!

GYRFALCON
FALCO RUSTICOLUS

This Arctic species is the largest of the around 50 species of falcon. It breeds on the tundra, hunting low to the ground in open country for ptarmigan and other birds. It also preys on hares and rodents.

Different colors
The coloring of these birds varies greatly. Some are white—useful in the snowy north—while others are gray or dark brown. The adult gyrfalcons have heavy barring on the back, wings, and tail.

The **Andean condor** has an **impressive** wingspan of **10.5 ft (3.2 m)**.

Andean condor hunting

The high life
The Andean condor lives high in the Andes mountains, gliding with little effort while looking for carrion. It nests on bare rocky cliffs or ledges, laying one or two eggs at a time.

ANDEAN CONDOR
VULTUR GRYPHUS

This South American bird is the largest vulture in the world and among the heaviest of all birds. It can reach 33 lbs (15 kg) and stand 4 ft (1.2 m) tall. It scavenges for dead animals, but also raids other birds' nests for eggs and hatchlings.

Bald head and neck with feathered collar

COMMON KESTREL
FALCO TINNUNCULUS

A small falcon that hunts rodents and insects, the kestrel is a familiar sight hovering above the verges of roads or farmers' fields, a master of stationary flight.

In the woods
Kestrels hunt for small mammals such as mice and voles. They nest in holes in trees, with both parents looking after the four or five chicks until they fledge.

LAMMERGEIER
GYPAETUS BARBATUS

Unlike other vultures, the lammergeier has feathers on its head and neck. They live in the high mountains of southern Europe, Africa, and central Asia, and specialize in digesting bones.

No waste
Known as the bearded vulture because of the dark feathers around its beak, this bird knows how to get everything from a tough carcass. As well as eating the skin, it drops bones from a height to break them, so that it can eat the marrow inside.

WHITE-BACKED VULTURE
GYPS AFRICANUS

The most common of Africa's vultures, the white-backed is adept at scavenging. They circle for hours watching for prey. Their bare heads and necks mean they can reach inside prey without feathers matting in the blood.

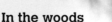

A feast for many
These vultures feed on the soft parts of large carrion—an elephant carcass can attract up to 1,000 birds to feast on it. There is a strict pecking order—larger birds with strong beaks feed first.

Marked presence
These giant birds grow up to 4 ft (1.2 m) in height and have a wingspan of 9 ft (2.7 m). Their territory size is enormous, up to 155 sq. miles (400 sq. km) in which a pair will live and breed.

Eagle-eyed predator

The bald eagle has a very sharp and wide field of vision, so can spot prey from a great height. It is also very fast, pulling in its wings and diving at up to 100 mph (160 km/h). It hunts mainly fish, but also ducks and other waterbirds in both fresh and salt water. It swoops feetfirst, sometimes striking and stunning the prey before snatching it up. It is also a scavenger, stealing food from other eagles or birds of prey, and eating any carrion that it finds.

BALD EAGLE
HALIAEETUS LEUCOCEPHALUS

The bald eagle is so called because its name is derived from "piebald," an old English word that means "white-headed." It is one of the largest of all raptors and soars with stretched-out wings and slow wingbeats in the skies over North America. In the 1970s, there were only 500 nesting pairs in 48 states—the birds had been destroyed by hunting and the use of pesticides during most of the 20th century. However, this is a conservation success story. Today there are at least 9,789 nesting pairs in 48 states, and around 70,000 birds in North America.

Scientific name: *Haliaeetus leucocephalus*

Group names: congregation, convocation

Size: up to 3.6 ft (1.1 m) long

Weight: up to 14 lbs (6.4 kg)

Diet: fish and waterfowl, carrion

Lifespan in wild: up to 30 years

Location: North America, from Alaska and Canada to Mexico

Chick and egg in nest

Mother feeding older chicks

Family living
Bald eagles usually mate for life. They take it in turns to sit on their eggs and feed the young. Their large nests are 6 ft (1.8 m) across and 4 ft (1.2 m) tall, and weigh up to a ton.

Majestic symbol
On June 20, 1782, the bald eagle was chosen as the national emblem of the United States. It is a powerful symbol representing freedom and strength. The bird has also appeared on various coins, including gold coins dubbed the eagle, half eagle, quarter eagle, and double eagle.

The **wingspan** of a **female bald eagle** can be up to **8 ft (2.4 m)**.

Worn with pride
To many Native American peoples, the feathers of this bird are symbolic of many things, including honor, trust, wisdom, and freedom. For centuries, they have proudly worn the feathers in their headdresses.

Sharp beak
The hooked beak is used to tear at food and for preening.

Distinctive features
Juvenile bald eagles have brown feathers mottled with white. It takes about five years for them to develop black and white adult plumage. They have a very odd call that is a series of high-pitched whistling notes.

Flying power
The wings are long, broad, and streamlined, perfect for soaring and gliding.

Lightweight bones
Eagle bones are light because they are hollow—the entire skeleton of a bald eagle only weighs 9.5 oz (270 grams).

Fishing for food
The bald eagle takes fish near the surface, only immersing its feet and legs, and carries it to a perch. It can eat 1 lb (0.45 kg) of fish in only four minutes, holding its prey with one talon and tearing off chunks with its hooked beak.

Killing tools
The sharp talons are used for hunting and killing prey, as well as for defense.

GAMEBIRDS
GROUND-NESTING BIRDS

These birds have plump bodies, short wings, and strong legs that sometimes have a sharp spur. They nest on the ground, where they feed mostly on seeds, insects, and berries, so they need short, heavy-duty beaks. The more than 290 species are not called gamebirds because they love to play—the word describes the fact that for hundreds of years people have enjoyed hunting these birds for food or for sport.

Bright color
The blue peafowl male has stunning metallic blue head and chest feathers.

BLUE PEAFOWL
PAVO CRISTATUS

One of the most spectacular birds, the male peafowl, a native of Asian forests, does not begin to grow its magnificent tail until it is three years old. Peafowls are ground feeders, searching forest floors for insects, small mammals, seeds, and wild fruit.

Razzle-dazzle
The peacock's tail is a real statement at more than 60 percent of its total body length. It fans and vibrates the tail when it is courting the peahen.

Broad wings
This is one of the largest and heaviest flying birds but cannot stay airborne for long.

Scientific name: *Pavo cristatus*

Common names: Indian peafowl, peacock

Group name: muster, bevy, ostentation, pride, party

Size: up to 5 ft (1.5 m) long including train

Weight: up to 13 lbs (6 kg)

Diet: omnivore

Lifespan in wild: up to 20 years

Location: India, Sri Lanka

Contrasting
The brilliant iridescent green-and-blue colors and long tail of the peacock contrast vividly with the brown-and-white colors and short tail of the peahen. The male's tail feathers are tipped with an "eye."

RED GROUSE
LAGOPUS LAGOPUS

The red grouse's habitat is the high moorlands, where it is easily camouflaged against the heather. If startled, it will suddenly leave the ground with distinctive whirring wingbeats. It is in danger from habitat loss and hunting.

Bird of the heather
This northern British plump-bodied bird is about the size of a small hen. It has a hook-tipped beak that is perfect for eating the shoots, seeds, and flowers of the heather.

WILD TURKEY
MELEAGRIS GALLOPAVO

Wild turkeys will travel a mile or more each day to find food, scratching for seeds and bugs in leaf litter. These North American birds are great communicators, with 28 distinct calls. They eat anything they find, from acorns and seeds to insects and lizards, in daytime. At night, they roost in trees.

Turkey names
The male wild turkey with his red wattle and beard hanging from his chin (below) is called a "tom" or "gobbler," while the female is a "hen."

Dancing style
The male fans the 18 feathers that make up his tail, throws his head back, drags his wings on the ground, and struts to attract a mate.

CRANES AND RELATIVES

LONG-LEGGED WATERBIRDS

Cranes, like many of their relatives, have long neck and legs, and long wings on which they soar and glide so expertly. This group of birds mostly live near water or marshy ground. When they fly, their necks are held out straight and their legs usually trail behind them.

Family life
Japanese cranes mate for life, bonding with a synchronized courtship dance. From a clutch of two eggs, one chick is usually reared successfully.

JAPANESE CRANE

GRUS JAPONENSIS

In Japan, this bird is known as the bird of happiness and long life, fabled to live for 1,000 years. It is up to 5 ft (1.5 m) tall with a wingspan of 8 ft (2.5 m). It forages in fields, rivers, and rice paddies for animals and plants.

GREAT BUSTARD

OTIS TARDA

This Eurasian bird is one of the heaviest flying animals, at up to 46 lb (21 kg). It roams open plains, feeding on plants and insects.

Male displaying

Feathered display
The male attracts a female by flipping its tail over onto its back, so the head is hidden.

Female great bustard

Adult and chick
Coots build nests of reeds and grasses in shallow water or on tree stumps. The chicks have red faces, and orange down is scattered around their heads.

COMMON COOT

FULICA ATRA

A freshwater bird of Eurasia, Africa, and Australia, the coot has a white beak and black plumage. It dives for the plants and animals it eats.

WADERS

SHOREBIRDS

These birds inhabit beaches, wetlands, lagoons, rocky shores, and mudflats. Here they find the mollusks, worms, and other small creatures that they eat—their bills may be short or long and pointed, depending on their diet. As the seasons change, most of these shorebirds gather in large flocks to migrate between the Arctic, Europe, South America, Asia, and Australia.

PIED AVOCET

RECURVIROSTRA AVOSETTA

This bird walks steadily through shallow water, searching for small animals and plants with its long, sensitive beak. It lives on lagoons and lakes, on salt-pans, and in estuaries, and nests in large colonies on muddy islands.

Food finder
The unique sharply upturned beak is swept from side to side just below the water's surface to find food.

In the thousands
These birds migrate to find warmer weather in Africa and southern Asia. In winter, tens of thousands gather on some lakes in east Africa.

Floating lifestyle
African jacanas live on lagoons, and in swamps and marshes with a lot of floating vegetation. They mainly eat insects, but will also hunt crabs, snails, and small fish.

AFRICAN JACANA

ACTOPHILORNIS AFRICANUS

This wader has very long toes and claws that help spread its weight as it hops and flutters across the water's surface, using lilypads and leaves as stepping-stones. It is a good diver and strong flier.

Wildebeest

Every year, during the "Great Migration," more than two million wildebeests, zebras, and gazelles move across the Serengeti and Masai Mara in Africa to find green pasture. The pattern of their movement is dependent on and triggered by the rainfall in the area. Here they are crossing the Mara River between Tanzania and Kenya.

MIGRATION

When a habitat gets too hot, cold, wet, or dry, animals must move on or die. Some travelers follow the sun's warmth, others track the green growth spurred by the rain. Their journeys are usually round trips and are called migration. This might be a short pond-to-pond hop for frogs, or a trek from pole to pole for the Arctic tern. Many of these trips are to breed, but some are just because the food is better elsewhere!

Arctic tern in flight

Monarch butterfly
In North America, some of these butterflies travel more than 3,000 miles (4,800 km) between winter quarters in Mexico and their breeding grounds in Canada. The journey there and back takes so long that no one butterfly completes the round trip.

Congregating en route

Monarch butterfly

Bar-headed goose
Some of these birds have been recorded at more than 23,000 ft (7,000 m) in their flight across the Himalayas – some have even been seen flying over Everest, at more than 29,000 ft (8,840 m)! Bar-headed geese live in India, Mongolia, and areas of west and central China. Many travel over the Himalayas to migrate between their breeding grounds in Tibet and their winter sites in India.

Bar-headed geese in formation

Arctic tern
The longest of all bird migrations is the 50,000-mile (80,000-km) round-trip marathon of the tiny Arctic tern from the top to the bottom of our planet. It breeds north of the Arctic Circle, then flies south to Antarctica, where it is able to use the long daylight hours to feed.

Humpback whales feeding

Caribbean spiny lobster
Once a year, Caribbean spiny lobsters line up and move in single file across the ocean floor in their march offshore to reach deeper water. This process is called queuing, and is thought to be triggered by autumn storms. Each lobster rests its long antennae over the shell of the lobster in front, and the queue moves to waters up to 100 ft (30 m) deep.

Lobsters following one another

Adélie penguin
Every year, these penguins move 8,000 miles (13,000 km) from Antarctica to warmer winter sites and back again. The Adélie are the smallest penguin in the Antarctic but they breed only on the continent's coast or on islands nearby. They undertake the long journey to northern pack ice to find the krill, mollusks, squid, and small fish that they take from the ocean.

Adélie penguins on pack ice

Humpback whale
One of the longest migrations by a mammal is that of the humpback whale. It travels more than 5,000 miles (8,000 km) from its warm breeding ground near the equator to the colder, krill-rich waters of the Arctic and Antarctic.

Humpback whales eat a **daily** diet of **1.5 tons** of **krill.**

SKUAS, GULLS, AND PUFFINS

BIRDS OF SEA AND LAND

Some gulls follow fishing boats at sea or whirl above fields, always on the lookout for an easy meal. Skuas take the scavenging a step further and raid other birds' nests for eggs and chicks. Terns stay in the air as they migrate huge distances to find food, while puffins prefer the seas as they are skilled swimmers and fliers.

HERRING GULL
LARUS ARGENTATUS

The ultimate scavengers, these large, noisy gulls are seen in seaside towns, and inland above garbage dumps or circling round tractors on farms. They hunt food both at sea and on land, and nest on clifftops, rooftops, or islands.

Color prompt
The herring gull's hooked beak has a red spot on the underside that acts as a prompt to the bird's chicks. The young birds react by pecking at it, causing the parent to regurgitate a meal for them.

Great travelers
Skuas live most of their lives at sea. They have an impressively long migration, breeding in the far north and wintering in the far south.

ARCTIC SKUA
STERCORARIUS PARASITICUS

This fierce pirate bird gets most of its food by chasing other seabirds such as puffins to make them drop fish. The skua will also eat dead birds and mammals, and eggs.

ATLANTIC PUFFIN
FRATERCULA ARCTICA

These small seabirds are often called "sea parrots" or "clowns of the sea" because of their brightly colored beaks and red feet. They live at sea, and can dive to depths of 200 ft (60 m) in pursuit of fish.

Scientific name:
Fratercula arctica

Common names: common puffin

Group name: colony, circus, puffinry, improbablity

Size: up to 10 ins (18 cm) height

Weight: up to 18 oz (500 g)

Diet: small fish

Lifespan in wild: up to 20 years

Location:
North Atlantic

Great fliers
Puffins reach spceds of 55 mph (88 km/h).

Bright color
The puffin sheds the colorful outer part of the beak after the breeding season.

Skilled fishers
Puffins catch up to 12 fish on each fishing trip. Waterproof feathers keep them warm as they "fly" underwater, flapping their wings and steering with the feet.

Nesting in high places
Puffins only land to mate and nest on cliff ledges or in burrows that they dig in the short grass at the tops of the cliffs. They mate for life and lay only one egg at a time.

KITTIWAKE
RISSA TRIDACTYLA

Named for their call, these medium-sized gulls live in large colonies near Pacific and Atlantic coasts in summer, and spend the winter months out at sea, looking for fish, shrimps, and invertebrates to eat.

Precarious perch
Kittiwakes nest together, sometimes thousands of them, on steep coastal rock ledges and clifftops. Many parents are established pairs that share the raising of the chicks. The chicks instinctively sit very still in their nests so they do not fall off.

PIGEONS AND DOVES

WILD STREET BIRDS

Two things make pigeons and doves different from other birds—they can suck up water without raising their heads, and they feed their young on a milky liquid made in their throats. Both have small heads that bob up and down on their thick necks as they walk.

ROCK DOVE

COLUMBA LIVIA

This is the wild ancestor of all the street pigeons. People caught and bred the wild birds for food, and later some escaped, learning how to find food and survive in towns and cities.

Pigeons—a familiar sight in cities

With green-purple neck

Appearance
Rock doves have plump bodies with thick plumage. The color of the feathers varies considerably. The common form has a blue-gray head, but some birds have green-purple iridescence on the neck.

SUPERB FRUIT DOVE

PTILINOPUS SUPERBUS

This colorful bird lives high in the rain forest canopies of northeastern Australia and New Guinea. It feeds on berries and fruit such as figs or palms.

Contrasting colors
The male is brightly colored, with a purple crown, orange feathers around the back of its neck, and a blue-black breastband. The female is green with a gray breast and underparts.

PARROTS

GREAT COMMUNICATORS

These are among the most colorful, noisy, and intelligent of all the birds. They use their hooked beaks for gripping and climbing, and to crunch up shells. Parrots mostly live in warm habitats and are popular pets that can learn to mimic sounds and use tools.

Easily identified
Contrasting with its gray plumage is a bright red tail. Like other large parrots, it has a patch of bare skin around its eyes.

GRAY PARROT

PSITTACUS ERITHACUS

A large bird, the gray parrot lives in forests and mangrove swamps in western and central Africa. It clambers from branch to branch to find seeds, nuts, fruits, and berries. It is expert at copying human speech, and is a popular pet.

SULFUR-CRESTED COCKATOO

CACATUA GALERITA

The best-known Australian parrot, this loud bird with its sulfur-colored quiff has adapted so well to human habitation that it was considered a pest for destroying crops. It is now a protected species.

Family life
These cockatoos eat berries, seeds, nuts, and roots, and nest in eucalyptus tree hollows, where both birds incubate and rear their chicks. They communicate with a distinctive loud screech.

RAINBOW LORIKEET

TRICHOGLOSSUS MOLUCCANUS

Widespread in eastern and northern Australia, these birds feed on nectar and flower pollen, which they lap up with the tips of their tongues. They lay their two or three eggs in a nest of chewed, decayed wood, usually in hollows high up in eucalyptus or palm trees.

Noisy crowd
Both sexes have the same bright coloration and they travel in loud, fast-moving flocks, roosting together at dusk. They inhabit rain forests, woodlands, and towns along the coastline.

RED-AND-GREEN MACAW

ARA CHLOROPTERUS

The red-and-green macaw is as colorful as the rain forests it inhabits in the tropics of northern and central South America. This bird is one of the largest of all the parrots but is under threat from habitat destruction and the pet trade. Like all macaws, it has a powerful beak to crack nuts and seeds, and a dry, scaly tongue that can pull kernels from shells and dig seeds from fruits. It flies well and rarely comes to the ground, preferring the shelter of the trees or the freedom of the skies.

In **lowland areas**, up to **30 red-and-green macaws** can be heard **noisily arguing** among themselves **as they roost**.

Scientific name:
Ara chloropterus

Size: body length of up to 3 ft (95 cm)—the tail adds more than half of this length

Weight: up to 3.8 lbs (1.7 kg)

Diet: fruit and nuts, supplemented by nectar and flower; clay

Lifespan in wild: up to 60 years

Location: northern and central South America

Unique pattern
The pattern of feathers on the bare patch of skin on a macaw's face are as unique as a fingerprint.

Contrasting colors
Brilliant blue and green feathers cover the lower wings.

Flexible toes
Macaws have two toes pointing forward and two pointing backward that they use like hands.

In flight
With broad wings and a wingspan of over 3.6 ft (1.1 m), scarlet macaws can reach speeds of 35 mph (56 km/h). They live in the rain forest canopy and understory, skimming over the treetops, screeching loudly with tails trailing.

One of a kind
As well as crushing nuts and seeds, the macaw uses its beak as a climbing aid. The brilliant red feathers are that color because of a combination of five pigments that are produced only in parrots.

Endangered species
There are around 17 species of macaws, and the red-and-green is among the best known. The destruction of its habitat is the main reason that its numbers are decreasing. Macaws are also caught illegally and sold to breeders because they are in demand as pets.

Tree habitat cut down for building

Aerial shot of deforestation in South America

Nests and chicks
Red-and-green macaws lay 1–4 eggs at a time in holes in trees or cavities in sandstone cliffs. They raise two or three chicks at a time, and the young stay with the parents for up to two years.

Chicks born bald and blind

Pair nesting in a hollow

Mealtime in the rain forest
This is not a very social species and lives in pairs or small family groups, each of which has its own large territory. But this does not prevent the birds gathering regularly to eat clay from riverbank cliffs, often in the company of other types of macaw. Why they do this is a puzzle. Some scientists say the clay acts as an antidote to toxins in their natural diet, which includes unripe fruits containing poisonous chemicals such as tannin and oxalic acid.

OWLS

SILENT AND DEADLY HUNTERS

Wings and tail
The barring on these shows the age and sex of the bird.

A flattened disk-shaped face holds two huge eyes that see even in the dark, while two huge holes in the skull form ears that pick up far-off sounds. Together with soft edges to the feathers that allow most owls to fly silently, these special features make these birds deadly to their prey. Owls are also so highly adaptable that they are able to live on every continent except Antarctica.

Tiny hunter
These owls hunt during both day and night for moles and mice as well as insects, frogs, and reptiles. They store any extras in their burrows until they are needed.

Burrowing owl with rotated head to see back

BURROWING OWL

ATHENE CUNICULARIA

Standing guard at the burrow in daylight

Found throughout the Americas, this tiny owl lives underground in burrows that it digs out, or adopts those of small mammals such as ground squirrels. If threatened it makes a call that sounds like a rattlesnake shaking its tail!

GREAT HORNED OWL

BUBO VIRGINIANUS

This is the largest owl in North America, a powerful bird that can kill birds and mammals larger than itself with its strong claws. Its large eyes provide excellent night vision. It has few enemies but may be injured by large prey, for example porcupines.

Horned appearance
The distinctive feathery tufts, or "horns," on top of this owl's head are not its ears—those are hidden beneath feathers on either side of the broad head.

Nocturnal hunter
Barn owls can find prey by sound alone, and it is normally swallowed whole. The indigestible parts—fur, bones, feathers, teeth etc.—are regurgitated in pellets.

BARN OWL

TYTO ALBA

At dusk, the ghostlike shape of this owl can be seen flapping slowly over open country and marshes as it searches for mice and other small rodents. It is one of the most widespread owls, found in all kinds of habitat on every continent except Antarctica.

It's in the name
This owl's Latin name means "white owl," but its common name, barn owl, comes from the fact that it often nests in old farm buildings. It also lays eggs in tree holes or rocky outcrops, but it does not build a nest.

Well-camouflaged
White feathers flecked with black and gray make it difficult to spot in the snowy Arctic.

Thick coat of feathers
Dense feathering protects the owl, including on its legs and toes. This helps the bird maintain a body temperature of 104°F (40°C) in very cold weather.

Scientific name:
Bubo scandiacus

Common names:
Arctic owl, great white owl

Group name:
parliament, wisdom, study, glaring

Size: up to 2.6 ft (75 cm) height; up to 5.5 ft (1.7 m) wingspan

Weight: up to 5 lbs (2.3 kg)

Diet: omnivore, but mainly eats rodents, birds, small mammals

Lifespan in wild: up to 17 years

Location: Arctic tundra of Alaska, northern Canada, and Eurasia

SNOWY OWL
BUBO SCANDIACUS

Found mainly inside the Arctic Circle, this is one of the largest species of owl. Unlike most owls, it hunts both day and night over the frozen ground. These owls are solitary but may gather in pairs or small groups when they move north to their breeding grounds in spring. They have few predators, but may be killed by Arctic foxes, wolves, and other large birds.

Silent hunter
Snowy owls need to eat at least five lemmings or mice a day, around 2,000 a year. In good lemming years, snowy owls may raise 10 or more chicks in ground nests on ridges or other raised areas.

Gray ghost
This bird is a mottled gray color and has a large facial disk that directs the sounds made by prey into its ears. Its eyes are small to avoid heat loss, and fixed in place to spot prey that is far away.

GREAT GRAY OWL
STRIX NEBULOSA

The largest flying bird across the northern hemisphere, this elusive owl lives in dense evergreen forests. It has a number of different calls, including a hoot, shriek, or wail if it is excited. It has been known to growl and spread its wings when threatened.

ELF OWL
MICRATHENE WHITNEYI

The smallest owl in the world lives in deserts and woods in the southwestern United States and Mexico. It is only about 6 in (15 cm) tall, weighs less than 1.5 oz (43 g), and has a wingspan of 10.5 in (27 cm).

Living space
Elf owls hunt moths, crickets, and spiders at dusk. They also take some lizards and mice and an occasional scorpion, with stinger carefully removed. The owls often roost and nest in woodpecker holes, and in desert regions are found in a saguaro cactus (right).

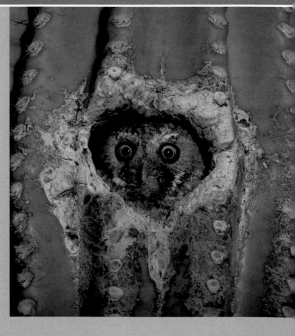

NIGHTJARS AND FROGMOUTHS

BIRDS OF THE NIGHT

These species and their relatives have gray-and-brown coloring to blend in during the day, before emerging big-eyed at night to scoop up insects. However, nightjars nest on the ground and fly up to hunt in midair, while frogmouths live in the trees and move down to feed mostly at ground-level.

TAWNY FROGMOUTH
PODARGUS STRIGOIDES

The tawny frogmouth lives in forests and wooded areas in Australia and Tasmania, and is rare in that it can adjust its temperature to save energy. It hunts at night, catching prey in flight or by sitting motionless to ambush it.

Now you see it!
This extraordinary bird has a great defense if it is threatened by day. It flattens its feathers, points its beak toward the sky, and stays stock-still, looking just like the branch of the tree it is roosting in!

Perfect coloring
The color of the feathers merges brilliantly with this tree's bark.

Frogmouth with chick

Scientific name: *Podargus strigoides*

Size: up to 21 ins (53 cm) height

Weight: up to 1.5 lbs (0.7 kg)

Diet: insects and centipedes, worms, spiders, and frogs

Lifespan in wild: up to 14 years

Location: Australia, Tasmania

Camouflaged tawny frogmouth

COMMON POTOO
NYCTIBIUS GRISEUS

This close relative of nightjars and frogmouths spends its daytime roosting high up in trees in Central and South America. It is also named "poor-me-one" because of its call.

Night hunter
In the night, the potoo flies silently and quickly short distances from its perch when it spots its insect prey. Its small, hooked beak is accompanied by a wide, gaping mouth that sweeps up large flying insects.

Dark home
Oilbirds roost and breed in noisy colonies deep inside caves. They make their nests out of regurgitated seeds mixed with their own guano, or droppings.

OILBIRD
STEATORNIS CARIPENSIS

A unique bird in this group, the oilbird is the only nocturnal fruit-eating bird in the world. It feeds mainly on the nuts of oil palms, ranging up to as much as 150 miles (240 km) in a single night.

EUROPEAN NIGHTJAR
CAPRIMULGUS EUROPAEUS

Breeding in Europe and central Asia, this bird migrates to winter in Africa. Some people believe that its call is the sound made by witches.

Ground nester
Nightjars roost on the ground by day, flying up to feed on insects over heath and scrubland at night. They nest with one or two eggs on the ground, usually in dry, open country.

CUCKOOS AND RELATIVES

A DISPARATE BUNCH

A gathering of these birds would be pretty strange. The cuckoos would be deciding in which other bird's nest to lay their eggs. The turacos and hoatzin chicks would be clambering up trees using tiny claws on their wings. And the roadrunners would be on the ground moving fast enough to catch a rattlesnake.

COMMON CUCKOO

CUCULUS CANORUS

Famous for the call it is named after, this European and northern Asian bird is easier to hear than it is to see. The "cuckoo" call is made by the male, and has been copied for cuckoo clocks. Cuckoos eats insects, particularly hairy caterpillars, that it hunts in woodlands and marshes.

Adult common cuckoo

Cuckoo chick in marsh warbler nest

Cuckoo in the nest
This cuckoo lays its eggs in the nests of small birds such as warblers. The single chick is fed by the hard-working host birds. When the cuckoo chick has hatched, it pushes the other eggs out of the nest so it can eat all the food.

ROADRUNNER

GEOCOCCYX CALIFORNIANUS

This fast-running ground cuckoo lives in scrub and semidesert in the southwestern United States and Mexico. It can run at more than 20 mph (32 km/h) and is able to kill a rattlesnake.

Roadrunner rock art
Roadrunners are the subject of several petroglyphs, or rock art carvings, in the United States. At the Painted Rock Petroglyph Site in Arizona, there is one (far right) that shows a roadrunner catching its favorite lizard food.

A greater roadrunner

Petroglyph, Arizona

RED-CRESTED TURACO

TAURACO ERYTHROLOPHUS

An African native, the red-crested turaco lives in tropical forests where it clambers around the branches like a parrot, eating fruit, berries, flower buds, shoots, and insects.

Real colors
The beautiful red and green colors come from the turacin and turacoverdin copper pigments in their feathers, which are unique to turacos.

HOATZIN

OPHISTHOCOMUS HOAZIN

Also known as the reptile bird, this is an inhabitant of swamps and mangroves along the edges of lakes and slow-moving rivers in northern and central South America. It eats nothing but leaves and buds that ferment in a foregut, a rare digestive system that only ruminants have. It is often called the stinkbird because of the smell this process makes.

Safe nesting
Hoatzins nest in trees over water, and the young drop into the water if they are threatened. The chicks have claws on their wings that help them scramble up branches.

MOUSEBIRDS

ACROBATIC MICE

These African birds get their name from the way they scurry around like mice—and they are brown and gray like rodents. But they could be called "acrobat birds" for their ability to hang upside down with food in their feet.

Long-tailed flier

Half the length of this mousebird is its mousy-brown tail, which often gets damaged as it flits through the trees. These mousebirds live in small flocks and are very social.

SPECKLED MOUSEBIRD

COLIUS STRIATUS

This omnivore feeds mainly on fruit, both ripe and unripe, but actively searches out termites and ants. They breed whenever there is enough food.

BLUE-NAPED MOUSEBIRD

UROCOLIUS MACROURUS

Marked out by the turquoise patch on the back of its nape, this mousebird eats fruit, seeds, leaves, and flowers. It also eats soil and swallows pebbles to grind up the vegetation as it is digested.

Adaptable feet

Mousebirds have outer toes that can be turned to point forward or backward. This comes in useful when clinging to thin branches.

RED-FACED MOUSEBIRD

UROCOLIUS INDICUS

This mousebird lives in the savanna regions of southern Africa, roosting in thickets and scrub, and feeding in small groups on fruits, flowers, berries, seeds, and nectar.

Easy identification

With its crested head and red bill and eye mask, this mousebird is instantly recognizable.

HUMMINGBIRDS AND SWIFTS

AERIAL ACROBATS

These very small birds with pointed wings and bare-skinned feet can cling to rough surfaces but not stay long, so they spend most of their lives flying. Swifts can beat each wing at a different rate to change direction incredibly fast, while hummingbirds stay still in the air and also fly backward!

Longest beak

Nearly as long as its body and tail, the beak of this hummingbird collects nectar. The bird hovers underneath a flower, pushing the beak and its equally long tongue up inside.

Beak

The Latin name ensifera means "sword wielder."

Strong muscles

Around 30 percent of a hummingbird's weight is in the pectoral muscles it uses for flight.

SWORD-BILLED HUMMINGBIRD

ENSIFERA ENSIFERA

With its record-breaking beak, this bird is able to reach nectar inside flowers that are too big for other hummingbirds. It is one of the largest hummingbirds, and is a solitary bird. The males do not take part in building nests or looking after the chicks.

Scientific name: *Ensifera ensifera*

Group name: charm, hover, shimmer, glittering

Size: up to 4.4 ins (11 cm) long body and tail, and 4 ins (10 cm) long bill

Weight: up to 0.4 oz (12 g)

Diet: nectar from flowers; insects that are regurgitated by female for chicks

Lifespan in wild: up to 12 years

Location: South America

Agility controlled by wings and the forked tail

EURASIAN SWIFT
APUS APUS

When they are not nesting, the swifts spend all their time in the air, sleeping and mating on the wing, even at 6,000 ft (1,830 m). These birds gather in large, screaming flocks when they feed and before they migrate. They breed in Eurasia and winter in Africa.

Feeding habits
Swifts zip through the air, their scythe-like wings helping them twist and turn, snapping up insects as they go. They gather the insects in their throat to feed nestlings, which are often hatched out in roof spaces, although they also nest on cliff ledges and in tree hollows.

Drinking water in flight

BEE HUMMINGBIRD
MELLISUGA HELENAE

This Cuban bird is the world's smallest bird at only 2.24 ins (57 mm) long. It is so small that it competes with hawk moths and bumblebees for food.

Fast feeder
You can see the beautiful iridescent hummingbird flitting from plant to plant, at a rate of 1,500 flowers a day, to find nectar to eat.

BOOTED RACKET-TAIL
OCREATUS UNDERWOODII

A native of South America, this bird lives in the Andean cloud forest. The male's tail ends in two elongated feathers tipped with broad blue-colored "rackets."

Contrasting plumage
The long tail rackets and prominent white leg puffs show that this is an adult male racket-tail. The female has a short tail and bill, and white underparts.

TROGONS
ELUSIVE FOREST BIRDS

Trogons are named after the Greek word for "nibble," because they gnaw holes in high rain forest trees to make their nests. Their first and second toes face backward and the third and fourth face forward, which helps them cling vertically to trees.

GUIANAN TROGON
TROGON VIOLACEUS

This trogon lives in the tropical forests of the Amazon basin of South America and on the islands of Trinidad and Tobago. It lays its eggs in the tree nests of ants and termites. The insects help to incubate the bird's eggs.

Perching post
In the trees, the Guianan trogon perches upright without moving. It feeds on insects and fruit.

RESPLENDENT QUETZAL
PHAROMACHRUS MOCINNO

This bird is as spendid as its name. It lives in Central American forests and feeds on oil-rich fruit. Both sexes are iridescent green but the male has long tail coverts.

Male with its red chest

Quetzal in forest habitat

No room in the nest
These birds nest in holes in trees. The male's tail plumes will not fit inside the nest when he is helping to incubate the eggs. The plumes simply hang down outside!

Brilliantly colored fast feeder

This fawn-breasted, or lilac-throated, brilliant (*Heliodoxa rubinoides*) delicately sips nectar in the forests of Ecuador. The South American hummingbird likes flowers in its feeding territory that have the highest sugar content. These are usually red-colored and tubular—a shape that stops bees and butterflies feeding on them. The brilliant hovers next to the energy-giving flowers and extends its strawlike tongue, licking up the nectar at a speed of up to 13 times per second. The plants in turn rely on hummingbirds for their pollination.

KINGFISHERS AND RELATIVES

FAST AND ELUSIVE

These birds are very territorial and you are more likely to hear their rattling, whistling, or piping calls than you are to spot them flash by. Some fly over water, spearing fish with daggerlike bills, while others live on land, snatching up lizards and snakes at lightning speed.

HOOPOE
UPUPA EPOPS

Feeding tool
The hoopoe uses it long, curved beak to search in grass and dung for worms, beetles, and grubs. Its name comes from its soft, far-reaching song—it has song duels with rival hoopoes.

This ground-feeding bird is found across Europe, as well as in Asia and Africa. It has an impressive crest that it flicks up above its head when it is excited, and it flutters very like a butterfly in flight.

GREAT INDIAN HORNBILL
BUCEROS BICORNIS

Nest or prison?
To protect his chicks from predators, the male helps seal the female and her eggs inside their treehole nest with mud. He pushes food through a small hole until the chicks are ready to leave the nest.

One of the largest hornbills, this bird lives in the forests of India and southeast Asia. The large casque on its head contains air-filled bone and helps to amplify the hornbill's call.

COMMON KINGFISHER
ALCEDO ATTHIS

Beginning the dive

Kingfishers are well equipped to hunt for prey in rivers and lakes. They have monocular vision (each eye is used separately) in the air, and binocular vision (both eyes are used together) in the water.

Scientific name: *Alcedo atthis*

Common names: Eurasian kingfisher, river kingfisher

Group name: concentration

Size: up to 7 ins (17 cm) long; up to 10 ins (25 cm) wingspan

Weight: up to 1.6 oz (46 g)

Diet: fish, insects, crustaceans

Lifespan in wild: up to 21 years

Location: Eurasia, northern Africa

Lifting prey out of the water

Hunting technique
The kingfisher perches in branches over water and watches for its fish prey. It dives in a flash of blue, snatches the prey from the water, then takes it back to its perch to eat.

Favorite prey
Common kingfishers eat mainly minnows and sticklebacks, but will also take insects, shrimps, and tadpoles.

Colorful bird
The iridescent turquoise blue wings and bright orange breast are instantly recognizable.

LAUGHING KOOKABURRA
DACELO NOVAEGUINEAE

The world's largest kingfisher is most famous for its laughing call. It lives in the forests of eastern Australia, where it hunts small birds, frogs, mammals, and small reptiles. It stuns small prey before swallowing it.

Comical appearance
This thickset bird is 18 ins (46 cm) long, and has a large head set on a short neck. It uses its large, two-colored beak to crush its prey.

WOODPECKERS AND TOUCANS
LIFE IN THE TREES

These birds head for different parts of the tree to eat. Woodpeckers use their tough beak like a drill to blast through tree bark and slurp up hidden insects with their long tongues. Toucans stay on top of branches, reaching out with their beaks to grip and peel fruits.

BEARDED BARBET
POGONORNIS DUBIUS

A close relative of the toucan, this strange-looking African bird with a large head has a strong bill that it uses to pound holes in dead trees for its nest. It uses its tail feathers as a prop like a woodpecker.

Bearded bird
The hairlike feathers that fringe the base of the bill make it look like this bird has a beard. Its upper bill has two grooves that help it break open fruit to eat.

MAGELLANIC WOODPECKER
CAMPEPHILUS MAGELLANICUS

The bright crimson head of the male of this species is highly visible in South American forests. The woodpeckers' diet includes grubs, insects, beetles, and small vertebrates.

The male woodpecker

Family group
These woodpeckers mate for life. Both hollow out the nest, incubate the eggs, clean the nest, and feed the chicks. The two adult birds travel together, sometimes accompanied by their chicks, which stay with them for up to two years.

The female woodpecker

CHESTNUT-EARED ARACARI
PTEROGLOSSUS CASTANOTIS

A social bird, this toucan roosts with up to five adults and their offspring in the same hole, beaks folded over their backs.

Daily life
These rainbow-colored birds live near water in South American forests and swamps. They feed on fruits, but also eat flowers, nectar, insects, and eggs.

TOCO TOUCAN
RAMPHASTOS TOCO

This South American bird is the largest toucan of all, with a beak that is one-third of its length that it uses to pick and peel the fruit it eats. It is a poor flier and spends most of its time in the trees.

Cooling down
Scientists have discovered that by adjusting the flow of blood to their enormous beaks, toucans are able to release heat so that they can keep cool.

GREEN WOODPECKER
PICUS VIRIDIS

Instead of feeding in the trees, this European bird searches the ground for ants. Its spiny and sticky tongue is perfect for pushing into an anthill and scooping up the insects.

Different behaviors
Instead of communicating by drumming on trees, these woodpeckers call to each other. They do, however, use trees to excavate their nest holes.

PASSERINES
PERCHING SONGBIRDS

These birds have feet that are perfectly adapted for holding onto a tree or a cliff. They have three forward toes plus one at the back, and muscles that tighten if they start to fall. This is why they are known as perching birds. They are also called songbirds because so many have adapted to communicate with sounds, sometimes a song, sometimes a rasped warning.

Feather crest
The large disk-shaped crest extends over the bill.

Showing off
The males gather together in leks—courtship sites—to squawk loudly, bob up and down, and hop around in displays that attract the females.

Feminine looks
The female cock-of-the-rock is brown-orange all over and has a smaller orange crest. She is much harder to spot in the cloud forest.

ANDEAN COCK-OF-THE-ROCK
RUPICOLA PERUVIANUS

The national bird of Peru, this spectacular species is distinctive for the male's brilliant orange feathers and fan-shaped crest. They construct cup-shaped mud nests on rocks and ledges in ravines, hence the name.

Scientific name: *Rupicola peruvianus*

Common names: tunki

Size: up to 13 ins (32 cm) long

Weight: up to 11 oz (312 g)

Diet: mainly fruit, also insects, amphibians, reptiles, and small mice

Lifespan in wild: maybe up to 7 years

Location: in the Andean cloud forests, South America

RUFOUS HONERO
FURNARIUS RUFUS

This insect-eating ovenbird of eastern South America is the national bird of Argentina. It is a ground forager, looking for insects and their larvae, but will also eat seeds and fruit.

Bird builder
Rufous horneros are amazing architects, building oven-shaped nests with two chambers from wet mud and straw. The domed nests are 12 ins (30 cm) in diameter.

BARN SWALLOW
HIRUNDO RUSTICA

Swooping through the air and catching insects on the wing, this is a bird of open countryside. It makes its nests out of mud and grass and often sticks them to the walls of farm buildings, hence "barn" swallow.

Barn swallow on the wing

Flock of swallows

En route
You can often see flocks of these birds lined up on electricity cables when they migrate. Barn swallows breed in the northern hemisphere and winter in the southern hemisphere.

GREAT GRAY SHRIKE
LANIUS EXCUBITOR

The largest of the European shrikes, these birds are mobbed by other birds that see them as the predators they are. Shrikes perch in trees or on fences to spot prey.

Gruesome larder
These songbirds are just 9 ins (23 cm) long. They catch beetles, small mammals, and birds, storing surplus food in a "larder," by impaling the corpses on thorns or even on the spikes of barbed-wire fences.

SUPERB LYREBIRD
MENURA NOVAEHOLLANDIAE

This ground-dwelling Australian bird is great at mimicking whatever it hears, including other birds and chainsaws! It scratches through leaf litter on forest floors for insects, worms, spiders, and seeds to eat.

Superb dance
A male lyrebird has a beautiful courtship display. It tips special curved feathers and lacy plumes forward over its head to take on the shape of an ancient Greek lyre.

Lyrebird with folded tail

Full-feathered display

NORTHERN CARDINAL
CARDINALIS CARDINALIS

A large, long-tailed North American songbird, the northern cardinal has a short, thick bill that it uses to open up large seeds. It lives in woodlands and in vegetation near gardens.

Contrasting couples
The male is a splendid red, and the female pale brown with red on wings and tail. Both males and females sing, and pairs use their own phrases.

GREEN-HEADED TANAGER
TANGARA SELEDON

Small flocks of up to 20 of these brightly colored birds forage for fruits and insects in rain forest canopies in South America. They hop with ease from branch to branch.

Small but colorful
Only around 5 ins (12 cm) long, this male bird packs in a lot of color to a small space—turquoise, yellow, dark blue, light blue, black, green, and bright orange.

Mixed diet
A ground-feeder, the meadowlark uses its sharp beak to probe in the grass for worms, insects, and seeds. In summer, it eats grasshoppers, beetles, ants, and caterpillars, as well as spiders.

EASTERN MEADOWLARK
STURNELLA MAGNA

The whistle-like song of the meadowlark can be heard across the grasslands and meadows across the Americas. The bird nests on the ground, and the male defends the nest by singing, flicking his wings, and spreading his tail.

BLUE TIT
CYANISTES CAERULEUS

Common in woodland and hedgerows, as well as gardens, this perky little Eurasian bird flits from tree to tree to look for insects, caterpillars, seeds, and nuts. It has a high-pitched song that ends in a trill, and the males sing at any time in the year.

Blue tit in flight

Nesting habits
Blue tits usually nest in tree holes, but their nests have been found in many unusual places, including streetlamps. They lay large clutches—up to 13 eggs at a time.

Has small, compact wings

RAGGIANA BIRD-OF-PARADISE
PARADISAEA RAGGIANA

Native to the tropical forests of New Guinea, these birds feed on fruits such as figs, and use their feet as tools to extract the seeds. They also forage for insects in bark crevices and on leaves.

Spectacular display
Male birds-of-paradise have some of the most flamboyant and colorful displays of all the birds. The raggiana bird-of-paradise shows off his feathers in the treetops.

RAVEN
CORVUS CORAX

The largest passerine, this bird has a 5 ft (1.5 m) wingspan. The raven is one of the most intelligent animals, and has been able to solve problems set by scientists.

Adaptable
These birds can live in a wide range of habitats, from the Arctic Circle to hot deserts. It is a scavenger and predator, feeding mainly on carrion although it will kill small animals.

Grooming companions
Oxpeckers' bills are specially adapted to comb through the coats of African animals such as buffaloes (left). The birds' legs are short, which allows them to grip onto their moving hosts.

RED-BILLED OXPECKER
BUPHAGUS ERYTHRORHYNCHUS

These extraordinary small birds sit on terrifyingly large mammals such as buffaloes, rhino, and giraffes for one purpose—to eat the parasites and ticks from the skin of these animals.

BLUE JAY
CYANOCITTA CRISTATA

This bright blue and noisy bird is native to North America. It is called the thief of the bird world because it often raids nests from other birds and preys on nestlings and eggs. Its diet mostly consists of fruits, nuts, seeds, and insects.

Scientific name:
Cyanocitta cristata

Group name: party, band, scold, cast

Size: up to 12 ins (30 cm) long; 17 ins (43 cm) wingspan

Weight: up to 3.5 oz (100 g)

Diet: omnivore, acorns a favorite

Lifespan in wild: up to 17 years

Location: eastern North America

Cobalt blue color
The blue is the result of the inner structure of the feathers, which distort the reflection of the light, making the bird look blue.

Feeding hungry chicks

In the nest
The blue jay nest is made with twigs and other material such as lichen and moss. Both parents build it and take care of the young.

Feather pattern
The wings and tail have bold black bars across the blue.

Perched blue jay

COMMON STARLING

STURNUS VULGARIS

At a distance, these birds look black, but when seen closer they are glossy with patches of purple and green. They feed mainly on the ground, using their beaks to find insects and earthworms.

Aerial stunt
During early evenings in winter, up to 100,000 starlings may gather over a roosting site and wheel and swoop in unison. They do this for protection from predators and also to keep warm at night.

Iridescent feathers

Murmuration of starlings

Nomadic birds
Gouldian finches are seed-eaters that move regularly to find food and water. There may be several hundred birds in a single flock.

GOULDIAN FINCH

ERYTHRURA GOULDIAE

These pretty Australian birds are also known as rainbow finches for obvious reasons. They are never far from water and build their nests inside tree hollows.

CRESTED OROPENDOLA

PSAROCOLIUS DECUMANUS

Also called the yellow-tailed cornbird, this weaver bird of Central and South American rain forests has a yellow beak and a bright yellow tail with two black central feathers. It raises its black crest when it is excited.

Bird of the trees

Lifestyle
The bird lives on forest edges and nests in tall trees. It forages for insects, fruits, nectar, and seeds on the ground and high up in the trees.

Unusual bright blue staring eyes

Nesting together
The oropendolas' nests are shaped like giant teardrops and are more than 3 ft (1 m) long. Big flocks of up to 100 birds may build dozens of these nests in a single, very tall tree.

TREE SPARROW

PASSER MONTANUS

Eurasian tree sparrows are smaller relatives of the house sparrow (*Passer domesticus*). They move around in small flocks foraging for seeds and insects on farmland, pastures and gardens, often nesting in buildings just like house sparrows.

Family success
Tree sparrows build grass nests in cavities in old trees or rocks, or in holes in buildings. They lay up to six eggs at a time, and the parents may raise two or three families a year.

SATIN BOWERBIRD

PTILONORHYNCHUS VIOLACEUS

This medium-sized Australian bird has glossy blue-black feathers and a bluish bill. It mainly eats fruit, but in summer it also eats insects. It is best known for collecting blue-colored objects such as clothes pegs, drinking straws, bottle tops, feathers, flowers, and shells.

Attraction
Male bowerbirds make bowers to attract a mate. The satin bowerbird arranges his sticks like an avenue with two walls. Inside he colors it with a "paint" made from saliva and fruit, and decorates it with his blue objects.

REPTILES

REPTILES

These scaly sun-seekers have been crawling, slithering, and swimming for around 320 million years. They are cold-blooded so they need to bask in warm sunlight or on hot rocks to get themselves going, but that means they can last on less food than mammals—some only need one good meal a year. Reptiles are mostly carnivores and use a variety of methods to ambush, paralyze, or trap prey.

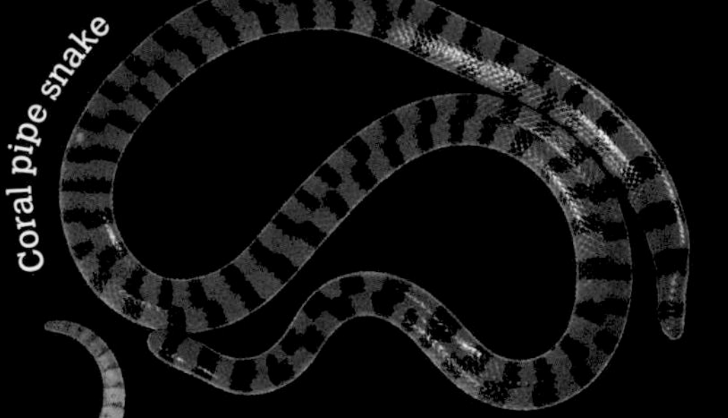

Coral pipe snake

American alligator

Giant day gecko

Royal python

Eastern worm snake

Corn snake

Pacific rattlesnake

Spectacled caiman juvenile

Lizard

Box turtle

Frilled-neck lizard

Horned viper

Armadillo girdled lizard

Gharial

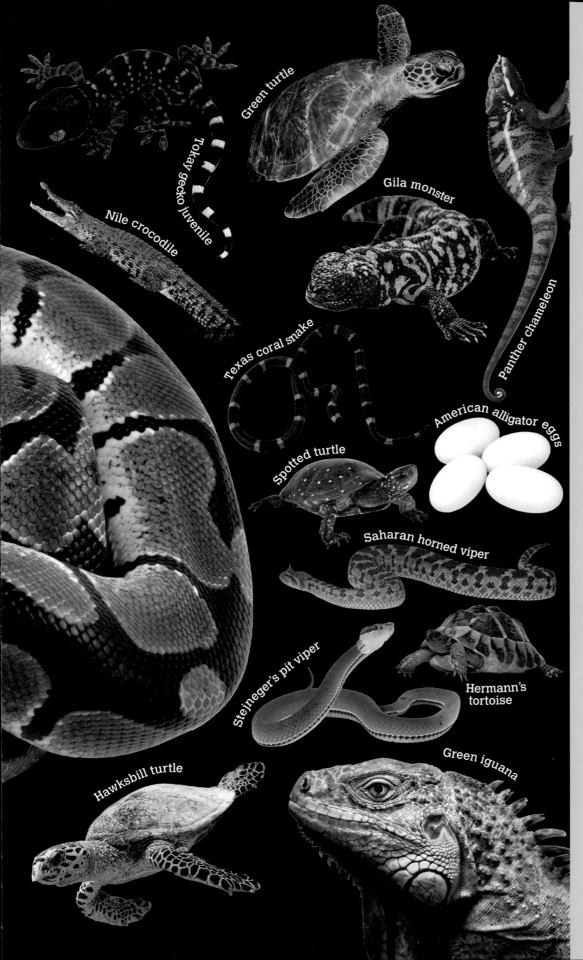

Tokay gecko juvenile

Green turtle

Nile crocodile

Gila monster

Panther chameleon

Texas coral snake

American alligator eggs

Spotted turtle

Saharan horned viper

Steineger's pit viper

Hermann's tortoise

Hawksbill turtle

Green iguana

SKIN AND BONES

The more than 10,700 species of reptile all have a bony skeleton with a backbone—even turtles, in their shells. Reptiles have tough, waterproof skin covered with flat, thick scales made of keratin that block attackers' blows, keeping water out and moisture in. Reptiles' scaly bodies do not dry out, so they do not need to drink much and are able to live in extremely dry habitats, including the hottest deserts. In fact, the warmer it is the better, because reptiles are cold-blooded and need to bask in the sun's rays or lie on warm rocky surfaces to heat their bodies in order to be able to move, hunt, feed, and digest. They also have to seek shade or water to cool down when the temperature is really high—that tough skin does not allow sweating, which is what mammals would do.

STORY OF THE EGG

Nearly all reptiles lay eggs with waterproof shells. Some are soft and leathery, but tortoises, crocodiles, and geckos lay hard-shelled eggs. The eggs are usually laid in holes burrowed into the sand or soil. Unless they are very well hidden, they attract predators. Some reptiles guard their nests, but most leave the eggs and young to take their chances. Inside the eggs, the babies grow a special tooth or horny growth that becomes their tool for breaking out. They hatch as tiny adults, and are up and about almost immediately with no help from their parents. The exception to this is the crocodile, which carries her young to water. A small group of reptiles in colder regions bear live young because their babies would not survive as eggs—it is warmer inside their mother's body.

Red-eared slider

CROCODILES AND ALLIGATORS
WATER DINOSAURS

So what's the difference between these crocodilians? Alligators and caimans have wider and more rounded noses, plus their teeth are hidden when the jaws are shut. In contrast, the fourth teeth on the lower jaw stick out in a creepy grin on crocodiles. Alligators live near freshwater, while crocodiles prefer the salty life—some have special glands on their tongue that get rid of salt. These reptiles are among the very few that take care of their young after hatching.

Teeth and jaws
Crocodiles have pointed snouts (left), while alligators' snouts are broad and the jaws of gharials are very long and narrow. Crocodilians have up to 80 teeth in their mouth at one time.

In and out of water
The eyes and nostrils are on the top of the head and poke out above the surface of the water to allow the crocodile to see, smell, and breathe, while its body is hidden in the water. When it dives, muscles close the nostrils, and the throat is shut off by a flap of skin.

SALTWATER CROCODILE
CROCODYLUS POROSUS

The largest species of crocodilian, the "saltie" is also the heaviest reptile in the world. It lives in estuaries, mangrove swamps, and the open ocean, as well as freshwater rivers. A fully grown saltwater crocodile can kill animals as large as water buffaloes, and will attack people—between 2005 and 2014, 14 people died in northern Australia.

Sunning on a rock

Warning sign

Scientific name: *Crocodylus porosus*

Common names: estuarine crocodile, marine crocodile, Indo-Pacific crocodile

Group name: bask, float

Size: up to 20 ft (6 m) long

Weight: up to 2,200 lbs (1,000 kg)

Diet: carnivorous

Lifespan in wild: more than 65 years

Location: northern Australia, Bay of Bengal (India), southeast Asia

Tough life
A saltwater remains motionless for very long periods and may be mistaken for a log. They are a danger to people, because they eat anything that comes close, including fish, birds, mammals, crustaceans, turtles, and lizards.

Look out!
Crocodilians swim fast but they can also sprint short distances on land. They have sharp teeth and an incredibly powerful jaw—they are dangerously well-equipped killers.

Strong teeth
These are designed to grab and hold onto prey and are constantly replaced throughout its life.

Muscular tail
The tail is flattened on both sides to push through the water at speed.

The **saltwater crocodile** can **swim** at up to **15 mph** (24 km/h).

NILE CROCODILE
CROCODYLUS NILOTICUS

This freshwater crocodile mainly eats fish, but also takes animals coming to drink at the rivers, lakes, and freshwater marshes in which it lives. It drags them into the water and rolls its body in a death roll until the prey is drowned. It is the largest crocodile in Africa.

Cool hunter
Ancient Egyptians worshipped the crocodile god Sobek and the Nile River was said to have been formed from his sweat. In fact, crocodiles do not sweat. Instead they "mouth gape" to keep cool. They do, however, produce crocodile tears!

Ancient Egyptian god Sobek

Mouth gaping

GHARIAL
GAVIALIS GANGETICUS

The freshwater gharial lives in India and Nepal, but is critically endangered. Since the mid-1900s, its numbers have declined by 98 percent, partly because of the damming of rivers—it does not move well on land so finds it difficult to relocate. The gharial lies in wait in the water and uses its long snout to catch fish to eat, flicking them back into its mouth.

Long-nosed reptile
The male gharial has a "ghara," or bulbous lump, at the end of its snout. This is thought to amplify the buzzing sounds that it makes when defending its territory. The gharial's snout houses up to 110 needlelike, razor-sharp teeth.

Night hunting

Day and night
This caiman's name comes from the bony ridge between its eyes. During the day, groups can be seen on the shore, but they take to the water to hunt at night.

Group basking on the riverbank

SPECTACLED CAIMAN
CAIMAN CROCODILUS

Also known as the common caiman, this small crocodile lives in Central and South America and can tolerate salt as well as fresh water. It is a fast water predator, taking fish, amphibians, reptiles, and water birds, as well as insects. It is able to survive droughts by burrowing into the mud.

AMERICAN ALLIGATOR
ALLIGATOR MISSISSIPPIENSIS

The largest reptile in the western hemisphere, this alligator lives in the rivers and swamps of the southeastern United States. During the summer, it can be found keeping cool in a "gator hole," a water-filled hollow that it digs out. There is only one other alligator species, the Chinese alligator.

Courtship moves
Male alligators display to attract females by making low-frequency sounds that people cannot hear. These infrasonic vibrations are accompanied by head-slapping and nuzzling.

Good start
Female alligators lay around 35 to 50 eggs. The females aggressively defend the nest and the young, but only about 20 percent survive.

Alligator eggs

Safe ride

Menace on the green
In Florida, gators are a common sight crossing fairways. Most of the states in the southeastern US have alligator management plans or protocols to deal with these reptiles.

Portrait of a hunter
The tail of the alligator accounts for half of its length, which can be up to 14.5 ft (4.4 m). With strong jaws that can crack a turtle shell, it also eats fish, snakes, small mammals, and birds.

TUATARAS
LIVING FOSSILS

Tuataras are unusual reptiles found only on a few New Zealand islands. They are born with a "third eye" on the top of the head that is soon covered by scales. No one is sure why it is there. These ancient animals have a double row of teeth in their upper jaw and a single row below. These do not regrow, so tuataras switch to softer food toward the end of their long lives. The name comes from the local word for the spiny back and crest of spiky scales.

Keeping warm
Green iguanas (*Iguana iguana*) are native to Central and South America. They are agile climbers, but when it is cold, they will group together on the ground.

LIZARDS
FAST-MOVING SCALED REPTILES

Most lizards have small heads, long tails, and long slim bodies with four same-size legs, each with five toes. They prefer warm habitats, and the ground- or tree-dwellers are brightly colored while the desert lizards tone it down to blend in with the sand and rocks. Lizards grow all their lives, but their skin does not, so they shed it every so often. If attacked, part of their tails can drop off to distract the predator—it grows back later.

COMMON TUATARA
SPHENODON PUNCTATUS

These nocturnal animals are of huge interest to scientists because their species' origins can be traced all the way back 200 million years. Tuataras are New Zealand's largest reptiles today with the slowest growth rate—they keep growing until they are middle-aged, around 35 years old. Their diet includes beetles, seabird eggs, and spiders.

TOKAY GECKO
GEKKO GECKO

This southeast Asian gecko is a regular visitor to houses, scuttling up walls after insects. The name comes from the loud "tokay" call they make during mating season—they also squeak and bark. The tokay gecko is nocturnal and its diet includes locusts, crickets, and scorpions.

Underside of the tokay gecko's foot

Sticking to things
Geckos are able to run up walls and across ceilings because their feet are covered by a million tiny microscopic hairs that help them to stick to the surface.

Tokay gecko scampering up a wall

Third eye

Science puzzle

Putting on a display
The tuatara has a large head with the third eye on top and a crest of spines running along the neck and down their back and tail, almost its entire length of 1.6 ft (0.5 m). The crest is fanned out to attract females or when fighting another male.

Tuatara on forest floor

Great hunter
This chameleon has eyes that move independently, and a long, lightning-quick tongue that shoots out to pull in the small insects that it eats.

JACKSON'S CHAMELEON
TRIOCEROS JACKSONII

This three-horned chameleon lives in east Africa, although it has also been introduced to Hawaii. It moves slowly, letting prey get close before striking. Unlike most chameleons, Jackson's chameleon gives birth to live offspring, which are independent and hunt within a few hours of birth.

Color change
Like all chameleons, Jackson's chameleon has color-changing skin. This provides great camouflage for it in the forests in which it lives.

KOMODO DRAGON

VARANUS KOMODOENSIS

The Komodo dragon is the largest lizard in the world and is the perfect carnivore. It hides and waits for prey, such as monkeys, wild boar, or deer, then attacks with its claws and 60 short, sharp teeth that cut and tear flesh. Groups of dragons often quarrel over kills. They are able to swallow 5.5 lbs (2.5 kg) in just one minute.

Scientific name: *Varanus komodoensis*

Size: up to 10 ft (3 m) long

Weight: up to 365 lbs (165 kg)

Diet: carnivorous

Lifespan in wild: up to 30 years

Location: Lesser Sunda Islands in Indonesia

Portrait of a dragon
This massive lizard has a flat head and heavy body supported by sturdy legs that end in long, sharp claws. They can run quite fast and swim long distances from island to island. Juveniles are agile climbers.

Dangerous bite
When a Komodo dragon bites, it is injecting its prey with venom. Venom glands in its mouth are loaded with toxins—even its drool is venomous.

New life
Male Komodos fight each other for the attention of the females. However, if there are no males on a particular island, the females can still lay a clutch of eggs that will hatch out, in a process called parthenogenesis.

Bowed legs
The stout, bowed legs support the massive torso of this heaviest of lizards.

Forked tongue
This flicks in and out, helping the lizard to pick up smells in the air.

Huge tail
To reach prey, the dragon may stand on its hind legs using its muscular tail as support.

ARMADILLO GIRDLED LIZARD

OUROBORUS CATAPHRACTUS

Found in sandstone crevices in the mountain slopes and shrub lands of western South Africa, this lizard is active during the day. It looks mainly for termites, but also eats other insects, spiders, and scorpions, as well as some plants.

Armadillo lookalike
When threatened, this lizard curls up, gripping its tail in its jaws and turning itself into a tight armored ball.

Fierce defense
Gila monsters open their mouths very wide and hiss when they want to warn off predators such as coyotes.

GILA MONSTER

HELODERMA SUSPECTUM

This lizard of the deserts of the southwestern United States and northern Mexico is up to 22 ins (56 cm) long. It lives in underground burrows, coming out to feed at night on small mammals and other lizards that it injects with venom.

Food storage
A carnivore, this lizards's food includes nestlings, rodents, frogs, and carrion. Like a camel, it stores fat—in its tail—and can go months between meals.

Dinosaur of the seas

A marine iguana feeds on algae, moving along the seabed off the coast of the Galapagos Islands in the Pacific Ocean, where each island is host to its own unique reptile. The marine iguana is the only lizard that is able to live and forage in the ocean, helped by the fact that its heartbeats slow to half the normal pace in the water to conserve energy. This one's head and crest are usually white with the excess salt that it expels from glands near its nose. Despite its fierce, prehistoric looks, the marine iguana is a gentle lizard.

SNAKES
SLITHERING REPTILES

They are not slimy and most are not poisonous. Snake skin is smooth and dry and covered in keratin scales, and of the over 3,700 types of snake, only around 600 have venom that they inject through fangs to kill prey. Others wrap around an animal, squeezing it to death. They swallow it whole, opening the jaw wider for anything large. Still scared?—there are no snakes in Antarctica, Iceland, Ireland, Greenland, or New Zealand.

Losing sight
When it is an embryo, the blind snake has eyes like other snakes. By the time it hatches, the eyes have reduced in size and it is blind.

LINEOLATE BLIND SNAKE
AFROTYPHLOPS LINEOLATUS

A native of Africa, this brown or gray snake is oviparous, laying eggs like a bird, as opposed to viviparous like the green anaconda (below), which gives birth to live young. The blind snake's body is covered in smooth, shiny scales. It spends most of its life underground feeding on the eggs and larvae of ants and termites, and on other invertebrates.

GREEN ANACONDA
EUNECTES MURINUS

One of the largest snakes in the world, the green anaconda can move on land and climb trees, but is most at home in the water of rivers, swamps, and marshes. Its eyes and nostrils are on top of its head so that it can stay submerged.

Scientific name: *Eunectes murinus*

Common names: water boa, common anaconda

Size: up to 30 ft (9 m) long

Weight: 550 lbs (250 kg)

Diet: carnivorous

Lifespan in wild: more than 10 years

Location: Trinidad, tropical South America

Open wide
The jaws are unhinged to swallow large prey whole.

Constrictor
This member of the boa family uses its teeth and powerful jaws to hold onto prey. It wraps its body around the animal either to suffocate it or drag it underwater to drown.

Stocky body
Powerful muscles contract to crush and push prey along.

Aqua killer
The anaconda spends its time in water, ambushing and asphyxiating animals such as tapirs and capybaras when they come to drink.

Bright green adult boa

Color changes
This bright green boa is resting, its looped coils draped over a branch with its head in the middle. The young snakes are different colors, changing to green after a year.

Brick-red young boa

EMERALD TREE BOA
CORALLUS CANINUS

This snake uses heat-sensitive pits in its lips to detect the presence of warm-blooded prey at night in the South American rain forests. It then lures its food to it by sitting very still on a branch and dangling its tail until the curious prey comes close enough to be caught.

BLACK MAMBA

Danger signal
The mamba opens its mouth wide to show the black inside as a warning. Just two drops of its venom can kill a person.

DENDROASPIS POLYLEPIS

This poisonous snake is frighteningly fast, moving at up to 12 mph (20 km/h) in short bursts. It is aggressive and unpredictable when threatened, and is one of the most feared snakes in Africa.

OLIVE SEA SNAKE

AIPYSURUS LAEVIS

Sea serpent
The snake's paddle-shaped tail drives it through the water. It is viviparous, giving birth to live young at sea.

This venomous sea snake lives in shallow, tropical waters on coral reefs and around the rocky coastlines of Australia. It can spend up to two hours between breaths at the surface, because its one lung extends for almost the entire length of its body and it takes oxygen from the water.

SIDEWINDER

CROTALUS CERASTES

Also known as the horned rattlesnake, this snake is a small, venomous pit viper that lives in the deserts of the southwestern United States and northern Mexico. The "horns" keep the sand out of the eyes.

Sidewinding
The sidewinder slithers at up to 18 mph (29 km/h). It throws its body from side to side, which allows it to move on loose sand and also keeps it cool.

SURINAM CORAL SNAKE

MICRURUS SURINAMENSIS

This semiaquatic snake is found in the equatorial forests of northern South America. It hunts fish in the water at night, biting to inject venom before letting go and waiting until the prey is weak. At this point, it goes in for the kill.

Venomous coral snake

Brazilian false coral snake

Lookalike
The burrowing venomous coral snake is brightly colored but can be mistaken for the nonvenomous false coral snake, a pipe snake also found in South America.

Stout snake

GABOON VIPER

BITIS GABONICA

The largest viper in Africa, this snake is up to 7 ft (2 m) long and weighs around 25 lbs (11 kg). Its broad head can measure 6 ins (15 cm) across. It is an ambush hunter, lying in wait to bite and hold onto the small mammals and birds it eats.

Charmers' favorite

Distinctive hood

Big display
When the Indian cobra spreads its ribs, the hood it forms is impressively wide, so it used to be popular with snake charmers (see p.127). It has distinctive markings.

INDIAN COBRA

NAJA NAJA

There are around 60 highly venomous snakes in India, and this one, also known as the spectacled cobra, is one of the most deadly. It bites quickly, paralyzing rodents, lizards, and frogs with its venom. Its color forms range from creamy white, through gray and yellow, to red and black.

On the forest floor

Camouflaged assassin
The brown and black wedge-shaped marks on the gaboon viper's broad back make it very difficult for passing prey to spot among the fallen leaves on the rain forest floor.

Kings of their realms

King cobras are very adaptable—they live in fields or bamboo thickets, up in the trees or in mangrove swamps. Their coloring is best camouflaged in dense rain forests, and they are great climbers and very good swimmers. They move swiftly along the ground and through trees and water, using their excellent eyesight to spot moving prey up to 300 ft (100 m) away. They can also track animals by sensing their vibrations as they run away.

KING COBRA
OPHIOPHAGUS HANNAH

This is the world's longest venomous snake at 18 ft (5 m). The king cobra has its own genus, *Ophiophagus*, which is Greek for "snake-eating," because, believe it or not, snakes are its main food. Most snakes nest in burrows, but the female king cobra builds her own shelter from sticks and leaves and lies on them to keep her eggs warm. If the nest is threatened, she uses the cobra defense, rising up, hissing, and spreading her neck into a hood using special ribs and muscles. Cobras strike at lightning speed, injecting powerful venom through short fangs.

The **king cobra** rarely **attacks** people—it **prefers** to **feast** on **other snakes**.

Scientific name:
Ophiophagus hannah

Common name:
hammadryad

Group name: quiver

Size: up to 18 ft (5.5 m) long

Weight: up to 20 lbs (9 kg)

Diet: snakes, lizards, eggs, small mammals

Lifespan in wild: up to 20 years

Location: India, southern China, southeast Asia

Extracting venom
King cobra venom is produced in special salivary glands just behind its eyes. By making it bite a glass, it is possible to "milk" it of this venom. A protein in its venom has been found that may be very effective as a painkiller.

Charmed snakes
Snake charmers made it look like the snakes were dancing to music, when they were simply following the moving flute. Today, this form of entertainment is dying out because a law banning ownership of snakes in India is being enforced.

Snake-eater
The king cobra preys on other snakes, including rat snakes, pythons, other cobras, and venomous kraits. It will also eat lizards, eggs, and small mammals. Its jaws can open to swallow large prey whole, and it can go for months without food.

Naga King guarding the entrance to Angkor Wat, Cambodia

Snakebite
The bite is so powerful that elephants have died within three hours when bitten on the toe or trunk.

Colored throat
The throat is either light yellow or beige in color.

Rising up
When prey is swallowed, it can take 3–5 days for the very strong acid in the stomach to digest it.

Striking an attitude
This snake is not aggressive, but if it is threatened or cornered, one-third of its body rises up, its hood is spread, and it growls. It can still move forward to attack while maintaining this stance.

Muscular system
The cobra moves by contracting and relaxing muscles to push it along.

Kolam cobra mask

Cobra as symbol
Through the ages, the king cobra has been equally revered and feared. In Cambodia, the Naga King was depicted as a cobra-shaped serpent with multiple heads. In Sri Lanka, actors performed the Kolam dance wearing different masks, including that of the cobra.

Box jellyfish
All box jellyfish like this one, the Bonaire banded box jellyfish (*Tamoya ohboya*), are highly venomous, with tentacles covered in venom-injecting capsules. The Australian sea wasp (*Chironex fleckeri*) is one of the most deadly creatures on Earth. Each of its 15 tentacles, which are up to 10 ft (3 m) long, is laced with enough venom to kill 60 people.

DEADLY ANIMALS

Watch out where you tread or swim! The world is a dangerous place, made all the more so by animals that have developed fatal self-defense mechanisms. And a number of these poisons and venoms can be deadly to humans. Some animals on these pages are poisonous, delivering toxins if touched or eaten by another animal, while others are venomous, injecting toxins via teeth, fangs, spikes, or harpoons.

Puffer fish

Many puffers and porcupine fish are highly toxic. However, some of the most dangerous, such as this one, *Sphoeroides nephelus*, are eaten as a delicacy. The chef must remove the poison sacs, or the customer may die.

Golden poison arrow frog

Phyllobates terribilis of Colombia is only 2 ins (5 cm) long, yet it has enough venom in glands beneath its skin to kill ten humans. Local people would dip their blow-darts in the poison before using them to hunt and kill prey.

Inland taipan

The most venomous snake in the world, *Oxyuranus microlepidotus*, lives in central east Australia. It has a lightning strike when threatened and often bites several times in a row. It is said that one drop of its venom can kill 100 people, but it seldom comes in contact with anyone as it lives in very remote areas.

Brazilian wandering spider

Phoneutria fera is highly venomous. A native of Central and South America, it was first discovered in Brazil. There are several venomous spiders in this group and they are fast-moving animals that live on the jungle floor, stalking prey at night. During the day, they hide in dark, moist places, which could be piles of wood, garages, or shoes!

Stonefish

Anyone who accidentally stands on the *Syanceia verrucosa*, a reef stonefish, will be injected with painful and deadly venom through its 13 dorsal spines. This fish is very well camouflaged, covered in algae and blending in perfectly with the corals and rocks in which it lives in warm seas and oceans. A stonefish will only use its venom as a defense, releasing it when pressure is applied to its spine.

Deathstalker scorpion

Also known as the Naqab desert scorpion, *Leiurus quinquestriatus* is found in Africa and the Middle East. Its sting is used defensively and delivered through a stinger at the end of its arched tail at an amazing speed of up to 3 mph (5 km/h)

Blue-ringed octopus

The blue rings are a warning signal. This tiny octopus (*Hapalochlaena lunulata*) is found hiding in crevices or shells in the waters off the coast of Borneo. Its venom is the same as that found in pufferfish and it uses it to hunt. The octopus's painless bite can inject a venom 1,000 times more powerful than cyanide that can kill a human in minutes.

Marbled cone snail

This sea snail, *Conus marmoreus*, lives in the shallow water of reefs in the Indo-Pacific and is a deadly hunter. When it attacks, it uses a harpoon-like tooth to deliver venom that paralyzes its fish prey. The toxins are produced in the venom duct and pushed into the harpoons. Once fired, the harpoons are discarded, together with any undigestible material.

Asian giant hornet

The largest species of hornet in the world, this insect, *Vespa mandarinia*, has a stinger that is 0.2 ins (0.5 cm) long but is not barbed, so remains attached to its body. This means it is able to sting again and again, injecting a venom that contains eight different chemicals.

TURTLES AND TORTOISES

REPTILES WITH BODY ARMOR

Don't be fooled by the clumsy way they move—turtles are masters of the oceans. They cruise around the world powered by long feet that have become flippers and protected by a 60-bone tough shell that sees off most predators. Tortoises are turtles that only live on land and are mainly vegetarian—turtles will eat anything.

Leather amulet
In many Native American belief systems, turtles were thought to look after women. This beaded turtle-shaped amulet was worn by girls to ward off illness.

Portrait of a terrapin
This terrapin has a broad head and short snout, while its neck is long and muscular. Its paddlelike front feet and webbed back feet all have five sharp claws.

COAHUILAN BOX TURTLE

TERRAPENE COAHUILA

Only 2,000 of these Mexican turtles are believed to have survived in the wild. They are threatened by habitat destruction and horses grazing on the grass they rely on. They spend much of their lives in water.

Omnivore
This medium-sized box turtle eats both in and out of the water, hunting fish, insects, and worms.

Memorable marks
This tortoise has a beautifull shell, with bold, black markings. It has a strong, horny beak and scaly limbs.

HERMANN'S TORTOISE

TESTUDO HERMANNI

Living in southern Europe, Hermann's tortoise supplements its plant diet with earthworms, slugs, and insects. It spends the winter months hibernating, buried in a bed of dead leaves.

HELMETED TERRAPIN

PELOMEDUSA SUBRUFA

Terrapins are freshwater turtles, and this small African species is adapted to live in many different habitats. It is most active in the wet season and cold winter months. It may estivate (see p. 143), burrowing underground to escape summer droughts.

LOGGERHEAD TURTLE

CARETTA CARETTA

These turtles live in all the oceans, but not in the coldest seas near the poles. They are the most common turtle in the Mediterranean and are a familiar sight swimming or nesting on sandy beaches.

Large and lumbering
The largest tortoises of all, these animals weigh more than 500 lbs (250 kg) and only move at a slow 0.17 mph (0.27 km/h).

Cooling off

Slow mover

GALAPAGOS GIANT TORTOISE

CHELONOIDIS NIGRA

This dome-shelled tortoise lives on the Galapagos Islands—*galapágo* is an old Spanish word for tortoise. It spends up to 16 hours a day resting, and the rest eating grasses, fruit, and cactus pads.

Loggerhead looks
This turtle has a large head that houses powerful jaw muscles, which easily crush the crabs, sea urchins, clams, and other shellfish that they eat. Its four flippers have two, or sometimes three claws on each.

ALLIGATOR SNAPPING TURTLE

MACROCHELYS TEMMINCKII

This is the largest freshwater turtle in North America and spends most of its time underwater—it is able to hold its breath for up to an hour at a time! Only the females haul themselves on shore in order to lay eggs.

Swamp habitat

Ambush predator
With their shells often covered in algae, these turtles look just like the rocks in their muddy habitat. Their camouflage means that prey that ventures near stands no chance.

Carapace
The three high ridges of shell are quite unlike other species.

Algae-covered

Ready to go
The long, springlike neck is very mobile.

The eyes have it
Unique among snapping turtle species, this turtle has eyes on the side of its head, giving it greater peripheral vision.

Scientific name: *Macrochelys temminckii*

Group name: bale, dole

Size: carapace (shell) up to 32 ins (80 cm) long

Weight: up to 200 lbs (90 kg)

Diet: carnivorous

Lifespan in wild: up to 70 years

Location: Mississippi Basin, southern US

Beaklike jaws
This turtle has the most powerful jaws of any reptile and can crush anything it bites.

Hunting tactic
This reptile lies motionless in the water to catch prey. It waves a red wormlike lure on the tip of the tongue to attract fish into the mouth.

Female leatherback arriving in French Guiana to lay eggs high up on a beach

Egg-laying

Hatchlings digging their way out of a sand nest

Hatching out
Female leatherbacks return to the same beach to lay their eggs. When the hatchlings emerge, they run for the sea as fast as possible.

LEATHERBACK TURTLE

DERMOCHELYS CORIACEA

This sea turtle is the world's largest turtle, with a shell that is up to 9 ft (2.8 m) long. And it can weigh an impressive 2,000 lbs (960 kg). The leather-like carapace (shell) is scaleless and has grooves running from front to back.

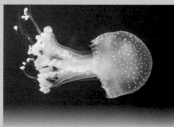

In search of food
Leatherbacks migrate extremely long distances. They may travel 10,000 miles (16,000 km), for example from Japan to California, to find jellyfish-rich waters.

GREEN TURTLE

CHELONIA MYDAS

These turtles spend nearly all of their lives at sea. They migrate up to 1,000 miles (1,600 km) between feeding areas and nesting sites. They nest every two years, with an average of 115 eggs per nest that hatch out after 60 days.

Sea and shore
With their paddle-like flippers, green turtles are powerful swimmers. They warm themselves near the surface in shallow waters, but also regularly sunbathe on beaches in Hawaii.

AMPHIBIAN

S

AMPHIBIANS

Amphibians are named from the Greek words for "both" and "lives" because they live in water and on land. Indeed, amphibians are thought to be descended from the first backboned animals that moved from water to dry land about 400 million years ago. However, they cannot live just anywhere on land. They are cold-blooded, so small variations in temperature can kill them—they need to stick to warm and wet habitats.

Dyeing poison frog

American toad

Edible frog

Chinese fire-bellied newt

Eastern tiger salamander

European common toad

Tomato frog

Alpine newt

Vietnamese mossy frog

American bullfrog

Axolotl

Long-nosed horned frog

Fire salamander

Black-legged poison frog

Awarape dyeing poison frog

Red salamander

Australian green tree frog

Troschel's tree frog

Surinam horned frog

Palmate newt

Red-eyed tree frog

Common spadefoot toad

Eastern red-spotted newt

Green paddy frog

European common frog

European tree frog

Greater siren

Asian painted frog

Smooth-sided toad

Lemus leaf frog

Red-headed poison frog

Kaiser's spotted newt

Yellow-banded poison dart frog

Smooth newt

European green toad

Yellow-striped caecilian

WHAT MAKES AN AMPHIBIAN?

Amphibians have smooth skin with no scales, feathers, or hair. Most have four limbs with four toes on the front legs and five on the back. Their thin skin can absorb water and allows air to pass through, which is how some of them breathe. Amphibians do not have proper teeth and jaws able to chew, so they have to swallow food whole. Most, however, have a long, sticky tongue that can flick out lightning-fast to grab and hold onto prey, snapping it back into the mouth. To avoid becoming prey themselves, the first thing amphibians do is to plunge into the safety of water. Many, however, can produce poisons from glands that taste so bad or are so harmful that predators steer clear—the brighter the skin color, the more powerful the poison the amphibian is likely to exude.

TRANSFORMATION

Most amphibians change dramatically to become adults in a process that is called metamorphosis. Just as a caterpillar becomes a butterfly, so simple creatures called larvae transform into a frog, toad, salamander, or caecilian. Nearly all amphibians lay jelly-covered eggs in water. These eggs hatch into larvae that can swim and breathe through gills. The larvae eat plants and vegetation, although some eat meat. As they grow, they lose their tails and gills, developing legs and lungs. Then they are ready to live on land, where their diet is wholly carnivorous and the transformation is complete. Some amphibians may only return to the water to breed.

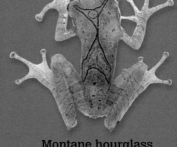

Montane hourglass tree frog

FROGS AND TOADS

HOPPERS AND CRAWLERS

Around 90 percent of all amphibians are frogs or toads. They live in every kind of habitat and all like to be near water, although toads cope better with dry conditions. Both frogs and toads have wide mouths for catching insects and other prey. Frogs have smooth skin, narrow bodies, and long hind legs that they use to hop. Toads have dry, bumpy, and thicker skin on their wider bodies and are more likely to crawl than hop.

SPRING PEEPER
PSEUDACRIS CRUCIFER

These North American amphibians are able to freeze their bodies when winter temperatures dip below freezing. When they thaw out, they provide a nightly chorus to signal that spring has arrived.

Calling all females
The males "peep" by closing their nostrils and mouths and squeezing their lungs, which makes the vocal sac puff up. The sound happens as the air leaves the lungs.

RED-EYED TREE FROG
AGALYCHNIS CALLIDRYAS

This bright green frog lives in the moist canopy of rain forests and is completely nocturnal, eating mostly insects, including crickets, moths, and grasshoppers. Its scientific name is taken from the Greek words *kallos* for "beautiful" and *dryas* for "tree nymph."

Left hanging
The female red-eyed tree frog's 20–50 eggs are laid on leaves that hang above water to avoid predators. After 5–8 days, the tadpoles hatch and fall into the water below.

Skin color
According to mood, the skin may become dark green or reddish brown.

Sticky-toed
Cuplike footpads help the frog climb and cling to leaves.

Color combo
This frog relies heavily on its green color to provide camouflage. If it is threatened, it opens wide its red eyes to startle and distract any predator long enough for it to leap away.

Leaflike looks
The upper eyelids and snout are elongated, so it looks as if it has horns. The females can reach 5 ins (13 cm) in length, with the males half the size.

LONG-NOSED HORNED FROG
MEGOPHRYS NASUTA

This remarkable frog lives in the rain forests of southeast Asia, looking just like the leaves on the forest floor. It is an ambush predator, lying in wait, then engulfing spiders, rodents, and lizards.

TOMATO FROG
DYSCOPHUS ANTONGILII

Found only in Madagascar, tomato frogs spend much of their time burrowed under leaves and mud. They inflate themselves and can release a toxin through their skin to deter predators.

Island life
Females are a bright red-orange color, while the males are yellow-orange. They breed in freshwater pools, laying black eggs in protective jelly on the surface.

Scientific name: *Agalychnis callidryas*

Common names: red-eyed leaf frog, gaudy leaf frog

Group name: army

Size: up to 3 ins (7.7 cm) long, female; up to 2 ins (5 cm) long, male

Weight: up to 0.5 oz (15 g)

Diet: insects, smaller frogs

Lifespan in wild: 5 years

Location: Central America

PAINTED REED FROG

HYPEROLIUS MARMORATUS

Also known as the marbled reed frog, this African amphibian lives in low trees near pools. The adults estivate (*see p.143*) in the dry season, hiding under logs or in vegetation and slowing down their metabolism to 50 percent of its normal resting rate.

Lots of variety
The colors and patterns of adult painted reed frogs vary considerably, from dark brown to yellow and bright green, and from stripes to dots and splotches.

RETICULATED POISON FROG

RANITOMEYA VENTRIMACULATA

This frog forages for insects on the forest floors of Ecuador and Peru. This group are called "dart frogs" because local people used their toxins to coat their blow darts.

Family life
Females lay eggs on the forest floor. When they hatch, the male frogs carry the tadpoles to tree holes or bromeliads off the ground.

Bright blue skin
They have a sticky skin that holds in moisture and allows tadpoles to cling to them. Their unique pattern of spots is like a fingerprint.

DYEING POISON FROG

DENDROBATES TINCTORIUS

This frog was not discovered until 1969 because it lives in very remote areas of the rain forests of Suriname and Brazil. Toxins in its skin can paralyze predators.

Voracious eaters
Bullfrogs eat anything they can fit in their huge mouths, flicking their tongues out to seize prey that includes small mammals and birds, frogs, and reptiles.

AFRICAN BULLFROG

PYXICEPHALUS ADSPERSUS

This is the largest amphibian in southern Africa, with a weight of 3 lbs (1.4 kg). It is also one of the few with a male that watches over and defends its eggs—although it eats many of the tadpoles!

Hunting mechanism
The bullfrog's tongue is folded over inside the mouth. When it is hunting, it drops its lower jaw, which causes the tongue to flip over and out.

ARGENTINE HORNED FROG

CERATOPHRYS ORNATA

These large horned frogs live in the grasslands of Argentina. They bury themselves in damp earth and wait to ambush animals that can be as large as themselves. Their jaws have toothlike projections that grip invertebrates, snakes, mammals, and other amphibians.

Deceptive looks
This horned amphibian appears inactive. However, it is simply lying in wait for prey.

The **Argentine horned frog** is also known as the **"Pac Man" frog** after the **computer** eating **game**.

GLASS FROG

CENTROLENIDAE

There are around 145 species of glass frog living in the rain forests of Central and South America. Most live in treetops above water and some species are endangered because of habitat loss. They are nocturnal and eat insects and spiders.

See-through body
Most glass frogs have translucent, or semi-transparent, skin. This means that some of their internal organs can be seen.

Nighttime gathering

In the rain forests of New South Wales in eastern Australia, these three orange-eyed tree frogs (*Litoria chloris*) have gathered together at night, hoping to find a mate. Orange-eyed tree frogs spend most of their lives high in the trees and are only seen when they come down to breed. They do this during and after very heavy spring and summer rains, and they call for females in a series of long "aark"s that end with a soft trill or chirp. The fertilized eggs are laid in clumps or singly beside streams or in the vegetation of shallow pools.

GOLIATH FROG

CONRAUA GOLIATH

This giant is the world's largest frog, with a body up to 12.5 ins (30 cm) long, and a legspan of 34 ins (87 cm). It can leap 10 ft (3 m) forward. It does not have a vocal sac, but makes a whistling noise.

Patient fisher

Goliath frogs live near the rivers and waterfalls of tropical western Africa. They come out at night and sit on river rocks to look for the insects, crustaceans, fish, and other amphibians they eat.

Life in the water

This toad spends its entire life in water. Unlike other toads, its eyes and nostrils are on top of its head, allowing it to see and breathe. It is a scavenger, feeding on insect larvae, fish, and small crustaceans such as water fleas.

AFRICAN CLAWED TOAD

XENOPUS LAEVIS

African clawed toads like warm, stagnant streams where they stir up the silt and mud in search of prey. They only leave the water if there is a drought, when they burrow into mud. Today, they are found in many countries of the world.

HARLEQUIN TREE FROG

RHACOPHORUS PARDALIS

This small frog from southeast Asia lives high up in the canopy of rain forest trees and only comes down to breed. Its eggs are laid in a foam nest attached to leaves hanging over water.

Big-toed frog

Large, heavily webbed fingers and toes act as parachutes that the frog uses as it glides from branch to branch as it forages for insects.

CENTRAL COAST STUBFOOT TOAD

ATELOPUS FRANCISCUS

This toad lives in the wetlands and rain forests of French Guiana, in South America. Males compete noisily with several frog species by streams and creeks, in which the toads lay their eggs. Their tadpoles use suction lips to cling to rocks in the fast-flowing water.

Calling time

This species does not have an external vocal sac, so produces calls only over a short distance.

SURINAM TOAD

PIPA PIPA

With its flattened body and triangular head, this South American toad is an unusual amphibian. In the rivers and streams in which it lives, the females give birth to up to 100 tiny but fully formed toads.

Female with eggs on her back

Life cycle

The female's body is a nursery for her eggs. The male presses them into the skin on her back, which then grows over them for protection. Around four months later the eggs hatch.

Close-up of eggs

MIDWIFE TOAD

ALYTES OBSTETRICANS

Midwife toads are nocturnal, hunting invertebrates, including beetles, bugs, maggots, and snails. The females lay their eggs on land, at which point the males take over the care of them.

Midwife male

The male wraps the eggs around his back legs and carries them for a month or more, protecting them and keeping them moist.

AMERICAN TOAD

Color variety

Sometimes called hop toads, these amphibians vary a lot in color, from olive and red to brown or gray. Their dry backs are densely covered in warts. Males are smaller than females.

ANAXYRUS AMERICANUS

Living in many different habitats, this toad is a useful visitor to backyards, where it eats many garden pests, including insects and slugs.

EUROPEAN TOAD

BUFO BUFO

This nocturnal toad is widespread on the European mainland. It migrates to breed, traveling a mile or more to reach a pond and produce long strings of eggs.

Moist habitats

This carnivore lives in forests, woodlands, and marshes, where it eats slugs, worms, insects, and dragonfly larvae.

Food larder

This toad exudes a sticky substance from its skin to protect itself against insect bites. The insects stick to it and the toad eats them later.

CRUCIFIX TOAD

NOTADEN BENNETTII

In dry seasons, this Australian toad burrows underground, creating a cocoon for itself to keep in moisture. When the rains come, it eats the cocoon and digs its way out.

CANE TOAD

RHINELLA MARINA

The world's largest toad, this amphibian is nocturnal and adaptable to very different habitats. These toads originally lived only in the American tropics but they have been introduced to other parts of the world because they eat so many insects. However, a single female cane toad can produce up to 35,000 eggs a year, and in Australia this has proved disastrous for many of the native species.

Skin oozing toxins

Predator lineup

Despite the fact that the cane toad's skin secretes toxins, it has several predators, including the broad-snouted caiman and the banded cat-eyed snake. Eels and ibis, as well as the kookaburra, eat them as well.

Kookaburra with dead toad

Scientific name: *Rhinella marina*

Common names: giant toad, marine toad

Group name: knot, nest

Size: up to 9.5 ins (24 cm) long

Weight: up to 3 lbs (1.3 kg)

Diet: insects, carrion

Lifespan in wild: 15 years

Location: South America, United States, Australia

Bony ridges

All cane toads have bony M-shaped ridges over their eyes.

Bumpy back

The skin is covered with warts—males have more than females.

Parotoid glands

The cane toad's toxins are secreted as a milky liquid from these glands on either side of the shoulders.

Overhead view

Toad portrait

The cane toad is large and heavily built, with a dry, warty skin. Bony ridges over the eyes meet in the center. It sits upright and moves in short hops.

Front view

Super-chilled frog

In winter, in the north of its North American range, the eastern wood frog (*Rana sylvatica sylvatica*) buries itself in a shallow burrow and freezes. Up to 70 percent of its body turns to ice, and its blood flow, breathing, and heartbeat stop altogether. Its body cells, however, are protected by glucose that acts as antifreeze, so it thaws out safely.

DORMANCY

In winter, some animals go into a deep sleep called hibernation to survive the long cold months. Estivation is another form of dormancy, but this snooze helps different animals from drying out in the summer heat. Creatures as varied as brown bears, ladybugs, rattlesnakes, and lungfish find a safe spot and go into a state of torpor. Their body functions slow down so they use less energy and therefore need less food.

African lungfish (*Protopterus annectens*)

Digging deep
The African lungfish is able to survive drought through estivation (torpor during a hot or dry period). It burrows into muddy ground and spreads a mucus cocoon around itself. As well as having gills to take oxygen from water, its lung means it is able take oxygen from air.

Timber rattlesnake

Reptile chill
Timber rattlesnakes (*Crotalus horridus*) hibernate in dens during winter. However, scientists have observed many of them emerging at regular intervals during that time to bask and warm their bodies.

Group protection
In autumn, when the weather gets colder, ladybug beetles (*Coccinellidae*) search for a place to hibernate—usually under the loose bark of a rotting log, under a rock, or in fallen leaves. They like to group together and the colonies can sometimes contain thousands of ladybugs.

Ladybug colony

Brown bear (*Ursus arctos*)

Laying down the fat
Bears do not actually hibernate during the winter, but black, grizzly, and brown bears do go into a deep sleep known as torpor to escape the cold. They can go for more than 100 days without eating, drinking, or passing waste and wake up if threatened by predators. To prepare for this, they build up fat reserves in autumn.

Hibernating colony

Hibernating lesser horseshoe bat

Bats in winter
The lesser horseshoe bat (*Rhinolophus hipposideros*) hibernates in caves, mines, tunnels, and cellars that have a high humidity. It wraps its wings around its body as it hangs upside down. In colonies, the bats hang a little apart from their neighbors.

The **common poorwill** is the **only** bird to **hibernate**.

Camouflaged hibernation
Instead of migrating like other birds, the North American common poorwill (*Phalaenoptilus nuttallii*) hibernates. Its diet of flying insects dies out in winter so it finds a hollow log or some rocks to lie in and survives several weeks without eating.

Hibernating among the rocks

Common poorwill

Drying out
The all-female bdelloid rotifers are small invertebrates that have been around for 80 million years. If the water they live in evaporates, they completely dry out, living in a dormant state until the rains fall and they are rehydrated.

Bdelloid rotifer

CAECILIANS
BLINDWORMS

Never seen one? No surprise, because caecilians mostly live underground, pushing their hard, thick skulls with pointy snouts to burrow through dirt or mud. The head and backbone mean they cannot be worms, and the lack of scales is why they are not snakes.

Eel-like
The broad yellow stripe makes this caecilian very recognizable. It has a flat head, and it has no need for eyes so they are covered with skin.

KOH TAO ISLAND CAECILIAN
ICHTHYOPHIS KOHTAOENSIS

A limbless native of southeast Asia, this amphibian is also known as the Koh Tao snake frog. It lives underground in forests and marshes, but comes above ground during the rainy season. It is a favorite prey of snakes and monitors.

BOETTGER'S CAECILIAN
SIPHONOPS PAULENSIS

This caecilian lives below ground or in rotting logs in forests and grasslands in South America. It is also frequently found in termite mounds. It has sensitive tentacles between its nostrils to find its way around.

Well equipped
The shiny skin of the caecilian is ringed with folds of skin called annuli. An organ in the ear of caecilians helps them detect prey such as worms, termites, frogs, small snakes, lizards, and other caecilians.

SALAMANDERS AND NEWTS
MOISTURE-LOVING AMPHIBIANS

Salamanders look like a mash-up of a frog and a lizard. They have slender bodies, short legs, long tails which may have fin-like edges to help them swim, and well-developed toes for digging. Most adult salamanders stay on land except when they mate or lay eggs. Newts are a type of salamander with webbed feet and a paddle-like tail that they need because they mostly live in the water.

AXOLOTL
AMBYSTOMA MEXICANUM

Most of these salamanders stay "babies" their whole lives—they are able to reproduce without growing up. They live in the lakes and canals of Mexico City's Xochimilco district, where they are under threat from pollution.

White variation

Always young
Unlike other salamanders, some axolotls do not exchange their feathery gills for lungs, and they stay in the water. They may be white, brown, or black in color.

Brown variation

Tiger features
Stout-bodied with a broad head and small eyes, the tiger salamander is the largest salamander that lives on land.

EASTERN TIGER SALAMANDER
AMBYSTOMA TIGRINUM

This large North American species—up to 13 ins (33 cm) long—spends most of its life underground. On warm, rainy nights in winter, it emerges and migrates to special breeding pools to lay its eggs.

OLM
PROTEUS ANGUINUS

Deep in underwater caves in a limestone region of western Europe is a blind salamander. It lives in darkness and relies on its hearing and sense of smell to get around and find food. It eats worms, water insects, larvae, and snails.

Long-lived cave "dragon"
This cave-dwelling salamander has pale pink skin. It never grows up, retaining the red, feathery gills of its larval form. It can live for more than 100 years.

CHINESE GIANT SALAMANDER

ANDRIAS DAVIDIANUS

Meet the world's largest amphibian, with a tail that is around 60 percent of the length of the body. This nocturnal species lives in the mountain streams of China. It spends its time entirely in water but does not have gills. Instead, it absorbs oxygen and releases carbon dioxide through its skin.

Scientific name: *Andrias davidianus*

Size: up to 6 ft (1.8 m) long

Weight: more than 110 lbs (50 kg)

Diet: fish, invertebrates

Lifespan in wild: up to 200 years

Location: China

Family life
Male Chinese giant salamanders compete fiercely for the females and many die from injuries. The survivors prepare underwater breeding dens in which several females lay up to 500 eggs each. The male guards the entrance until the larvae hatch.

Open-mouthed trap for prey

Biting strength
The salamander uses a sit-and-wait strategy to catch prey. It pulls prey to the back of the jaw where the bite is stronger.

Teeth on both jaws

Chinese culture
For thousands of years, the Chinese have revered these animals and they are the subjects of myths and legends. This carving was done at the end of the 17th century and is one of four carvings of salamanders on Yujin Bridge in Yunnan Province.

Strong tail
The large, flattened tail pushes the salamander through the water.

Tiny eyes
These are so small that the salamander relies on smell and touch to find prey.

Short limbs
These and the tail are used to push sand out of the breeding den.

Prehistoric relative
The salamander is described as a "living fossil" because it is so similar to a relative from the Miocene era more than 5 mya.

Warty pattern
The newt has bony ridges on top of its head and back, and a row of warts down each of its sides.

EMPEROR NEWT

TYLOTOTRITON SHANJING

This rough-skinned newt lives in mountain rivers in China. The males and females perform a courtship dance underwater, turning in circles, snouts almost touching.

ALPINE NEWT

ICHTHYOSAURA ALPESTRIS

Native to central Europe, this newt is active at night. It lives in the water but forages for food and hibernates on land. It is prey to hedgehogs, snakes, and rats.

Colorful newt
The iridescent blue mottling on this beautiful newt's back contrasts with the bright red underside, which has no spots.

Crested males
When breeding, the males have a large crest that runs from the neck to the tip of the tail.

MARBLED NEWT

TRITURUS MARMORATUS

This large newt can often be found under dead and rotting logs in its native woodlands of western Europe. It is nocturnal and may estivate in the summer if its breeding pond dries out.

FISH

FISH

Some have dagger-like teeth, others little suckers for nibbling. Some are predatory giants, others floating specks in the ocean. But fish have some things in common—they are all cold–blooded, they breathe through gills, and they have fins and scales.

Blacktip reef shark

Warty frogfish

Yellow multi-

Powder-blue tang

Titan triggerfish

Bullethead parrotfish

Leopard torpedo ray

Two-barred rabbitfish

Common carp

Black-spotted moray eel

Copperband butterfly fish

Harlequin ghost pipefish

Clownfish

Weedy sea dragon

Flowerhorn cichlid

Yellow tang

Jewel cichlid

Atlantic herring

Giant frogfish

Tasselled wobbegong

Rockfish

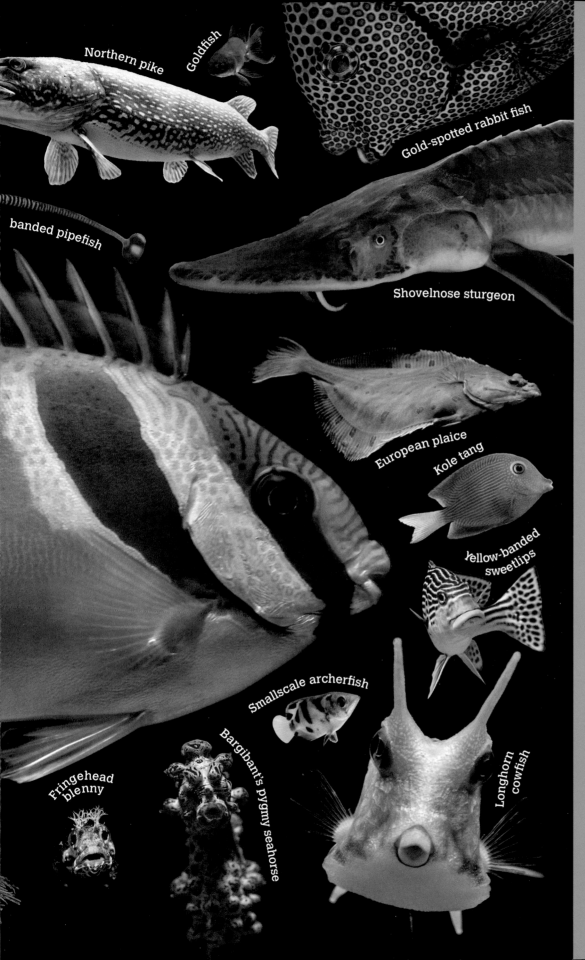

Northern pike

Goldfish

Gold-spotted rabbit fish

banded pipefish

Shovelnose sturgeon

European plaice

Kole tang

Yellow-banded sweetlips

Smallscale archerfish

Fringehead blenny

Bargibant's pygmy seahorse

Longhorn cowfish

WATER CREATURES

Nearly three-quarters of our planet is covered by water and this is a massive habitat for the more than 32,000 different species of fish in the world today. Water is a strange environment that can be either light or dark and where sounds, smells, and electricity travel faster than on land. Fish have adjusted so that some rely on good eyesight, others use mostly smell or taste or sense movement, and a few use electrical charges to know what is around them. The majority can only survive in salty water, but around 46 percent live in the freshwater of rivers, lakes, and streams. All these creatures cope with environments as different as coral reefs, kelp forests, fast-running rivers and streams, and small, calm pools. Some live in complete darkness and under pressure down on the ocean bed, while others inhabit the sunlit surface.

BODY PARTS

Fish bodies are covered in overlapping rows of thin, flexible plates called scales that protect against injury and infection and are covered in slimy mucus that helps reduce friction in the water. They breathe through gills that contain thousands of tiny blood vessels that transfer oxygen into the bloodstream. Most fish also have a special internal organ called the swim bladder that allows them to adjust their depth so they do not have to swim all the time. And most fish have paired fins (pelvic) on the bottom of the body and paired fins (pectoral) on the sides. These have various functions, including helping the fish move up and down. The top fin (dorsal) and bottom fin (anal) stabilize the body, keeping it level, and the tail fin (caudal) propels the fish forward.

Grouper

JAWLESS FISH
PRIMITIVE VERTEBRATES

These simple, eel-like fish have a notochord—a rod-like set of cells—along their backs and are descended from the first vertebrates, most of which died out 300 mya. Lampreys and hagfish suck up their food with jawless mouths.

PACIFIC HAGFISH
EPTATRETUS STOUTII

Also known as the slime eel because it exudes defensive slime, this hagfish has no true eyes and no stomach. It lives in burrows in the ocean floor.

Finding food
Hagfish are nearly blind and use tentacles around their mouths to sense for food such as worms and small invertebrates. They also scavenge on dead and dying fish.

Gill openings along side

Mouth studded with teeth

Eating technique
Lampreys attach themselves to fish with their rasping mouths and suck out tissues and fluids. One lamprey eats around 40 lbs (18 kg) a year.

SEA LAMPREY
PETROMYZON MARINUS

Lampreys do not have scales or gill covers. They breathe through seven pairs of gill openings along their sides. The sea lamprey is native to the northern and western Atlantic Ocean.

EUROPEAN BROOK LAMPREY
LAMPETRA PLANERI

These lampreys live in fresh water. They travel upstream to spawn and the female lays her eggs in the gravel of the stream bed. After they spawn, the adults die. Their larvae take five years to grow.

When to eat
Adult brook lampreys do not feed at all. Brook lamprey larvae, however, are filter-feeders, eating organic matter from the water.

CARTILAGINOUS FISH—SHARKS
STREAMLINED SWIMMERS

Our ears are tough but bendy because they are made of cartilage. The same stuff forms the skeletons of cartilaginous fish. Flexible cartilage helps these fish twist and turn, and glide easily through water, because it is less dense than bone. Sharks are the best-known type. Most have to keep moving to force water through their gills. If they stop, some drown. Sharks have a bloodthirsty image, but some eat plants or swallow zooplankton, just like whales.

LEOPARD SHARK
TRIAKIS SEMIFASCIATA

These leopards of the sea live near the west coast of the United States. They swim near the ocean floor, where they use suction to pull crabs, fish eggs, and worms into their mouths.

Surface feeding
This small shark grows to around 6.5 ft (2 m) in length. It sometimes swims near the surface with its mouth open, and fish prey swims straight in!

Hard to spot
The shark has a beautiful metallic blue back and white underside. This countershading provides perfect camouflage for the open ocean.

BLUE SHARK
PRIONACE GLAUCA

These torpedo-shaped, powerful sharks hunt both inshore and in the open ocean worldwide. They are active predators feeding on small fish and squid, sometimes herding the fish in packs or undertaking feeding dives to hunt in deeper waters.

SHORTFIN MAKO
ISURUS OXYRINCHUS

Scientific name:
Isurus oxyrinchus

Common names: blue pointer, mackerel shark

Group name: frenzy, shiver

Size: up to 14.8 ft (4.5 m) long

Weight: up to 1,100 lbs (500 kg)

Diet: bony fish and squid, other sharks, sea turtles

Lifespan in wild: up to 35 years

Location: worldwide, mainly in warm waters

The fastest shark, the mako is thought to have a top speed of 56 mph (90 km/h). It can hunt fast-moving prey in bursts of speed because, unlike most sharks, the mako is endothermic, or partially warm-blooded.

Versatile tail
Large tail helps the mako produce spectacular bursts of speed when swimming.

Toothy grin
The mako's tilted, dagger-like teeth stick out even when the shark's mouth is closed. They are long and razor-sharp.

Built for speed
Streamlined shape minimizes water resistance.

Apex predator
This top predator feeds on prey such as swordfish (*see pp. 164–165*), tuna, and mackerel. When it attacks, it often bites off the tail of the prey so that it cannot swim away.

Hunting on the seabed
The shark is a nocturnal feeder on crustaceans, mollusks, sea urchins, and small fish. It crushes the shells of its prey with flattened back teeth.

PORT JACKSON SHARK
HETERODONTUS PORTUSJACKSONI

A bottom-dwelling shark found in temperate waters near Australia, the Port Jackson lays egg capsules that are sometimes eaten by other sharks.

Ocean-going shark
This distinctive shark can grow up to 20 ft (6 m) long, and weigh as much as 1,100 lbs (500 kg). It is found in both open and coastal waters in oceans worldwide.

COMMON THRESHER SHARK
ALOPIAS VULPINUS

The common thresher uses a tail almost as long as its body to hunt. It catapults its tail tip over its head to hit a shoal of sardines or mackerel, wounding the prey.

Losing the stripes
When these sharks are born they are dark brown with pale yellow stripes. By the time they are adults, they have lost the stripes and their pale brown body is covered with small dots.

ZEBRA SHARK
STEGOSTOMA FASCIATUM

This carpet shark lives in the warm waters of the Indo-Pacific, often around coral reefs, and is threatened because of fishing.

SPOTTED WOBBEGONG
ORECTOLOBUS MACULATUS

The wobbegong, a carpet shark, lies in wait for prey, perfectly adapted to life on the seabed. It is very well camouflaged with its flattened body, the fleshy tassels along its jaw, and its shape broken up by the pattern of markings on its back.

Warm habitats
These sharks are found in warm, shallow waters, including algae-covered reefs and sandy areas around the coast of southern Australia.

BULL SHARK
CARCHARHINUS LEUCAS

This shark gets its name from its short, blunt snout and its aggressive behavior. It cruises warm waters everywhere, particularly along tropical coastlines and up rivers far inland.

People hunter?
In spring, the bull shark moves into freshwater rivers to have its young. This often brings it into contact with people, so it is one of the most feared sharks, alongside the great white and the tiger.

TIGER SHARK
GALEOCERDO CUVIER

A large shark that swims in tropical seas, the tiger is a voracious hunter and notorious for its attacks on divers and surfers. Its notched teeth can shear through almost anything, including old oil drums!

Fast mover
Tiger sharks have asymmetric tails, with a very long upper lobe and a short lower lobe. This helps them twist and turn, and accelerate quickly when they are chasing prey such as turtles and other sharks.

WHALE SHARK
RHINCODON TYPUS

This gentle giant is the largest fish on Earth, but it is still a bit of a mystery. One female was found with more than 300 embryos, but little is known about how the young sharks develop—there are few sightings of any less than 10 ft (3 m) long.

Scientific name: *Rhincodon typus*

Group name: aggregation

Size: up to 41.5 ft (12.5 m) long

Weight: up to 24 tons

Diet: mainly plankton, sometimes crustaceans, squid

Lifespan in wild: up to 70 years

Location: tropical seas worldwide

The **whale shark** is the **size** of a **school bus**.

Big mouth
The cavernous mouth is 5 ft (1.5 m) across, and large enough inside to hold a car. The shark has more than 600 rows of tiny teeth, but does not use them to eat.

Hangers-on
Remoras attach themselves and eat parasites from the shark's skin.

Filtering food
There are only three sharks that filter-feed—the whale shark, basking shark, and megamouth. They swim forward with open mouths, scooping up anything in their path. Water is pushed through the gills, and prey filtered by gill-rakers is swallowed.

BASKING SHARK
CETORHINUS MAXIMUS

The basking shark is a slow mover, traveling at 1.9 mph (3 km/h) when feeding, and only speeding up to 2.4 mph (4 km/h) when swimming in cool seas worldwide. As it moves, its bulbous snout, dorsal fin, and tail tip are often visible above the water.

Feeding method
As the shark cruises near the surface, its mouth wide open, the white gill arches with the bristly black gill-rakers between are clearly visible. At intervals it closes its mouth and swallows the plankton it filters out of the water.

GREAT HAMMERHEAD SHARK
SPHYRNA MOKARRAN

At 20 ft (6 m) long, this is the largest of the hammerheads. As it swims, it swings its head from side to side to give all-around vision from the eyes at the end of the hammer.

Wide head provides lift

Finding food
This is an aggressive hunter, pinning down stingrays with its head while biting off their wings. It uses its wide head to stir up sand on the seabed to find prey.

Foraging for food

SMOOTH-BACK ANGEL
SQUATINA OCULATA

Also known as the monkfish, this shark is found in the tropical, warm waters off the West African coast. It is severely threatened by the activity of trawlers.

Lying in wait
This young smoothback angel shark has been lying on the seabed, hidden by the sand on its back. It is an ambush predator, waiting for the squid, mud shrimp, crabs, and small fish (such as goatfish and codlets) that it eats to come close enough to grab.

Nose twitching
Bottom-feeding nurse sharks use the barbels on their noses to find prey such as sea urchins, crabs, and squid. Then their throat acts like a powerful pump to suck it up.

NURSE SHARK
GINGLYMOSTOMA CIRRATUM

Small groups of nurse sharks rest under reef overhangs in the Atlantic and eastern Pacific oceans during the day and forage for food at night. They breathe by opening and closing their mouths to push water through the gills.

BLACKTIP REEF SHARK
CARCHARHINUS MELANOPTERUS

This small shark patrols its territory in coral lagoons and around the edges of reefs in search of its preferred fish prey but also crustaceans, octopuses, squid, mollusks, and sea snakes. It is viviparous, giving birth to between two and four live young per litter.

Distinctive feature
This powerful swimmer is named for its brilliant black fin tips, particularly the one on the dorsal fin, which is commonly seen above the surface of the water in Indo-Pacific reefs.

Dangerous cousins
The blacktip reef shark is vulnerable to attacks by larger reef sharks, including the gray reef shark, sicklefin lemon shark, and great hammerhead (*above*).

GREAT WHITE SHARK
CARCHARODON CARCHARIAS

The great white is a fearsome predator. Superbly equipped for hunting, it is able to sense blood from miles away, and senses vibrations as well as the electrical signals given off by other creatures. This is the only shark able to lift its head above the waves, but it shares with its relatives scarily powerful jaws lined with up to seven rows of teeth. Films and stories sometimes include attacks by great whites, but these are so rare that you are far more likely to die from a bee sting or being struck by lightning.

Great white sharks move through the water **very quickly**—they can accelerate to **more than 35 mph (56 km/h)**.

Scientific name:
Carcharodon carcharias

Common names: white shark, white death

Size: up to 20 ft (6 m) long

Weight: up to 4,300 lbs (1,950 kg)

Diet: marine mammals such as seals and dolphins; sea turtles; fish; seabirds

Lifespan in wild: more than 70 years

Location: warm waters worldwide

Dorsal fin
This stabilizes the body and stops the shark rolling.

Breaching with seal in mouth

Eating machine
The great white's bite is twice as strong as that of a lion. It stabs prey first with the teeth of the lower jaw, then clamps down the upper jaw. It then shakes its head from side to side, tearing off pieces of flesh.

Breaching
There is nothing more spectacular than the sight of this huge shark leaping right out of the water while hunting. It approaches prey such as the Cape fur seal—a favorite meal—from underneath at speed, and the impetus carries it into the air.

Cape fur seal

Vision protection
The eyes can roll backward into the sockets if the shark is threatened.

Sensitive nose
The shark's most acute sense is smell—it can detect one drop of blood in 175 pints (100 litres) of water.

Teeth
The front row of five rows of teeth do most of the biting. The up to 300 teeth in the shark's mouth have serrated edges, just like those of the prehistoric shark Megalodon.

Great white tooth

Prehistoric fossil tooth of Megalodon

Up close and personal
Shark cage diving is a popular way to observe great whites from a safe place, but many divers learn more by being in the water with the sharks. Stainless steel mesh suits, chemicals, and electrical devices are used for protection.

Long-distance voyager
Great whites migrate very long distances and scientists try to tag and track them. In 2004, a female great white completed a journey from South Africa to Australia and back, a distance of 13,670 miles (22,000 km) in less than nine months.

Dangerous beginnings
Female great white sharks are ovoviviparous, like the majority of sharks. Their eggs are hatched inside the mother and feed on unfertilized egg yolk and sometimes other pups. When any pups have developed enough to survive—usually three months later—between 2 and 12 babies are born. They swim away very fast from the danger of being eaten by their own mother.

Tropical predator

One of the most common sights near the islands of Fiji in the south Pacific, a white-tip reef shark *(Triaenodon obesus)* swims slowly over a shallow coral reef. It has a short, blunt snout and a slender gray body, with a brilliant white tip to its first dorsal fin. During the day, it often rests under coral ledges or the sand of the seabed. At night, it feeds on fishes, octopuses, lobsters, and crabs, and will wriggle into crevices and under the coral to find its prey, often breaking off the sharp coral and cutting itself in the process.

CHIMERAS

MONSTER FISH

Chimeras are named after a mythical monster that was made up of different animals, and the lines on their skin do look like something stitched together. Looking for a creepier name? Chimeras are also called ghost sharks because their pale, silvery bodies almost vanish in deep, murky waters.

SKATES AND RAYS

GRACEFUL BOTTOM-DWELLERS

Closely related to sharks, skates and rays have flattened bodies suited to their bottom-dwelling lifestyle. Their mouth, nostrils, and gill slits are on the underside of their bodies. On the top are the eyes and spiracle breathing-holes. Rays have kite-shaped bodies and give birth to live young. Skates' rounder bodies have thorn-like growths to deter predators and they lay eggs.

RATFISH

CHIMAERA MONSTROSA

Also known as the rabbitfish, this fish occurs in groups in the northeastern Atlantic and the Mediterranean Sea. It is a sluggish bottom-feeder, feeding on the mollusks and invertebrates it finds.

Rat or rabbit?
The ratfish has a long rat-like tail and a rabbit-like mouth, hence the two names. It is oviparous, laying eggs enclosed in long, slender cases. When they hatch, the young look like the adults.

Keep away!
The luminous blue spots act as a warning to predators. The short tapering tail usually has one stinging spine one-third of the way from the tip.

Spot the ray
In the shadows its blue-and-tan coloring hides the stingray quite well. However, when it is not swimming along the seabed looking for prey, it prefers to cover itself with soft sand that hides it from predators.

BLUE-SPOTTED STINGRAY

TAENIURA LYMMA

Also known as the blue-spotted ribbontail ray, this bottom-dwelling species is around 14 ins (35 cm) across. It hunts crustaceans and small fish on reefs and may move into the sandy shallows with the tide.

SPOTTED RATFISH

HYDROLAGUS COLLIEI

A native of the northeastern Pacific, the spotted ratfish spends most of its time near the seabed in depths below 330 ft (100 m). It has a sharp dorsal spine that may protect it from the bite of predators such as sharks.

Built to eat
This ratfish has a short, blunt snout and strong teeth to break apart hard-shelled prey such as crabs, clams, and mollusks.

COMMON SKATE

DIPTURUS BATIS

Despite its name this skate is not common any longer—it is critically endangered. It is the largest skate in the world, but it is under threat mainly from getting caught in the nets of trawlers in the northeast Atlantic and Mediterranean Sea.

Wingspan of up to 9 ft (2.7 m)

Good camouflage
The skate's is difficult to spot on the seabed, where it feeds on crustaceans and mollusks. It takes flatfish such as dabs, flounders, and plaice, but also hunts mackerel and herring.

Blending in with the ocean floor

Big brain
This ray has the biggest brain to body ratio of any fish and can recognize its image in a mirror.

Gliding through the water
Using its elongated wing-like pectoral fins to push it through the water at a steady 9 mph (14 km/h), this magnificent ray travels with mouth open to pull in prey. If threatened, it is able to escape with a burst of speed of up to 22 mph (35 km/h).

Fleshy funnel
Two cephalic lobes funnel food into the mouth as the giant manta ray swims along.

GIANT MANTA RAY
MOBULA BIROSTRIS

This slow-growing filter-feeder is the largest ray in the world. It is migratory, traveling large distances to follow its plankton prey or to find a mate, or perhaps reacting to sea temperature or tidal patterns.

Scientific name:
Mobula birostris

Common names: devil ray, giant Atlantic manta

Group names: squadron, fever

Size: up to 22 ft (7 m) wide; 30 ft (9 m) wingspan

Weight: up to 5,300 lbs (2,400 kg)

Diet: plankton

Lifespan in wild: up to 40 years

Location: warm seas worldwide

Balletic ray
The manta ray often swims around and interacts with divers. It has the flexibility for a wide range of motion and is acrobatic, leaping spectacularly high out of the water.

THORNBACK RAY
RAJA CLAVATA

The thornback, mainly found in the coastal waters of the eastern Atlantic, varies greatly in coloration. Its tail is long and narrow, with rows of up to 50 spines running along its length.

On the seabed
At dusk, this ray begins to search the seabed for food, having spent the day partially buried in sand. It is an ambush hunter, lying in wait for shellfish, crabs, and fish. Up to 170 egg cases, each containing one embryo, may be laid on the seabed by a single female in a year.

Hunter and hunted
This ray flaps its wings to expose small animals such as shrimps, crabs, and worms on the seabed to eat. It has several barbed venomous spines in its tail that it uses for defense.

SPOTTED EAGLE RAY
AETOBATUS NARINARI

These graceful rays are often found in bays and around coral reefs, but may cross oceans. They swim near the surface, leaping out of the water, and often form large schools.

LARGETOOTH SAWFISH
PRISTIS PRISTIS

The sawfish is a ray, although it is often mistaken for a shark. It lives in warm coastal waters, estuaries, and freshwater worldwide. Females give birth to live young that have soft saws at first.

Striking
The extraordinary saw-like snout is edged with more than 50 teeth. It is used for defense, but also to sense where hidden fish prey is before swiping at it with hardly any water movement.

BONY FISH

DIVERSE FINNED FISH

Bony fish have a swim bladder that works inside the body like a float, allowing them to sink or rise without swimming. This group also has a skeleton of hard bones and other bony features such as a protective plate over the gills and a solid cranium that protects the brain just as our skulls do. Some bony fish move between fresh- and saltwater at different stages of their lives.

NORTHERN ANCHOVY

ENGRAULIS MORDAX

Prey and predator
These prey fish live in large shoals and are eaten by all kinds of animals, from bigger fish to seabirds to seals. The anchovies themselves eat by swimming with their mouths open, scooping up plankton.

Small and long, with a blue or black back and a silver belly, these fish are found in the Pacific off the coast of North America. They spawn throughout the year and play an important part in ocean life.

WEST INDIAN OCEAN COELACANTH

LATIMERIA CHALUMNAE

This species was once thought to have become extinct 65 mya, during the great extinction when the dinosaurs disappeared. But in 1938 a museum curator spotted one caught by fishermen. This is one of two known living species.

Colorful adult sockeye

Energetic journey
Sockeye salmon are powerful swimmers, swimming and leaping upstream to their spawning grounds. Females lay their eggs in gravel, then the adults die and the young fend for themselves.

A brown bear taking advantage of salmon returning to spawn

Fossil fish
This "prehistoric" coelacanth has a distinctive shape and lobed fins. It lives close to the coast in water up to 2,600 ft (800 m) deep, and feeds on fish, cuttlefish, squid, and octopuses. It has a unique "hinge" in its skull that allows part of the head to swing upward, enlarging the gape of the mouth.

SOCKEYE SALMON

ONCORHYNCHUS NERKA

These fish have a remarkable life cycle. They begin life in rivers, then swim downstream to the sea. After around two years, they use their sense of smell to navigate back to the rivers in which they were born in order to breed. They may lose more than half their weight on the return journey.

FANGTOOTH MORAY

ENCHELYCORE ANATINA

An ambush predator, this moray spends its time hiding in rocks waiting for small fish or crustaceans to come close. It is found in the eastern Atlantic at depths of at least 33 ft (10 m) and often seen with white-striped cleaner shrimps cleaning its mouth.

Double trouble
This eel is named for its extraordinary mouthful of fang-like teeth that are semi-transparent like glass. There are two rows of these teeth—the outer row are larger and the inner very sharp.

ELECTRIC EEL
ELECTROPHORUS ELECTRICUS

The electric eel can stun other fish or deter predators with a electric shock of up to 600 volts, enough to knock a person off their feet. Thousands of special cells called electrocytes in its muscles generate tiny currents that are stored until needed.

River swimmer
This eel is up to 8 ft (2.5 m) long. It swims slowly along in South American rivers, surfacing every few minutes to breathe. It mainly eats fish and fallen fruit.

Striped appearance
Its long, pointed nose is surrounded by sensitive barbels, and there is a sharp, defensive spine under each eye. One of the stripes runs vertically through its eyes.

CLOWN LOACH
CHROMOBOTIA MACRACANTHUS

A tropical freshwater fish, this bottom-dweller lives in rivers in Indonesia. It migrates to slow-moving waterways in flooded areas of rain forest to spawn.

Horns front and back
The two pairs of long horns are on the head and below the tail. It is thought that they developed because they make it hard for a predator to swallow the fish. A horn may break off but it grows back.

LONGHORN COWFISH
LACTORIA CORNUTA

Although it looks almost comical with its "horns" and pouting mouth, this fish has poisonous flesh. If it is threatened, it can release toxins that deter predators. It is also protected by its body's plate-like scales that are fused into a triangular shell.

RED-BELLIED PIRANHA
PYGOCENTRUS NATTERERI

Traveling in schools of 20 or more, these fearsome predators are scavengers, normally feeding on fish. They will go into a feeding frenzy to take down any large animal that threatens them.

Scientific name:
Pygocentrus nattereri

Common names: red piranha

Group name: school, shoal

Size: up to 12 ins (30 cm) long

Weight: up to 4 lbs (1.8 kg)

Diet: omnivorous, eating fish, animals, and plants

Lifespan in wild: over 10 years

Location: South American rivers

Family life
The red-bellied males woo the females by swimming in circles. They then make bowl-shaped nests where the females lay 5,000 eggs at a time in clusters.

Gray body
The body is flecked with small, bright, silvery green scales.

River life
The modern species of piranhas have lived in the warm waters of rivers and lakes in South America for 1.8 million years. It is preyed on by the pink dolphin and egrets.

Red underside
The red coloring extends from the chin to the belly.

Toothy fish
The blade-like teeth and underslung lower jaw are perfect for biting chunks out of the fins of larger fish and stripping a carcass in a few minutres.

An abundance of life

Around cracks in the planet's surface on the ocean floor there is a wealth of life, including huge clams, limpets, and shrimp that thrive in the warm, chemically charged waters where hot lava flows out. The giant tube worms (*Riftia pachyptila*), seen here with anemones and mussels, live several miles deep on the floor of the Pacific Ocean.

THE DEEP

Strange secrets lurk in the dark depths of the world's oceans, where sunlight cannot reach and the water hardly moves. Hidden creatures feast on plants, the sunken bodies of the dead—or each other. Some hide and ambush prey with unexpected speed. Others have learned to glow in the dark, a clever trick that is used to trick prey into venturing fatally close, warn off predators, or signal for a mate.

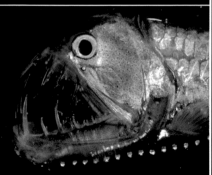

Female humpback anglerfish

Hairy frogfish

Camouflage is a great disguise for this fish living near coasts at depths of up to 720 ft (220 m). *Antennarius striatus* can change color and is covered in hair-like spines that make it look like coral or seaweed.

Hairy frogfish in the Indo-Pacific

Box jellyfish

In the deep ocean, where sunlight is very dim or absent, 90 percent of the animals emit light—an ability called bioluminescence. Some of the most beautiful of these animals are jellyfish. Scientists agree that most jellyfish light up to startle predators. Box jellyfish may use bioluminescence to attract prey into the reach of their long trailing tentacles that are lined with poisonous stinging cells.

Bioluminescent box jellyfish

Humpback anglerfish

This anglerfish (*Melanocetus johnsonii*) is found off the coast of Australia at depths of at least 6,600 ft (2,000 m). Growing from the female's snout is a modified fin ray. Millions of light-producing bacteria cause the globe at the end to glow and this lure attracts prey.

Fearsome viperfish

Viperfish

This deep-sea hunter has long fangs that are visible even when the mouth is closed. The viperfish (*Chauliodus sloani*) can swallow creatures almost as large as itself—it is 12 ins (30 cm) long.

The **fangs** of **viperfish** curve back **very close** to the fish's **eyes**.

Humboldt squid

This extraordinary species may only live for one year. During that time, a female Humboldt squid (*Dosidicus gigas*) grows to over 3 ft (1 m) and lays up to 20 million eggs, more than any other cephalopod. The squid dives to depths of 4,900 ft (1,500 m) in pursuit of prey and is covered in specialized cells that allow it to change color, either to communicate with others or as a warning color to large predators such as sperm whales.

Deep-sea octopus

Octopuses survive at great depths. This one (genus *Muusoctopus*) is at a depth of 8,850 ft (2,700 m) in the Bering Sea, which separates the continents of North America and Asia. In 2018, more than 1,000 *Muusoctopus robustus* were found by a remotely operated submarine in an octopus nursery "garden" 2 miles (3.2 km) down off the coast of California.

Long-distance travel

Swordfish migrate to warmer waters in winter and to cooler seas in summer. However, they also make another journey regularly—from near the surface to a depth of 1,800 ft (550 m) in pursuit of prey. In the cold ocean depths, where the temperature may be 37°F (3°C), swordfish have a unique muscle that helps them maintain the temperature of their eyes and brain at 66–82°F (19–28°C).

SWORDFISH
XIPHIAS GLADIUS

If you were creating a fish superhero, the swordfish would be a good place to start. They are among the fastest swimmers in the oceans, capable of fast sprints powered by streamlined bodies and a muscly tail. Special adaptations keep its brain warm and eyes supplied with blood in the coldest waters. Their top jaw is broad and tapers to a point, making a long "sword" that makes up a third of their body length. This is a great weapon for threatening rivals and slashing or beating prey so it cannot escape.

The **world record** for a **swordfish** is **1,182 lbs** (**536 kg**) set in **1952** for a **swordfish** caught off the coast of **Chile**.

Anatomy of a swordfish
This fast-moving fish has a bill, or "sword" that is longer than that of other billfishes, and the adults have neither scales nor teeth. The streamlined body helps it to travel fast through the water, and the stiff crescent-shaped tail makes it easier for the fish to change direction suddenly.

Dorsal fin
This tall first dorsal fin can often be seen sticking out of the water when the fish is basking.

All at sea
Swordfish travel alone, and they can do this at speed—up to 60 mph (97 km/h), which makes them one of the fastest fish in the sea. They often breach, leaping right out of the water to dislodge pests such as remora or lampreys.

Flattened sword *This strong weapon is the upper jawbone of the fish*

Scientific name:
Pongo pygmaeus

Common names:
broadbill, broadbill swordfish

Size: up to 15 ft (4.5 m) long

Weight: up to 1,430 lbs (650 kg)

Diet: carnivorous, mainly fish

Lifespan in wild: up to 9 years

Location: worldwide in warm seas

Swordfish top speed 60 mph (97 km/h)

Marlin top speed 50 mph (80 km/h)

Sailfish top speed 68 mph (110 km/h)

Squid

Herring

Common octopus

Prey and predators
Swordfish move through schools of fish, using their "swords" to slash at and injure prey so it cannot escape. They also take other prey including herring, octopuses, and squid. They are predated on by orca and large sharks.

Big game fishing
Fishermen tell tales of epic battles trying to land swordfish. They are powerful and athletic and one of the hardest billfish to catch, taking many hours to reel in, so they are a real challenge and one of the top species targeted by big game anglers.

Swordfish constellation
The Dorado constellation in the night sky of the southern hemisphere is most often called the Swordfish. It was identified at the end of the 16th century by two Dutch navigators. It is now one of the 88 constellations that are recognized by the International Astronomical Union (IAU).

ATLANTIC COD
GADUS MORHUA

The Atlantic cod has been heavily fished for centuries and is a popular food fish in North America and Europe. It spends most of its time near the seabed hunting bony fish, lobsters, and other invertebrates.

Saltwater fish
This cod is up to 4 ft (1.3 m) long and weighs more than 70 lbs (35 kg). It is a slow swimmer, moving in large groups and traveling up to 200 miles (320 km) to reach breeding grounds.

Reef stonefish

Danger underfoot
Stonefish live on rocky or coral seabeds. However, they also use their large pectoral fins to bury themselves in sand.

Stonefish in sand

REEF STONEFISH
SYNANCEIA VERRUCOSA

This is the most venomous fish of all. Its 13 dorsal fin spines can inject a venom that can kill an adult person in less than an hour. This master of camouflage uses its venom to deter predators in its rocky habitat in the Pacific and Indian oceans.

RED LIONFISH
PTEROIS VOLITANS

Native to Indo-Pacific coral reefs, this scorpionfish is a fierce ambush predator. It often hangs motionless until fish get close, then lunges at them, sucking them into its mouth and swallowing them whole.

In defense
The 13 long dorsal fin spines can deliver venomous stings for defense if the lionfish is threatened. Its predators include large bony fish and sharks. The males defend their territory fiercely.

Scientific name:
Periophthalmodon schlosseri

Size: up to 11 ins (27 cm) long

Weight: up to 9 oz (250 g)

Diet: small fish, insects, crabs, worms, algae

Lifespan in wild: up to 5 years

Location: tropical shores of eastern Indian Ocean and western Pacific

GIANT MUD SKIPPER
PERIOPHTHALMODON SCHLOSSERI

A native of mangrove swamps and mudflats of southeast Asia. It is remarkable for being a fish that is named for its ability to walk and skip on its pectoral fins when it is out of water.

Mudskipper skipping

Male mudskippers fighting

In and out of water
At high tide, mudskippers spend their time in burrows, coming out on land at low tide to search for insects, algae, crustaceans, and worms to eat. Courtship also takes place on land, with males facing off on the mud.

Pop-up eyes
These are on top of the head to help spot food and danger.

Amphibious fish
The mudskipper can survive for several hours on land. It breathes air through its gills and also absorbs air with its skin like an amphibian as it skips and climbs over tree roots.

Damp skin
The skin must be kept moist when it is out of water.

PYGMY SEAHORSE
HIPPOCAMPUS BARGIBANTI

A true master of camouflage, this tiny seahorse species is so well disguised that it was only found by accident in the 1960s! It lives on crustaceans that are even smaller than itself.

Home sweet home
The pygmy seahorse has adapted to look just like the particular sea fan on which it lives in the western central Pacific. It has only one gill opening on the back of the head.

Hunting together
There are usually around 20 of these barracuda in a school but some young fish make up schools of 200 or more. These aggressive fish may slash their fish prey into pieces before eating.

PELICAN BARRACUDA
SPHYRAENA IDIASTES

These long, torpedo-shaped fish have very sharp teeth along the side of each jaw and are ruthless pack-hunters. They live in warm Pacific waters.

LEAFY SEADRAGON
PHYCODURUS EQUES

Perfectly kitted out to hide in seaweed and kelp, the leafy seadragon lives in the waters off the coast of south and east Australia. It has an elongated pipe-like snout that sucks up plankton from the water.

Male nanny
Closely related to seahorses, the male leafy seadragon also broods its young. The female places around 120 eggs in a brood patch on the male. He carries the eggs for around a month until they hatch.

A **flyingfish** can "**fly**" more than **655 ft (200 m)** in **one go**.

In flight

Large pectoral fins for gliding

Flight technique
The two-wing uses its "wings," which are enlarged pectoral fins. It cannot change direction.

TROPICAL TWO-WING FLYINGFISH
EXOCOETUS VOLITANS

To avoid predators such as swordfish, tuna, and snake mackerel, this extraordinary fish can glide long distances above the surface of the ocean. In the water, it feeds on crustaceans, plankton, and other small invertebrates.

BETTA
BETTA SPLENDENS

Also known popularly as the Siamese fighting fish, this is a southeast Asian freshwater species. These fish are very popular aquarium fish, so have been bred in ever more wonderful colors over the years.

Fighting fish
The colorful males are very aggressive particularly when they are defending their territory. They will lunge at rival males, trying to bite off bits of their fins.

Lemon shark and remoras

Common remora

Looking after each other
Remoras get a free ride from a shark and eat scraps that their host drops. In return, they feed off parasites from the shark's skin and mouth.

COMMON REMORA
REMORA REMORA

Also known as suckerfish, these fish are found attached to sharks, whales, manta rays, and turtles. Their flat head has a sucking disk that is pressed against the host.

INVERTEBR

ATES

INVERTEBRATES

Nearly every creature on Earth is an invertebrate, meaning it has no backbone. Mammals, reptiles, amphibians, fish, and birds have backbones, but they make up around 3 percent of the planet's species. Invertebrates crawl, fly, swim, or float everywhere on Earth. Most live in watery habitats, including many parasites that thrive in the squelchy bits of other animals' bodies, including yours.

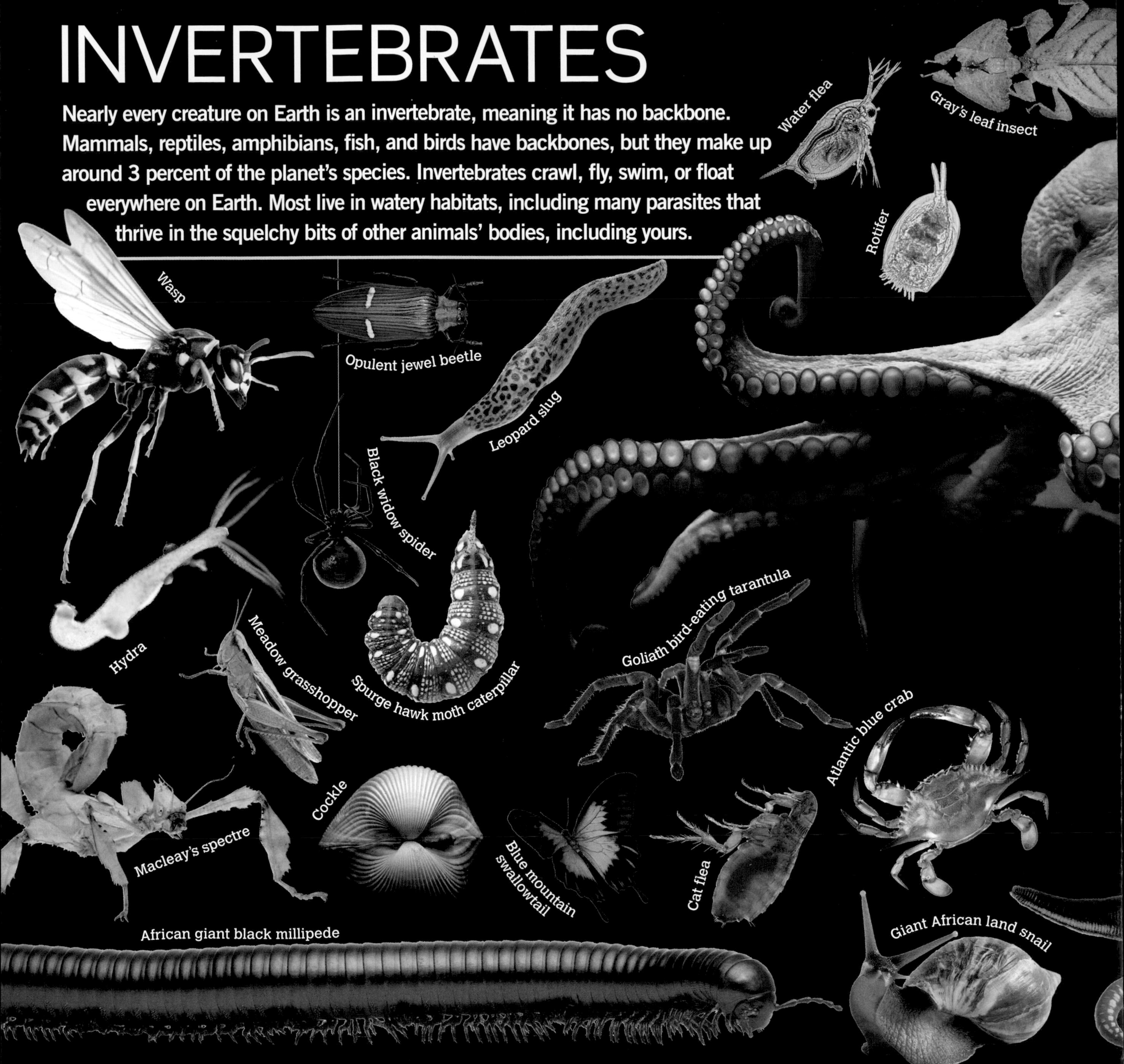

Water flea

Gray's leaf insect

Rotifer

Wasp

Opulent jewel beetle

Leopard slug

Black widow spider

Hydra

Meadow grasshopper

Spurge hawk moth caterpillar

Goliath bird-eating tarantula

Atlantic blue crab

Macleay's spectre

Cockle

Blue mountain swallowtail

Cat flea

Giant African land snail

African giant black millipede

Flatworm

Tardigrade

Pill bug

Common octopus

Atlantic sea nettle jellyfish

Dung beetle

European lancelet

Forbes' sea star

Seven-spotted ladybug

Sponge

Medicinal leech

Earthworm

European praying mantis

INVERTEBRATE ANATOMY

Invertebrate groups are only distantly related to one another and they vary hugely. Some, such as jellyfish, have a soft body. Others, like bugs, grow an exoskeleton, a hard outer shell that gives structure and protection to their body. Invertebrates do not have a backbone and are multicellular, with many cells each doing a job to keep the animal alive. They range from being relatively simple like sponges that lack tissues or organs to complex organisms like beetles that have well-developed senses and move in a rapid and coordinated way.

A DIVERSE KINGDOM

The range of invertebrates goes from sea corals to spiders, butterflies, and crabs. Some invertebrates spend most of their lives without moving, some do not have senses such as eyesight, and some do not have heads! However, many invertebrates have highly developed bodies. The largest invertebrate is the bootlace worm that is estimated to stretch 180 ft (55 m)—twice as long as two school buses. At the other end of the scale are tiny rotifiers or dust mites too small for us to see with the naked eye. Many invertebrates live in the seas or watery habitats such as lakes or puddles. The most numerous terrestrial group are the insects—there are about 200 million insects for every person on the planet.

SIMPLE ANIMALS
SIMPLY SURVIVING

These look like alien monsters, but you rarely see them, even if they are lurking in every wet or moist place (and possibly inside your body). They developed from single-cell creatures, changing as they gained more cells. Some live alone, others in colonies, and many are parasites in plants or other creatures. They include the blob-like trichoplax, pore-filled sponge, and barrel-shaped tardigrade.

ROTIFER
FLOSCULARIA RINGENS

These microscopic animals are common in ponds and puddles and are freshwater plankton. They help to clean up the water by eating fish waste, dead bacteria, and algae.

Tiny cleaners
These rotifers live in tubes that they build from many little circular pellets of bacteria and small pieces of detritus. They grow to around 0.06 in (1.5 mm) long.

TARDIGRADE
HYPSIBIUS DUJARDINI

Known as water bears or moss piglets, these remarkable eight-legged micro-animals live in puddles and freshwater pools. However, they are virtually indestructible and have even survived the low pressure and intense radiation of space.

Grazing on food

Egg
Once laid, eggs take around 10 days to hatch.

Female carrying six eggs

Hooked hand
Each hand has claws that are different lengths.

Mouth
This sucks juices from algae, lichens, and moss.

Reproduction
Female tardigrades produce 1–30 eggs per clutch, and the young fend for themselves. They molt their tough exterior 4–12 times in a lifetime.

Scientific name: *Hypsibius dujardini*

Size: up to 0.02 in (0.5 mm)

Diet: fluids of plants and animals

Lifespan in wild: up to 12 years; scientists say up to 100 years if dehydrated

Location: worldwide in lakes, rivers, streams, and puddles

TRICHOPLAX
TRICHOPLAX ADHAERENS

This is the simplest multicellular animal ever described. It is rarely observed in the wild, although it has been found in warm seas worldwide. It has no organs or internal structure. However, it is capable of forming social feeding groups, absorbing green algae with its underside.

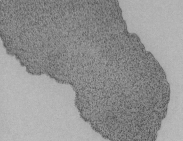

Primitive life
This flat, plate-like organism is only around 0.5 mm in cross-section. It moves on hair-like structures called cilia on its underside, and can change its shape to make itself tubular and elongated.

Boring sponge (*Cliona delitrix*)

Tube sponge (*Aplysina fistularis*)

SPONGES
PORIFERA PHYLUM

Sponges have been around for at least 600 million years and some may live for more than 200 years. These multicellular animals are found worldwide, mainly in seawater. They attach to rocks or surfaces on the seabed and filter water through small openings on their surfaces to get food.

CNIDARIANS
STINGING DRIFTERS

Cnidarians are big trouble in a spelling bee and a real danger in the warm seas they inhabit. Some carry stings strong enough to paralyze or even kill a person. They mostly drift about but some stick themselves to a surface and wait for passing food.

Polyps with stinging tentacles

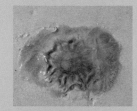

Branching out
Branching from the central column are the secondary polyps, each with eight stinging tentacles that are used to capture plankton.

Orange sea pen

SEA PENS
PENNATULACEA

A sea pen can look like an old-fashioned pen, a feather, or a worm. It can be anything from 2 ins (5 cms) to 6.6 ft (2 m) tall. Like corals, they are colonies of marine animals. The central stalk, anchored in sand or mud, is the primary polyp.

BOX JELLYFISH
CHIRONEX FLECKERI

Also known as the sea wasp or marine stinger, the venom of this jellyfish contains toxins that attack the heart, nervous system, and skin cells. Each tentacle has around 5,000 stinging cells. It uses the venom to stun or kill its prey that includes small fish and shrimp.

Box jellyfish

Fish prey in box jellyfish

Jellyfish hunter
Unlike other jellyfish that float along in the water, the box jellyfish actually hunts its prey. This box jellyfish has captured its fish prey with its tentacles, then swallowed it—you can see it inside the transparent box.

LION'S MANE JELLYFISH
CYANEA CAPILLATA

This brightly colored jellyfish is the largest jellyfish in the world, growing as long as 190 ft (58 m) with a bell that can be 7 ft (2.1 m) across. It lives near, or floats on, the surface of cold Arctic or north Pacific waters where it catches small fish, crustaceans, and other jellyfish. In the dark waters it is bioluminescent—it can produce its own light and glow.

All washed up
Jellyfish are around 95 percent water, so if they are stranded on a beach, the water evaporates and the jellyfish disappears.

Tentacle close-up

Mane killer
The "mane" of up to 1,200 long tentacles hangs from the underside of its colorful body. The venomous tentacles are used to stun prey.

Giant jellyfish

STINGING BUSH HYDROID
MACRORHYNCHIA PHILIPPINA

Often mistaken for a plant, the hydroid is in fact a colony of many little polyps that look like tiny ferns. It can form bushes of considerable size on coral and rocky reefs where there are currents and tidal surges.

Bushes in the water
Hydroids feed on plankton that they filter from the water. These stinging hydroids are in the Pacific near the coast of Misool Island in Indonesia. The polyps are very small and are carried on the stem and side branches.

GREEN HYDRA
HYDRA VIRIDISSIMA

This tiny freshwater hydroid with its delicate tentacles is found in slow-moving rivers and ponds, where it attaches to the stems and leaves of water plants.

Mutual benefit The green color comes from green algae that live inside its tissues. The algae supply oxygen to, and obtain food from, the hydra.

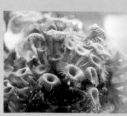

Coral flowers
These have short stalks topped with disks that have tentacles radiating out from the edges.

ZOANTHUS
GENUS ZOANTHUS

Also known as button polyps, these animals look like a bunch of tiny flowers. They range in color from brown to green, orange, and red.

PAINTED ANEMONE
URTICINA GREBELNYI

With a distinctive paintbrush coloring, this sea anemone can be up to 9 ins (23 cm) tall. It anchors itself to a rock crevice or ledge on its own or in a group and catches animals that swim past. It lives in the cold waters of the northwestern Pacific.

Defense and attack
Like all its relatives, this animal uses its venomous cells in the tentacles to both sting attackers, such as sea stars and snails, and stun and capture prey.

Above and below
The man o'war has a gas-filled float, or pneumatophore, that sits some 6 ins (15 cm) above the water. If threatened, it can deflate this and briefly submerge. Its long tendrils may extend as much as 165 ft (50 m) below the surface.

PORTUGUESE MAN O' WAR
PHYSALIA PHYSALIS

This is not a jellyfish—it is a siphonophore, a collection of cnidarians that work together as they float in warm ocean waters. Its poisonous tentacles have powerful stings to kill small fish and plankton. The loggerhead turtle, ocean sunfish, and blanket octopus think that the man o' war is a tasty treat.

GROOVED BRAIN CORAL
DIPLORIA LABYRINTHIFORMIS

This extraordinary coral grows in the shallow reefs of the Caribbean. It is deeply grooved and looks just like a giant brain. It is made up of rows of polyps that have their tentacles along the sides of each row, with their mouths forming the grooves.

Spawning
Grooved brain corals are hermaphrodites—they release both male and female reproductive cells, called gametes, into the water to form new corals.

Scientific name: *Diploria labyrinthiformis*

Common names: depressed brain coral, stony coral

Size: up to 6 ft (2 m) in diameter

Diet: plankton

Lifespan in wild: they may live hundreds of years

Location: the Caribbean, Bermuda

Polyps detail

Reef formation
Only the outer shell of these large reef-building corals is actually living tissue, the rest is a hard calcium carbonate skeleton.

Built to last
The brain coral only lives in areas where the light penetrates the water. It grows very slowly and the strong domed shape helps it withstand pounding waves.

Large brain coral

WORMS

NATURE'S RECYCLERS

Legless, worms wriggle around in lots of different habitats. Many live in water or damp soil but others prefer the warmth and darkness inside plants or other creatures. The three main types are flatworms that can regenerate lost parts; roundworms that live in soil; and segmented worms which include the leeches.

TAPEWORM
TAENIA SOLIUM

This flatworm is a parasite that lives inside a variety of animals including humans, in whom it is known to cause blindness, epileptic seizures, and even death. People eat the larvae in undercooked infected pork. The larvae then develop into adult tapeworms that can live in the gut for many years.

Attachment
The adult tapeworm attaches itself to the small intestine using the suckers and hooks in the scolex, or head region. There it feeds off its host's food.

NEMATODE WORM
CAENORHABDITIS ELEGANS

One handful of soil contains thousands of these microscopic worms. Some scientists estimate that four out of every five animals on Earth is a nematode.

Spawning
This species lives in the soil, particularly rotting vegetation, in many parts of the world. It feeds on microbes such as bacteria.

MEDICINAL LEECH
HIRUDO MEDICINALIS

This freshwater worm has a flattened body that is divided into 33 or 34 segments. Not all leeches suck blood but this species' talent is to create a wound that bleeds for hours and it is used in surgery today.

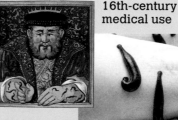

16th-century medical use

Leech treatment
For centuries, doctors have used medicinal leeches to bleed patients. The leeches produce a substance that stops blood clotting and are applied to clean wounds.

Modern use

Characteristics
The leech has suckers at both ends. The front one surrounds a mouth with sharp teeth with which it latches onto the host. The medicinal leech also has five pairs of eyes.

POLYCLAD FLATWORM
PSEUDOBICEROS FLOWERSI

This marine flatworm is found in the western Indo-Pacific. It is an active predator and scavenger, feeding on small invertebrates by covering them with its body before sucking them in.

Small mover
Up to 1.5 ins (4 cm) long, this flatworm undulates fast along the sea bed by beating tiny hairs that act like millions of feet.

Nightmarish
This bobbit worm can grow up to 10 ft (3 m) long. It has five antennae that it uses to sense passing prey, which it yanks back into its burrow to eat.

BOBBIT WORM
EUNICE APHRODITOIS

A predator that lives buried beneath the seafloor of the tropical Indo-Pacific oceans, the bobbit worm has jaws so strong that they can cut a fish in half.

PILE WORM
ALITTA SUCCINEA

This marine worm has up to 160 segments, four pairs of tentacles, two pairs of eyes, and one pair of antennae. It can grow up to 7.5 ins (19 cm) long.

Bottom-feeder
The pile worm emerges from its U-shaped mud or sand burrow at night to feed on plant material and small crustaceans that it finds on the seabed.

Conservation success

Jellyfish Lake is a saltwater lake on the uninhabited Eil Malk island in Palau in the western Pacific. It is 1,310 ft (400 m) long and 100 ft (30 m) deep and, in 2005, was home to an extraordinary 30 million non-stinging golden jellyfish (*Mastigias papua etpisoni*), a unique subspecies only found here. After a serious drought in 2016, hardly any of these medusa survived and the lake was closed to visitors to allow the population to recover. A survey in December 2018 established that there are now around 630,000 jellyfish, a number that shows the population is well on its way to recovery.

MOLLUSKS
SOFT-BODIED SHELLFISH

Mollusks have soft bodies, usually protected by a hard shell. They grow this casing inside a cloak of skin called a mantle. Every mollusk is different—the chiton is the only mollusk with an eight-piece shell, while the tusk shell's covering looks like an elephant's tusk and has an opening at both ends. They live in many different habitats, from deep oceans to ponds and sometimes dry land.

GIANT CLAM
TRIDACNA GIGAS

This is the largest mollusk of all with one found that measured 4.6 ft (1.4 m) and weighed 550 lbs (250 kg). The species is mainly found in the Indo-Pacific.

The eyes have it
These bivalves have hundreds of eyes along the edges of their mantles. The eyes detect shadows and warn of predators. The clams either filter-feed or rely on algae for nutrients.

GIANT AFRICAN LAND SNAIL
ACHATINA FULICA

The biggest group of mollusks are gastropods, a diverse group that includes slugs and snails. This African species is one of the largest land-living snails. It moves its up to 8-ins (20-cm)-long body with a muscular "foot" that releases a slime to help it slide along.

Sensing the world
This snail has a pair of short tentacles that sense smells and two long ones that carry its eyes. Its shell is cone-shaped with spirals on its surface. Inside its mouth is a rasping tongue called a radula, with toothlets to scrape and cut up its plant food.

LINED CHITON
TONICELLA LINEATA

Moving along
Lined chitons move slowly over rocks feeding on the coralline algae that they like to eat. If their foot fails to hold them in place, they can roll into a ball to protect their soft underbelly from any predators.

Chitons are the only mollusks with shells made of eight separate plates. The lined chiton lives on rocks in shallow Pacific waters.

BLUE GLAUCUS
GLAUCUS ATLANTICUS

This nudibranch, a sea slug, is also known as the blue dragon. It stores a bubble of air in its stomach and floats with the currents on the surface of the sea, belly side up. It is only 1.5 ins (4 cm) long.

Under threat
The glaucus stores and concentrates stinging cells from its favorite prey, the Portuguese man o' war (*see p.174*). If the glaucus is threatened, it releases the stinging cells.

PHARAOH CUTTLEFISH
SEPIA PHARAONIS

This species gets its name from its shape like that of a pharaoh's crown. This master color changer has a flat body suited to life near the seabed hunting for fish and mollusks.

Moving along
It moves by undulating a fringe along its body. If threatened, it produces a cloud of sepia ink.

BIG FIN REEF SQUID

SEPIOTEUTHIS LESSONIANA

The "big fins" extend the length of its body. Its specialized skin cells, chromatophores, change in color and pattern to attract a mate, confuse predators, or camouflage itself. And it is a voracious feeder on shrimp and fish around coral reefs and in seagrass meadows throughout the Indo-Pacific.

Female squid and eggs

Newly hatched squid

Cycle of life
The female squid lays her eggs in well-protected areas of the reef, and once she has reproduced, she dies. The young squid stay close to the shore, usually in shallow turtle grasses near islands, only venturing into open water when they become adults.

Scientific name:
Sepioteuthis lessoniana

Common name: oval squid

Size: up to 16.5 ins (42 cms) long

Weight: up to 4.4 lbs (2 kg)

Diet: small fish, crabs, shrimp, other squid

Lifespan in wild: 1 year

Location: Indian and western Pacific oceans

Squid senses
Their eyes are the largest in proportion to their bodies in the animal kingdom and give them good night vision. Squid are sensitive to touch and taste sensors on their tentacles tell them about the prey they catch.

Mantle
When the mantle expands, oxygenated water is sucked in and helps the squid breathe.

Locomotion
The squid uses a combination of flapping its two fins and producing jets of water to move around.

Chromatophores
The squid communicates by controling the pigment in its skin, flashing a message with color.

Characteristics
This cephalopod has a torpedo-shaped body, eight short "arms" with suckers, and two longer tentacles. The mantle contains three hearts, the stomach, gills, ink sac, and the reproductive and digestive organs.

Tentacles
The eight short "arms" and two long tentacles are arranged around the mouth in a circle.

Lunchtime
Squid catch prey with their two long tentacles and pull it into their small, beak-like mouth; the strong beak cuts it up. In turn, these squid are preyed on by tuna, sharks, and dolphins.

BELLYBUTTON NAUTILUS

NAUTILUS MACROMPHALUS

Found in waters off northeastern Australia, this species spends the day at depths of up to 1,640 ft (500 m), rising at night to feed on fish and crabs.

Chambered shell

Tentacled nautilus

Feeling its way
The nautilus adjusts gases in its chambered body to allow it to move vertically up and down. These scavengers have poor eyesight and use scent and touch to find food.

REEF OCTOPUS

OCTOPUS BRIAREUS

The Caribbean reef octopus likes warm, shallow waters and coral reefs for its den. It has seven rows of denticles and each of its eight arms has two rows of suckers to grab marine snails and clams to eat.

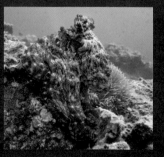

Now you see me
The octopus is superbly camouflaged against the reef rocks. It is typically green and blue, but changes color to blend in.

Zombie snail

Inside the eyestalks of this snail are the larvae of a parasitic flatworm, the green-banded broodsac (*Leucochloridium paradoxum*). The worm turns the snail into a zombie, mind-controlling it into the open where it can be found by a bird that eat its eyestalks thinking they are caterpillars. The worm then breeds in the gut of the predator bird and its eggs become part of the bird's droppings, which in turn are eaten by another snail and the whole cycle begins again.

MIMICRY

Not everything is always as it seems in the animal world. Those black-and-yellow stripes might be a wasp or a harmless insect. That green leaf might be an insect or a fish. Huge eyes staring out turn out to be . . . butterfly wings. Pretending to be something else is called mimicry. Some creatures even mimic others with sounds, or smells, or the way in which they behave. There are a lot of copycats out there!

Plant mimics
Many different animals mimic parts of plants. They do this to hide from prey or so that they can catch prey themselves. They may have the color and shape of petals or look like a stick, but the most common kind of plant mimicry is associated with leaves.

Hiding in the open
Some jumping spiders have long, slender legs and what appears to be a three-part body like an ant. They also raise their front legs in the air so that they seem to have a pair of antennae. It is likely they do this to put off predators that avoid ants because of their formic acid.

Carpenter ant (*Camponotus herculeanus*)

Ant-mimicking jumping spider (*Myrmarachne sp.*)

Hoverfly

Leaf insect

Is it dangerous?
The hoverfly, also known as the flower fly, is protected by its black-and-yellow markings. It looks enough like a bee, wasp, or hornet as it moves from flower to flower to deter bird predators. This tactic protects an insect that does not bite or sting.

Wasp

The leaf insects (family Phylliidae) are also called the walking leaves for good reason. When they walk they sway from side to side to mimic being blown by the wind. The lappet moth (*Gastropacha*

Lappet moth between two dead leaves

quercifolia) has brown creased or furled wings that make it look just like a dead leaf. And the Amazon leaf fish (*Monocirrhus polyacanthus*) mimics a leaf drifting in the water so that it can sneak up on prey such as small fishes or shrimp.

Monkey caller
The margay (*Leopardus wiedii*) wildcat of South America has developed a clever way of hunting. It has learned to imitate the calls of pied tamarin monkeys (*Saguinus bicolor*), luring them to their death.

Margay wild cat

Zone-tailed hawk's deceptive silhouette

Safe flight pattern
The zone-tailed hawk (*Buteo albonotatus*) of southwestern North America often flies with groups of turkey vultures (*Cathartes aura*). It is able to catch prey, including doves and lizards, that would flee the hawk's silhouette on its own.

Sound machine
The superb lyrebird of Australia is able to imitate even the most complex sounds. Up to 80 percent of its song is mimicry, and most birds can imitate 25 species.

Superb lyrebird (*Menura novaehollandiae*)

Amazon leaf fish

Devoted parent

A female giant Pacific octopus lays up to 100,000 eggs the size of rice grains in bunches of around 300 eggs. She guards them, not eating, until they hatch—for up to a year—and dies shortly afterward.

GIANT PACIFIC OCTOPUS
ENTEROCTOPUS DOFLEINI

This octopus grows bigger and lives longer than any other octopus. It is smart, agile, and well-equipped to hunt, grab, and wrap prey in its eight suction-cup-covered arms. Like other octopuses, its large head contains a well-developed brain—500 million neurons are located there and in its arms. In the laboratory, octopuses have learned to do many tasks, including opening jars, unscrambling Rubik's cubes, and solving maze puzzles. They have a working memory and can differentiate shapes.

The largest **giant Pacific octopus** had an **armspan** of **31.5 ft (9.6 m)** and weighed **600 lbs (272 kg)**.

Scientific name:
Enteroctopus dofleini

Size: up to 31.5 ft (9.6 m) armspan

Weight: up to 600 lbs (272 kg)

Diet: crustaceans, mollusks, dogfish sharks

Lifespan in wild: up to 5 years

Location: northern Pacific

Travel style
This jet-powered beast sucks water into its body, forcing it out of its siphon to push forward, long arms trailing behind. It lives in lairs on the seafloor, usually at depths of 360 ft (110 m), but it may also dive to depths of 5,000 ft (1,500 m).

Seafloor cruiser

Deep diver

Ambush hunter
Hiding under or on a rock, the octopus uses its chromatophores to change color and blend into the background. It is also able to look like the rock or vegetation with different skin textures.

Suction cup to identify objects

Complex eye

Siphon for expelling ink cloud

Body
The flexible body has no bones so it can squeeze into very small crevices.

Hearts
Under the mantle beat three hearts—one to circulate blood and two to pass blood over the gills to oxygenate them.

Suction cups
Ranged in pairs down the arms, these grab and hold prey, and can also be used for walking on the seabed.

Siphon
This muscular tube can be pointed to help the octopus change direction.

Efficient feeder
Octopuses hide during the day, emerging at night to hunt for prey. Their strong arms and more than 2,000 suction cups pry shells apart or their sharp beak drills holes in the shells to suck out the juicy contents.

Quick reactions
This octopus uses its excellent sense of touch to find out what it is touching and its very keen eyesight to spot trouble. If it does not have time to change color, it can release a cloud of ink from its siphon to confuse and disorient a predator.

CRUSTACEANS

SHELL-DWELLERS

Crustaceans are named after their exoskeleton, a carapace that grows around the body and is shed when it gets too small. The group includes crabs, shrimps, and barnacles, most of these living in water—although barnacles stick themselves to rocks—plus woodlice, which like damp places on land. Crustaceans have three-part bodies (head, thorax, abdomen) and some have eyes on stalks.

Egg sac
Some female copepods have egg sacs near the tail.

Essential food
Copepods are a major part of the plankton that feed so many larger sea creatures. Some use their legs to swim, others bend and straighten to move.

WATER FLEA
DAPHNIA MAGNA

This small, aquatic crustacean is only up to 0.2 ins (5 mm) long and lives in pools, swamps, and rivers throughout the northern hemisphere. Its body is covered by a transparent carapace, or body-case.

Microscopic
The water flea's antennae help to produce a current of water that carries food to its mouth and oxygen to its gills. This female has a clutch of eggs.

REMIPEDE
SPELEONECTES TANUMEKES

Out of some 70,000 species, this is the only class of venomous crustacean found so far. It was only discovered in the 1980s, living in coastal caves. The name "remipede" refers to its many pairs of swimming legs.

Finding food
The largest of these blind crustaceans has 40 segments. They swim slowly along on their backs in the cave waters looking for other crustaceans, and use their venom to soften the prey's shells.

COPEPOD
COPEPODA SPECIES

These small, free-swimming crustaceans are found in both fresh- and seawater. There are more that 4,500 species, and the word in Greek means "oar-feet." Some hunt prey, some filter the water, and some are parasites that suck blood from fish.

ANTARCTIC KRILL
EUPHAUSIA SUPERBA

These shrimp-like animals swim in the cold Southern Ocean around Antarctica. They feed on tiny plankton, using their legs to filter out microscopic algae. They are mostly transparent with a red tinge.

Antarctic krill

GOOSENECK BARNACLE
LEPAS ANATIFERA

A gooseneck barnacle does not move unless it is torn from the floating object it is attached to by its stalk, or peduncle. It often fastens itself to ships' hulls and driftwood, as well as plastic waste.

Feathered
The heart-shaped bivalve shell can grow up to 2 ins (5 cm) long. It filters water currents with its feathery legs for particles to eat.

Seabed life
The giant isopod feeds on dead whales, fish, and squid at depths of up to 7,000 ft (2,135 m), It rolls its 16 ins (40 cm) body into a ball for protection.

GIANT ISOPOD
BATHYNOMUS GIGANTEUS

This crustacean is the largest of around nine species of isopods. It is a deepsea scavenger that lives in the cold, deep waters of the Atlantic and Pacific oceans.

Food chain
Antarctic krill live in vast swarms and are one of the most important prey species. Large whales, leopard seals, penguins, and fish are among those sea creatures that eat huge numbers of the krill.

Humpback whale feeding

SCARLET CLEANER SHRIMP
LYSMATA AMBOINENSIS

This Indo-Pacific species lives in pairs or large congregations of up to 100. It sets up cleaning stations that fish visit regularly.

Scarlet cleaner shrimp

Moray eel at a cleaning station

Grooming
The shrimp feed by cleaning parasites, food particles, and bacteria from the fish that visit the cleaning stations.

Probing for food
The lobster probes its surroundings with its antennae for hermit crabs, whelks, worms, and mussels. It is also a scavenger on carcasses.

EUROPEAN LOBSTER
HOMARUS GAMMARUS

Usually found in shallow waters less than 130 ft (40 m) deep, this lobster is solitary. It shelters in burrows during the day and hunts for food at night. It has one claw to crush and the other for cutting.

Long-legged crustacean
The Japanese spider crab moves by walking over the seabed. It molts up to 20 times in its life, shedding its shell and growing a new one.

FIDDLER CRAB
UCA SPECIES

Fiddler crabs are found in large numbers on muddy seashores in the tropics. They live in saltwater-covered burrows and feed on algae. The largest are only 2 ins (5 cm) across.

Male display
Male fiddler crabs have one small pincer and one giant one, but females have two small pincers. The males use their large pincers during courtship to warn off rivals.

JAPANESE SPIDER CRAB
MACROCHEIRA KAEMPFERI

With the largest legspan of any crab at 13 ft (4 m), this spider crab does not worry about predators. It is found deep in the ocean near Japan, around 1,000 ft (300 m) down and can live for 100 years.

ROBBER CRAB
BIRGUS LATRO

This is the largest and heaviest land-living crustacean and the world's largest arthropod. It spends most of its time finding coconuts to eat on Indo-Pacific islands. It is also a scavenger and will catch chickens and other birds to eat. It has been hunted to extinction on some of the islands.

Land giant
Robber crabs use their long legs to scuttle, burrow, and climb coconut trees. They use their claws to break open coconut shells.

Scientific name: *Birgus latro*

Common names: coconut crab, palm thief

Size: up to 39 ins (1 m) legspan

Weight: up to 9 lbs (4.1 kg)

Diet: coconuts

Lifespan in wild: up to 60 years

Location: Indo-Pacific islands

Bone crusher
The two front legs have powerful claws capable of lifting 60-lb (27-kg) rocks.

Tough body
The outer body becomes hard and calcified.

Armored giant

Life process
The robber crab begins life in the sea, floating freely until it finds a shell to live in. Then it begins its move onto land. After a year of moving from shell to shell, it discards its adopted shell, its body hardens, and it takes to the open.

Climbing a coconut tree

Spring-loaded death machine

The peacock mantis shrimp (*Odontodactylus scyllarus*) is not only one of the most colorful animals on Earth, it is one of the swiftest of killers. Only up to 7 ins (18 cm) long, it can summon tremendous force with its front legs to stun or kill prey, punching crabs or clams with the force of a bullet shot from a .22-caliber gun! This very aggressive hunter lives in the warm waters of the Indo-Pacific, often near coral reefs, where it builds U-shaped burrows. It spots its prey with complex eyes on stalks that can move independently.

HORSESHOE CRABS AND SEA SPIDERS

MISNAMED INVERTEBRATES

Don't be fooled. Horseshoe crabs are not crabs—in fact they are more like spiders—while sea spiders are not spiders at all. Both animals, however, are related to arachnids. And like arachnids they do not have antennae and their bodies are divided into two parts.

ATLANTIC HORSESHOE CRAB

LIMULUS POLYPHEMUS

The horseshoe crab is named for the shape of its exoskeleton. It burrows into the sand in shallow waters near the northwest coast of the Atlantic.

Shoreline mover
The crab walks with five pairs of legs. A sixth pair are pincers that grab food such as clams and worms. Its tail acts as a rudder as it moves across the mud.

SEA SPIDER

PANTOPODA

Sea spiders are found scuttling along the bottom of oceans around the world. Most have eight legs, but some have 10 or 12. They are carnivorous, slurping out the insides of their sea sponge and worm prey with a trunk-like proboscis.

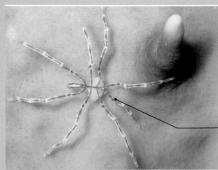

Alternative systems
Sea spiders do not really have a body, so their legs house some of their organs. They do not have a respiratory system. Instead they pump blood with the digestive system in their legs.

Breathing with legs
Sea spiders absorb oxygen through their exoskeletons.

ARACHNIDS

EIGHT-LEGGED INVERTEBRATES

The arachnid family includes spiders, scorpions, harvestmen, ticks, and mites. They all have four pairs of legs and most have two-part bodies. Spiders are the best-known arachnids and all of them carry venom to paralyze their prey. A few such as the black widow and the funnel-web have a bite that can kill people.

Web-builder
The golden silk orb-weaver (*Nephila* species) spins a strong web to catch its prey.

VELVET MITE

TROMBIDIUM SPECIES

This mite looks like a little red velvet cushion. Mites are found in almost every part of the world, and the adults feed on other insects, their eggs, and larvae.

Feeling the way
Only 0.12–0.47 ins (3–12 mm) long, velvet mites use their front legs as feelers to check where they are going and find food.

Leggy
Unlike other arachnids, this one uses only six legs for walking. The other two long legs are used like antennae.

TAILLESS WHIP SCORPION

ORDER AMBLYPYGI

By day, these arachnids hide under bark or leaf litter in the tropical forests of Asia, the Americas, and Africa. They emerge at night, walking in a crab-like fashion.

CAMEL SPIDER

GALEODES ARABS

Also called wind scorpions, these arachnids run like the wind on only six of their eight legs. They are a desert species that has large, powerful jaws and chases down insects, rodents, lizards, and small birds.

Desert life
Camel spiders are well adapted to desert life. They are covered in fine hairs that protect them from the heat, and sensory organs on the underside of the hind legs tell them about the ground they are traveling on.

FALSE SCORPION

ORDER PSEUDOSCORPIONIDA

Found all over the world, these tiny animals live in humid places such as cave floors, soil, and leaf litter. Some even take to the air on harlequin beetles!

Paralysis by touch
The arachnid has two large pincer claws with sensitive hairs to find prey and venom glands to immobilize it.

Killing machine
Scorpions can kill large prey such as mice and lizards with the sting in the tip of their tail, but most adults tear the prey apart with their strong pincers.

EMPEROR SCORPION

PANDINUS IMPERATOR

A native of west Africa, this impressive scorpion lives on open savanna and tropical forests, near to mounds that contain its favorite food, termites. It hides in burrows under rocks and litter.

Abdomen
Silk is exuded from glands in the abdomen.

Tough life
This species lays its hundreds of eggs underground encased in a silk sac. The spiderlings grow by molting their exoskeleton.

Little and large
The female spider is up to 2 ins (5 cm) long. The tiny red male, seen here on a female, is by contrast only up to 0.27 ins (7 mm) long!

Web of food
The female detects the slightest vibration from trapped insects in the web. She wraps victims in silk and keeps them until needed.

Pedipalps
These sensory organs are used to sense the presence of and hold prey.

Wide web

Eating a butterfly

GIANT GOLDEN ORB-WEAVER

NEPHILA PILIPES

Known for the golden 6.5-ft (2-m) webs she weaves, the female of this species maintains the web, while the tiny males sit on the outskirts, waiting for an opportunity to mate. The net is so strong it can catch birds or bats.

Scientific name: *Nephila pilipes*	1 in (2.5 cm) male legspan
Common names: northern golden orb-weaver	**Diet:** insects, birds, bats
	Lifespan in wild: up to 2 years
Size: up to 6 ins (15 cm) female legspan; less than	**Location:** India, southest Asia, Australia

GOLIATH BIRD-EATING TARANTULA

THERAPHOSA BLONDI

The biggest tarantula of all lives deep in the rain forests of northern South America. It is up to 4.75 ins (12 cm) long and has a legspan of up to 11 ins (28 cm). It is nocturnal, leaving its burrow to hunt for insects, small birds, or mammals.

Huge fangs

Irritating hairs

Self-defense
As a defense, the spider shows its fangs or rubs hairs together to make a hissing noise. It can also fire hairs at predators.

Living space
The North American spider likes dry, dark places, including rodent holes, garages, and barns. It wraps prey in silk, injecting it to liquefy the corpse so it can suck up the juices.

Spider home
This species lives in a deep burrow under the forest floor dug with its fangs and lined with silk.

Attack pose
When a tarantula rears up on its hind legs it is ready to attack.

BLACK WIDOW

LATRODECTUS MACTANS

If this spider bites you its venom is strong enough to kill, but it is not aggressive so this does not happen often. The male black widow spider is not so lucky. The female may kill and eat him after mating.

MILLIPEDES AND CENTIPEDES
LEGGY BUGS

Both have lots of legs on long bodies divided into segments, but their names are misleading as they do not describe leg numbers. Centipedes are flat-bodied carnivores that kill prey with venom injected from claws on the side of the head, while millipedes are usually longer, cylinder-shaped creatures that scavenge dead plant matter.

AMERICAN GIANT MILLIPEDE
NARCEUS AMERICANUS

This millipede of eastern North America lives in the soil of forests and farms. It also hides under moist dead leaves and sometimes in animal corpses.

Insect cowboy
Centipedes are active hunters. They use the two legs near their head to lasso prey. They then jump on it and wrap it up with the rest of their legs.

Self-defense
When the millipede is threatened it curls up. It can also release a poisonous fluid that irritates eyes or skin.

HOUSE CENTIPEDE
SCUTIGERA COLEOPTRATA

This animal is fast, scuttling up walls and under furniture. It has 15 pairs of legs and can cover 1.3 ft (0.4 m) in a second. However, it is harmless to humans and kills pests such as flies, cockroaches, silverfish, and termites.

GIANT CENTIPEDE
SCOLOPENDRA SUBSNIPES

A giant that has brightly colored legs and venomous claws, this centipede lives in eastern Asia, the Caribbean, and Central America. It is an aggressive nocturnal hunter, killing and eating insects, small mammals, arachnids, and reptiles.

Heads up
It has a pair of modified legs on its head with which it kills its prey.

Big beast
This centipede is among the largest of all, growing up to 8 ins (20 cm) in length.

In clouds
The black-veined white butterfly (*Aporia crataegi*) settles in groups of hundreds to feed in European meadows.

INSECTS
MYRIADS OF ARTHROPODS

On every square mile of land, there are more insects than there are people on Earth. Scientists estimate that there are some 10,000,000,000,000,000,000 (ten quintillion) species, but only around one million have been named. All have a three-part body, six legs, two antennae to sense the world, and an outer hard case called an exoskeleton. Insects breathe through a set of tiny tubes called tracheae and many have wings.

SILVERFISH
LEPISMA SACCHARINA

Also known as the bristletail, this small, wingless insect often lives in dark places inside houses. It is considered a pest as it likes to feed on sugar and starch, for example in paper and glue. It gets its name from its silver scales.

Voracious feeders
These silverfish are completely destroying the pages of an old book. They move like fish with a side-to-side movement.

BRISTLETAIL
DILTA HIBERNICA

Jumping bristletails are found all over the world, including in the Arctic. This one lives in western Europe and parts of north Africa. It is wingless, but can run very fast when it needs to.

Quick locomotion
To move quickly, this tiny insect thrusts muscles in its abdomen against the ground, forcing itself several inches into the air.

BANDED DEMOISELLE

CALOPTERYX SPLENDENS

This beautiful Eurasian damselfly flits above the waters of rivers, ponds, and lakes. The females lay their eggs by injecting them into plant stems under the surface of the water. The nymphs live underwater for up to two years.

Blue and green
The males (above) are metallic blue and the females metallic green, and they both have colored wings.

Fully grown adult

Reproduction
The female lays her eggs on floating plants. The nymphs emerge as adults after two years and leave the water.

Nymph

FOUR-SPOTTED CHASER

LIBELLULA QUADRIMACULATA

The large eyes of this common dragonfly easily spot insect prey near shallow ponds and lakes.

YELLOW MAYFLY

HEPTAGENIA SULPHUREA

Mayfly nymphs spend up to three years underwater, where they feed on plants. When they leave the water and transform into adults, they do not eat and, after scattering eggs, die within a few hours.

Flight of insects
These aquatic insects hatch in enormous numbers from spring to autumn (not just May). They are delicate, with smaller hindwings and large compound eyes.

Tough omnivore
This bush cricket has strong biting jaws to chomp happily into nestlings, plants, and insects, and even eats its own kind.

Feasting on an insect

Well-armored insect

ARMORED GROUND CRICKET

ACANTHOPLUS DISCOIDALIS

This flightless insect is a popular snack for many predators so its armored exoskeleton is covered in sharp spines. It is able to squirt haemolymph (insect blood) from seams in the exoskeleton.

Disguise
This insect relies on looking like the leaves of the trees it inhabits for protection. In addition, its head is confusing, looking like it is on back to front.

Tail
It is curled for defense.

Leaf-like legs
Spiky lobes that look like desert plant leaves.

Scientific name: *Extatosoma tiaratum*

Common name: giant prickly stick insect, Australian walking stick

Size: up to 5 ins (13 cm) long, males; up to 8 ins (20 cm) long, females

Diet: leaves of trees and shrubs, including eucalyptus

Lifespan in wild: up to 6 months

Location: northern Australia

MACLEAY'S SPECTRE

EXTATOSOMA TIARATUM

This stick insect inhabits the lowland rain forests of northern Australia. The female can lay more than 1,000 eggs that look so much like seeds that ants take them into their nest. When they hatch, the nymphs look very like ants and only begin to resemble leaves over time.

Gender differences
The males (left) are smaller than the females and only have little spines. The males have long wings and can fly, unlike the females.

Pink lady
The female of this Malaysian species is pink while the male is green. This is a nocturnal katydid that feeds on leaves, flowers, bark, and seeds.

PINK KATYDID

EULOPHOPHYLLUM LOBULATUM

This katydid is very rare. Most katydids are large and leaf-shaped, perfect for camouflage. This unusual color mutation means females can be easily spotted by predators such as spiders and frogs.

GRAY'S LEAF INSECT
PHYLLIUM BIOCULATUM

Leaf-alike
The large forewings have veins that look like the leaves in which the flattened insect lives.

This Malaysian leaf insect looks just like the leaves it lives in. It stays still for hours on end, and when it moves, it sways as if it is being blown by the wind. This confuses both predators and prey.

STRIPED EARWIG
LABIDURA RIPARIA

A voracious nocturnal predator found worldwide in the tropics and subtropics, this earwig likes dark, wet woodlands and damp spots near ponds and lakes. Earwigs' fat bodies end in a pair of forceps-like pincers, mainly used for defense.

Hindquarters
Earwigs use their pincers when hunting, for defense, and to court females. They scavenge and also eat insects, moss, fungi, and lichen.

On parade
These termites are named for the dark, pointed heads of their soldiers. A liquid squirted from the tip of the head stops lizards, frogs, birds, and other potential predators in their tracks.

CONEHEAD TERMITE
NASUTITERMES CORNIGER

This Caribbean termite does not tunnel underground like most termites. Instead, it forages for food on the ground and builds nests of chewed wood or mud there or in trees. The nest may be up to 3 ft (1 m) in diameter.

Antennae
The male's slender body is topped by feathered antennae.

Colors
These only show when it is in this defensive pose.

Defense
Body and legs are moved left and right to scare attackers.

DEVIL'S FLOWER MANTIS
IDOLOMANTIS DIABOLICA

This is one of the largest species of praying mantis. The adult mantis has impressive bright red, white, blue, and black markings. On its back is a huge shield that looks like a dry leaf. It can be very large and is an ambush predator on its fly food.

Baby devil
Females lay up to 50 eggs in an egg mass. Newborn nymphs are shiny black, probably to mimic ants.

Nymph

Colorful show
The males have an amazing display behavior, rearing up on their back legs for defense.

Adult

Scientific name: *Idolomantis diabolica*

Common names: n/a

Size: up to 4 ins (10 cm) long, male; up to 5 ins (13 cm) long, female

Diet: flies and other insects

Lifespan in wild: up to 12 months

Location: Africa, mainly Tanzania

Family portraits
Older nymphs are light brown or tan, a complete contrast to the colorful face and eyes of the adult flower mantis.

Spotty "beetle"
It is also known as the seven-spotted cockroach. It uses chemicals called pheromones to communicate with other cockroaches.

INDIAN DOMINO COCKROACH
THEREA PETIVERIANA

This unusual cockroach protects itself by mimicking an aggressive ground beetle that sprays stinging liquid at predators. The cockroach lives in Indian forests and burrows under leaf litter during the day.

RED ASSASSIN BUG

RHYNOCORIS IRACUNDUS

This eastern European bug has a narrow head and puts its beak to good use, piercing insect prey and sucking the fluids from its victim. And it will tackle prey that is much larger than itself.

Long-nosed
As well as feeding on prey, this assassin bug sometimes defends itself by stabbing predators with its proboscis.

Proboscis

Eating a honey bee

Infestation!
The aphids feed by sucking the plant juices and they can give birth to live young several times a day.

BLACK BEAN APHID

APHIS FABAE

A small black insect, this aphid is a common sight on many vegetables and flowers in northern hemisphere gardens. Ladybugs are effective aphid predators.

HEAD LOUSE

PEDICULUS HUMANUS CAPITIS

Lousy deal
As it cannot fly, the louse crawls from head to head. Its abdomen swells up with blood as the louse feeds. It lays eggs that it fastens to the hairs of the head.

This wingless parasite lives on the human scalp, where it feeds by sucking up blood.

Larva

Strong stance
The large male has two bifurcated horns that it uses to overcome rival males. When it is threatened, it makes a loud hissing sound.

BROWN RHINOCEROS BEETLE

XYLOTRUPES GIDEON

This shiny Indonesian scarab beetle can reach 2.8 ins (7 cm) in size. It is famous for its amazing strength, being able to lift objects that are hundreds of times its own weight. Its larvae develop from eggs laid in decaying plant matter, taking up to two years to become adults.

Large male

JEWEL BEETLE

CATOXANTHA OPULENTA

An exotic species from tropical Asia, this metallic green wood-boring beetle lives in forests and woods. Its larvae live inside plants.

Glowing
Jewel beetles measure up to 2.5 ins (6 cm). They are active on sunny days and quick to fly if they are threatened.

GOLD-SPOTTED TIGER BEETLE

CICINDELA AURULENTA

This predatory insect has long slender legs and moves at speed over the ground in pursuit of its insect prey. It lives in burrows 3 ft (1 m) deep along sea and lake shores in China and southeast Asia. Its larvae are efficient ambush hunters.

Pacy predator

Killing machine

GIRAFFE WEEVIL

TRACHELOPHORUS GIRAFFA

Extension
The weevil lives on trees in Madagascar, and its neck helps it reach the leaves that it eats and nests in.

The aptly named giraffe weevil has a hinged neck that is nearly twice as long as its body.

Creature features
This beetle has startlingly prominent compound eyes to spot prey and large mandibles to catch it. Its bright colors often have a metallic sheen.

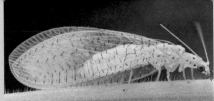

Hindquarters

Green lacewings all have long antennae and large eyes. Their two transparent iridescent wings form a tent over the body when at rest.

COMMON GREEN LACEWING

CHRYSOPERLA CARNEA

An important garden predator—the larvae are called aphid lions—the adults feed on nectar, pollen, and honeydew.

CAT FLEA

CTENOCEPHALIDES FELIS

Found worldwide, this parasite likes warm environments and lays up to 50 eggs a day. It sucks blood from prey and cats are allergic to their bites.

Fast pest
Cat fleas have sharp mouthparts to suck blood and powerful hind legs for running and jumping through fur.

Scientific name: *Attacus atlas*

Size: up to 12 ins (30 cm) wingspan

Diet: caterpillars eat leaves including privet, citrus, and mango; butterfly does not eat

Lifespan in wild: the butterfly lives up to 14 days

Location: China, India, southeast Asia

Brief life
When the butterfly emerges from its cocoon it cannot eat because it has no mouth and the proboscis is too small. It looks for a mate, lays eggs, then dies.

ATLAS MOTH

ATTACUS ATLAS

This bright orange moth is one of the biggest insects on Earth, with a wingspan of up to 12 ins (30 cm). It lives in the forests of China, India, and southeast Asia. If it is threatened by a predator, it will drop to the ground, flapping its wings slowly to look like a snake moving its head.

Snakehead
Markings bear a resemblance to the head of a cobra.

Caterpillar

Camouflaged pupa

Metamorphosis
The atlas moth caterpillar secretes a strong silk to build a cocoon, inside which the pupa or chrysalis transforms into a moth.

Wingspan
This beautiful butterfly has a wingspan of 4.5 ins (12 cm).

BLUE PEACOCK BUTTERFLY

PAPILIO ARCTURUS

The family of swallowtail butterflies all have long "tails" on their hindwings and rest with their wings open. This swallowtail, with its spectacular iridescent markings, is native to the Indian subcontinent.

RED WOOD ANT

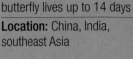

Worker ant

FORMICA RUFA

This ant is widespread in Europe and North America. It farms aphid honeydew and is very aggressive, spraying formic acid at predators.

Large nest

Nesting
The ants nest on logs in very large colonies with around 100 queens and 100,000 workers.

WESTERN HONEYBEE

APIS MELLIFERA

Honeybees are important pollinators of flowers and fruit, carrying pollen in baskets on their hind legs. They beat their wings 200 times per second and fly at around 15 mph (24 km/h).

Inside the hive
Honeybees live in hives, with a single queen that lays all the eggs and produces chemicals that guide the behavior of the other bees. Worker bees build the hive and forage for food.

FALL CANKERWORM MOTH

ALSOPHILA POMETARIA

This insect's caterpillar can strip the leaves off an entire tree. The name comes from the adult males, which feed in that season.

Walking moth
The female moth has lost her ability to fly and has no mouthparts. She simply lays eggs and dies.

ANNA'S EIGHTY-EIGHT BUTTERFLY

DIATHRIA ANNA

A native of the wet tropical forests of Central and South America, where it feeds on rotting fruit and dung, this butterfly has wings with a dark brown upperside.

Mystery number
On the startling red, black, and white underside of the wings are lines that look like the number 88, hence the butterly's name.

ROBBER FLY

FAMILY ASILIDAE

This fast-flying insect is an aggressive hunter, snatching other insects in midair. It is found worldwide, particularly in dry and sunny places.

Killing machine
The fly pierces its prey with hard mouthparts, first injecting toxic saliva to immobilize its victim, then sucking it dry.

ANOPHELES MOSQUITO

ANOPHELES SPECIES

The female anopheles is one of the most feared insects in the world because her bite may spread diseases, including malaria, yellow fever, and dengue fever.

Spreading disease
Only around 40 of the 430 species of anopheles mosquito are conveyors of malaria. The males are harmless, feeding on nectar.

ECHINODERMS

NATURE'S FIVE-PART PLAN

Most of these have five body segments each with a mouthpart and an arm ending in tube-shaped feet. Some are carnivorous, others feed on waste matter, while basket stars eat plankton.

RED KNOB SEA STAR

PROTOREASTER LINCKII

A native of the Indian Ocean, this sea star is found in shallow pools at low tide, although it likes to live on the seabed at depths of up to 100 ft (30.5 m). It has bright red protective tubercles and hundreds of tube feet to move it along.

Tentacles and mouth

Knobbly predator

Novel table manners
The sea star does not have teeth. It pushes out its stomach and engulfs its prey, pulling everything back in to finish digesting.

CHORDATES

PRIMITIVE LIFE IN THE SEAS

Most chordates are vertebrates, but lancelets and sea squirts are invertebrate chordates with a notochord instead of a backbone. These primitive animals are found in oceans worldwide.

Light micrograph of head with tentacles

Body core
The lancelet is 2.5 ins (6 cm) long. The strengthening notochord is not a backbone, so the animal is classified as an invertebrate.

Fish-like body

LANCELET

PROTOREASTER LINCKII

This most primitive of chordates is a long, thin marine invertebrate that looks like a fish, has light sensing organs, but does not have jaws. It lies half buried in the sand of the seabed filtering food from the water.

Looking into the future

This western lowland gorilla (*Gorilla gorilla gorilla*) is walking through a cloud of butterflies in the Dzanga Sangha Reserve in the rain forests of the southwestern Central African Republic. This critically endangered species is threatened by habitat loss, the bushmeat trade, and disease—in the last decade alone more than 5,000 western gorillas have been killed by the ebola fever. Reserves like this one do much to advance the knowledge of the life these fascinating animals lead and ensure they are protected. According to the WWF's Living Planet Report 2018, there has been a 60 percent decline in numbers of mammals, birds, reptiles, amphibians, and fish in the last 40 years. It is vital that people work with local communities to protect wild animals and their habitats to ensure that they will be around for future generations to enjoy.

abdomen
The part of an animal that contains organs used for digestion, getting rid of waste, and reproduction.

alga (pl. algae)
A simple plant that has no true roots or flowers. Most algae are microscopic but the largest, seaweeds, are many feet long.

antenna (pl. antennae)
A feeler on the head of an insect that it uses to sense the world around it.

arthropod
An animal that has a hard exoskeleton and jointed legs. Insects, spiders, and crustaceans are arthropods.

Antennae
(butterfly)

bacterium (pl. bacteria)
A microorganism; some bacteria cause diseases.

baleen
Long hair or fringed pieces of cartilage, hanging from the upper jaws of whales, used to filter small food items from the water.

barbel
A fleshy feeler on the head of a fish.

bioluminescence
The production of light by living things that live in dark places. It is found in fish and insects as well as simple animals that live in the sea.

bipedal
Moving on two legs.

bivalve
Having a hinged shell composed of two valves.

blowhole
A hole on a whale or dolphin's head that is used for breathing.

blubber
The layer of fatty substances under the skin of an animal that helps keep cold out and body warmth in.

breach
To leap out of the water into the air. Animals that breach include humpback whales and the great white shark.

camelids
A family of two-toed ruminants that have three-chambered stomachs. They include the camel, llama, alpaca, guanaco, and vicuna.

camouflage
Natural coloring that helps animals blend in with their surroundings. It is used by predators to ambush prey, and by prey to avoid being eaten by predators.

carapace
The hard protective case on an animal's back. Turtles and tortoises have carapaces.

carnivore
An animal that kills or scavenges and eats other animals.

carrion
The remains of a dead animal.

cartilage
A strong, lightweight, flexible material that makes up the skeletons of animals such as sharks, skates, and rays.

cephalopods
A class of marine mollusks that includes squid, cuttlefish, and octopuses.

cetaceans
An order of marine mammals that includes whales, dolphins, and porpoises.

**Exoskeleton
(cicada)**

chromatophores
Pigment-bearing cells, especially in the skin, that some animals use to change their color.

cloven-hoofed
Having a hoof divided into two.

cocoon
A silk case spun by an insect or spider to protect itself or its eggs.

cold-blooded
Unable to regulate body temperature. Reptiles are cold-blooded and need sunlight to warm themselves up and become active.

colony
A large group of the same kind of animal living together.

conservation
The active protection of animals and their habitat.

crustacean
An invertebrate with a hard outer shell, such as a lobster or crab.

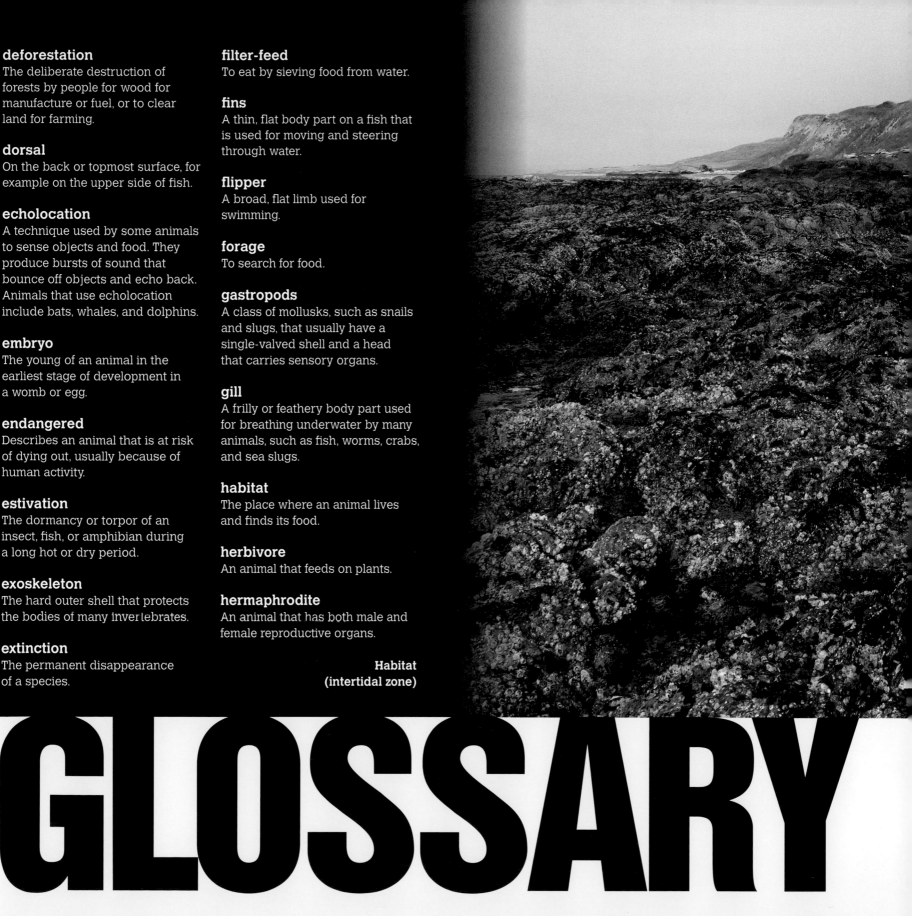

deforestation
The deliberate destruction of forests by people for wood for manufacture or fuel, or to clear land for farming.

dorsal
On the back or topmost surface, for example on the upper side of fish.

echolocation
A technique used by some animals to sense objects and food. They produce bursts of sound that bounce off objects and echo back. Animals that use echolocation include bats, whales, and dolphins.

embryo
The young of an animal in the earliest stage of development in a womb or egg.

endangered
Describes an animal that is at risk of dying out, usually because of human activity.

estivation
The dormancy or torpor of an insect, fish, or amphibian during a long hot or dry period.

exoskeleton
The hard outer shell that protects the bodies of many invertebrates.

extinction
The permanent disappearance of a species.

filter-feed
To eat by sieving food from water.

fins
A thin, flat body part on a fish that is used for moving and steering through water.

flipper
A broad, flat limb used for swimming.

forage
To search for food.

gastropods
A class of mollusks, such as snails and slugs, that usually have a single-valved shell and a head that carries sensory organs.

gill
A frilly or feathery body part used for breathing underwater by many animals, such as fish, worms, crabs, and sea slugs.

habitat
The place where an animal lives and finds its food.

herbivore
An animal that feeds on plants.

hermaphrodite
An animal that has both male and female reproductive organs.

**Habitat
(intertidal zone)**

GLOSSARY

hibernate
To spend the winter in a deep sleep or a sleep-like state called torpor.

incisor
A sharp, cutting tooth in mammals that is used for biting.

incubate
To sit on eggs to keep them warm.

infrasonic
Describes a frequency beyond the range of the human ear.

insectivores
An order of small, usually nocturnal mammals—for example moles, shrews, and hedgehogs—that feed mainly on insects.

invertebrate
An animal without a backbone or vertebral column.

iridescent
Having luminous colors that appear to change when seen from different angles.

keratin
The flexible material from which hair, fur, fingernails, hooves, birds' beaks, and reptile scales are made.

krill
Tiny, shrimp-like sea creatures that are an important part of the food chain in oceans and seas.

Marsupial (quoll)

larva (pl. larvae)
An insect in the second stage of its life, after it hatches from an egg and before it becomes an adult.

mammal
A warm-blooded animal that has fur or hair and breathes air. Female mammals produce milk to feed their young.

mandible
The lower jaw in mammals and fishes; either of the parts of a bird's beak; either half of the crushing organ in an arthropod's mouthparts.

marsupials
An order of mammals with pouches to carry young. They include kangaroos and opossums.

medusa
A free-swimming, bell-shaped form of a cnidarian such as a box jellyfish or sea nettle.

metabolism
The chemical and physical changes that take place in an animal's body, enabling it to grow and function.

metamorphosis
The changes in body shape that an animal such as a butterfly goes through as it becomes an adult.

migrate
To travel a long distance in search of food, to breed, or escape from cold weather.

molt
To shed an outgrown body part, such as feathers, an exoskeleton, or skin.

monotreme
An order of egg-laying mammals that consists of platypuses and echidnas.

mucus
A slimy liquid produced by some animals, for example snails use it to slide along and tree frogs often use it to make their nests.

musk
An oily, strong-smelling substance that is produced by some mammals.

mustelids
A family of carnivorous mammals that includes weasels, badgers, otters, and martens.

nectar
The sweet liquid made by flowers that bees make into honey.

nocturnal
Describes an animal that is active mainly at night and sleeps during the day.

notochord
A reinforcing rod that runs down the body of chordates.

nymph
A young insect that looks like its parents, but does not have fully formed wings or reproductive organs.

omnivorous
Describes animals that eat plants and other animals.

Prosimian (Senegal bushbaby)

oviparous
Producing eggs that develop and hatch outside the body of the mother.

ovoviviparous
Producing eggs that hatch inside the body of the mother.

parasite
An animal that feeds on or inside another living animal.

parthenogenesis
A form of reproduction in which an egg can develop into an embryo without being fertilized.

pellet
A wad of undigested bones and fur regurgitated by a bird of prey.

peripheral vision
The ability of an animal to see all around without turning their head.

pheromone
A chemical substance produced by an animal that stimulates other animals of the same species.

pincer
A claw of a lobster or crab and some insects.

pinnipeds
A suborder of marine carnivorous mammals that have flippers. They include seals and walruses.

plankton
Microscopic living animals and plants that drift near the surface of water rather than actively swimming.

plumage
The feathers of a bird.

pollen
A substance that flowers make to produce seeds. Many animals spread pollen from flower to flower.

polyp
An animal with a tube-shaped body and a ring of tentacles around its mouth.

predator
An animal that hunts and eats other animals.

prey
An animal that is hunted and eaten by another animal.

primates
An order of mammals that includes humans, apes, and monkeys.

proboscis
The long, flexible mouthparts or snout of an animal.

prosimians
A suborder of lower primates that includes lemurs and lorises.

Predator
(Indian water dragon)

GLOSSARY

**Raptor
(peregrine falcon)**

protozoan
A simple organism that is made of just one cell.

pseudopod
A growth that works like a temporary foot. Many protozoans use pseudopods to move.

pupa (pl. pupae)
The resting, non-feeding stage in the life of an insect, before it develops into an adult.

quill
A hollow shaft of a feather or the spine of a porcupine or hedgehog.

raptor
A bird of prey that kills and eats other animals for food.

rodents
An order of small gnawing mammals that have a single pair of incisors, such as a rat, squirrel, or beaver.

ruminant
A herbivorous hoofed mammal that chews the cud.

scales
Protective plates that cover a reptile's skin. In butterflies and moths, scales help to keep their body warm.

scavenger
An animal that eats the dead remains that have been left by predators.

sirenians
An order of aquatic herbivorous mammals such as the manatee, dugong, or Steller's sea cow.

species
A group of living things that look alike and can breed together

swim bladder
A gas-filled bag inside a fish that helps the fish stop itself from sinking or rising.

talons
The sharp claws of birds of prey that they use to snatch up quarry.

tentacle
Long, fleshy feeler that some animals use to catch their food.

tetrapod
A vertebrate that has two pairs of limbs.

**Venomous
(sting of the Brazilian
yellow scorpion)**

torpor
A state of reduced metabolism, heart rate, respiration, and body temperature in some animals that occurs in varying degrees during hibernation or estivation.

toxic
Poisonous to living things.

tusk
An enlarged tooth that projects when the mouth is closed and is used to dig for food or as a weapon.

ungulates
Herbivorous mammals, such as deer, elephants, or rhinoceroses that have hooves,

venomous
Describes an animal that injects poisons to kill prey.

vertebra (pl. vertebrae)
The backbones, or bones of the spine, in a skeleton.

vertebrates
Animals that have a backbone.

viviparous
Producing living young from within the body.

warm-blooded
Able to regulate body temperature independent of the surroundings. Mammals are warm-blooded.

GLOSSARY

INDEX

**Amphibians
(American
bullfrog)**

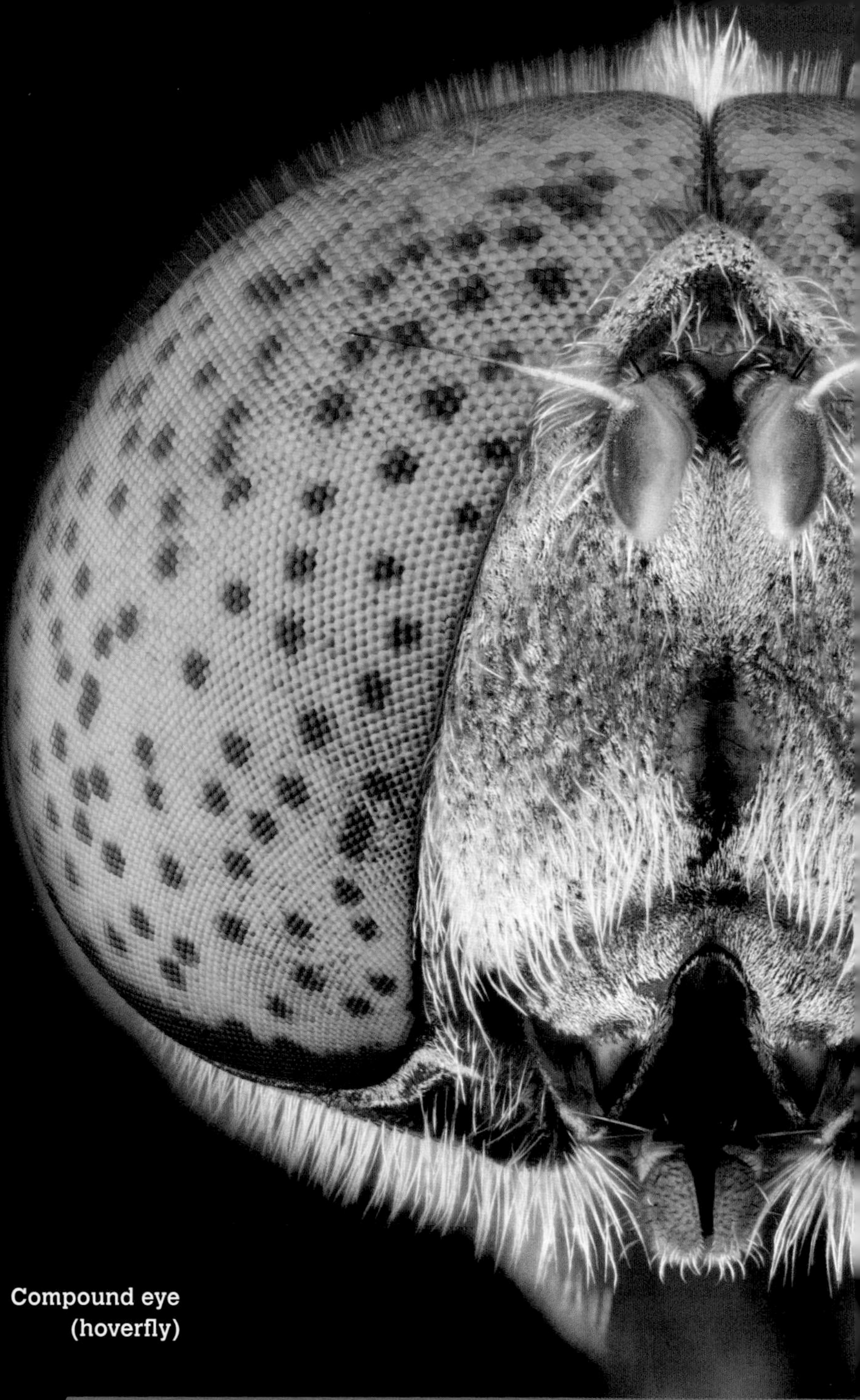

**Compound eye
(hoverfly)**

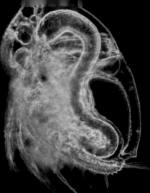

Crustacean (Daphnia)

D

E

F

G

Hyena (Spotted hyena)

H

The Hyena

Mongoose
(meerkat)

INDEX

**Shark
(great hammerhead)**

**Zooplankton
(copepods)**

INDEX

bottom = b, center = c, left = l, right = r, top = t

Photos ©: 123RF: 70 cr (Anan Kaewkhammul), 20 tl (Darryl Brooks); age fotostock/Norbert Wu/Minden Pictures:163 blb; Alamy Images: 163 blt (Amanda Cotton), 19 l (Arco Images GmbH), 43 norse wolf (ART Collection), 156-157 (BIOSPHOTO), 150 t (Brian Parker), 138-139 (cbstockfoto), 68 (Christopher Milligan), 155 (Cultura Creative), 167 tc (F1online digitale Bildagentur GmbH), 158 cl (Francisco Jesus Martin de la Sierra Hernandez), 180 (Frank Hecker), 99 (Frans Lanting Studio), 186-187 (Ger Bosma), 19 br (gerard lacz), 175 t (IanDagnall Computing), 55 (jvphoto), 12 bl (Life on White), 95 bl, 182 (Mark Conlin), 176-177, 196-197 (Nature Picture Library), 43 little red (Niday Picture Library), 164, 165 c (Paulo Oliveira), 146-147 (Poelzer Wolfgang), 39 br (Robertharding), 24-25, 46-47 (Steve Bloom Images). 94 (Steve Bloom Images); Dreamstime: 134 Eastern tiger salamander, 79 bl (Agami Photo Agency), 131 bc (Aleksandra Shutova), 36 tr (Alessandrozocc), 11 red-eyed tree frog, 135 red-eyed tree frog (Alptraum), 124 crb (Amwu), 34 cl (Anankkml), 119 tl (Andreanita), 67 t (Andreanita), 199 (Andreas Altenburger), 34 c (Anke Van Wyk), 124 crt (Anna Podekova), 13 tl (Anolis01), 195 cl (Anthony Paz), 31 (Aprison Aprison), 20 cl (Belizar), 118 c (Boitano), 137 br (Brandon Alms), 86 cr (Brian Lasenby), 192 bcbl, 192 bcbr (Cathy Keifer), 45 bc (Chris Alcock), 11 newt, 134 fire-bellied newt (Chrishowey), 191 tr (Christian Weiß), 131-tll (Christina Moreau), 10 slug, 170 leopard slug (Dave Bredeson), 134 American toad (David Anderson), 193 bl (Digitalimagined), 135 yellow-banded poison dart frog (Dirk Ercken), 73 drinking (Dndavis), 183 tr (Drew Collins), 65 cr (Duncan Noakes), 130 tr (Ecophoto), 120 cr (ePhotocorp), 134 long-nosed horned frog, 135 lemur leaf frog, 135 Kaiser's spotted newt, 135 Montane hourglass tree frog, 200 b (Farinoza), 129 cbr, 143 tr (Feathercollector), 163 br (Flinthard), 120 r (Forest71), 33 tr (Gidejor), 18 br (Holly Kuchera), 190 br (Ian Redding), 11 mouse (Icefront), 10 hermit crab, 11 alpine newt, 11 dormouse, 16 dormouse, 45 tl, 51 tl, 134 alpine newt, 145 br (Isselee), 37 t, 81 tl, 154 bcr (Izanbar), 40 ct (Jezbennett), 174 crbr (John Anderson), 18 bl (Johncarnemolla), 189 tl (Joyjoe), 22 bl (Kajornyot), 59 tr (Kcmatt), 183 blc (Kwerry), 188 cl (Leeta13), 200 t (Lizgiv), 64 bl (Lukas Blazek), 18 c (Martin Pelanek), 10 butterfly (Matee Nuserm), 125 tl, 127 br, 140 cr (Matthijs Kuijpers), 134 red salamander (Melinda Fawver), 22 cr (Michael Lynch), 65 b (Michael Migos), 35 house mouse, 188 cr (Morley Read), 30 tl (Omar Ariff Kamarul Ariffin), 23 br (Ondřej Prosicky), 45 bl (Peter Shaw), 35 Arctic hare (Photographerlondon), 35 (Przemyslaw Iciak), 131 (Qualityphotos1), 193 tr (Razvan Cornel Constantin), 131 cbr (Scottamassey), 10 red sponge, 172 cr (Seadam), 185 bl (Sean Pavone), 22 br (Sebastiangh), 154 tc (Sergey Uryadnikov), 69 bl (Simon Eeman), 131 bl (Stephanie Rousseau), 195 bl (Sukawal Radomkit), 41 br (Teresa Kenney), 160 cr (Tony Campbell), 194 bl (Vladimirdavydov), 191 tc (Whiskybottle), 95 br (Willtu), 19 tr (Woravit Vijitpanya), 119 tr, 149 European plaice; Getty Images: 32 (Björn Kleemann), 66 cl (Historical Picture Archive/Corbis), 106-107 (Jan van der Greef/Buiten-beeld/ Minden Pictures), cover (Koushik Chatterjee/EyeEm); iStockphoto: 69 tr (1001slide), 61 tr (33karen33), 11 hornbill, 29 tl, 77 hornbill, 78 bl, 104 cl (4FR), 167 bct (92/1 Moo3 Huai Yang Kham Chun Phayao, Thailand 56150), 49 tl (aaprophoto), 79 tl (AaronAmat), 149 pike, 206 r (abadonian), 84 ct (AbiWarner), 27 bl, 53 tl (abzerit), 198 l (Adisak Mitrprayoon), 11 Gila monster, 117 Gila monster, 121 br, 129 tr (adogslifephoto), 84 br, 87 tl (Adventure_Photo), 72 br (afhunta), 185 tcr (AHDesignConcepts), 29 ct (Alan_Lagadu), 135 smooth newt (AlasdairJames), 194 bc (AlasdairJames), 93 tr (AlbyDeTweede), 100 bl (AleksandarGeorgiev), 10 caterpillar, 170 caterpillar (AlekZotoff), 134 Australian green tree frog, 137 tc (aluxum), 130 blt (amwu), 109 tr (Anagramm), 16 capybara (anankkml), 16-17 rhino, 148 harlequin ghost pipefish (AndamanSE), 10 warty frog fish, 148 warty frogfish, 152 br, 179 bct (AndreaAstes), 51 cl (andreaskrappweis), 102 bl (Andrew Haysom), 108 c (Andrew_Howe), 121 tr, 81 br (AndreyGudkov), 125 br (andyKRAKOVSKI), 173 cl (anela), 190 tr (anna-utkina), 35 tl, 85 br (Anna39), 166 b (Annop Youngrot), 10 wasp, 10 ladybird, 134 edible frog, 170 wasp, 171 ladybug, 171 medicinal leech, 181 crbl (Antagain), 153 br, 174 tc (antos777), 56 br, 57 cl, 89 lammergeier (AOosthuizen), 151 tr (apomares), 134 fire salamander (arnowssr), 150 c (Arsty), 190 c (artiste9999), 165 cr (ARTKucherenko), 116 coral pipesnake (Atelopus), 33 bc (atese), 160 cl (Atypeek), 149 goldfish, 181 cl (Aukid), 144 tr (aureapterus), 193 ttt (Backiris), 11 quail, 77 quail, 85 l, 108 tr (bazilfoto), 48 br (bbossom), 151 cr (bearacreative), 69 l (BenLin), 168-169 (Bestwork), 57 tr (Binty), 11 bat, 16 bat, 64 c (BirdHunter591), 44 bl, 91 tc (BirdImages), 43 tl (birdy55), 117 red-eared slider (Birute), 10 eel, 148 black-spotted moray eel (bjdlzx), 50 tl (BlackAperture), 194 br (bo1982), 11 gecko, 116 giant day gecko (Bob_Eastman), 38 cr (Bobbushphoto), 98 c (borchee), 105 clt (BoukeAtema), 98 tr (Brasil2), 136 t (BrianLasenby), 170 cockle (busypix), 11 kingfisher, 76 kingfisher (Byshnev), 38 tl, 67 br (carstenbrandt), 111 cb (CathyDoi), 161 br (catshiles), 109 cl (CCeliaPhoto), 10 black grouper,

149 black grouper, 154 bl (cdascher), 85 r (Chantale Ouellet), 39 bl (Charlie Waradee), 194 tr (choja), 193 tr (Chris Mansfield), 148 clownfish (ChristianNasca), 44 t, 160 t (ChuckSchugPhotography), 119 clt (chuvipro), 84 bl, 166 ctr, 117 Hawkesbill turtle (cinoby), 141 c (Click48), 87 kites in sky (Connah), 64 tr (coolkengzz), 10 cat flea, 170 cat flea, 194 cbl (coopder1), 108 bl (CraigRJD), 9 tcr, 21 tr, 23 cr, 135 European common frog, 145 bc (CreativeNature_nl), 158 t, 159 cl (crisod), 28 cb (curioustiger), 76 egret (cyoginan), 172 br, 173 trb (Damocean), 112 cl (DanCardiff), 39 c (danielbenhaim), 79 bc (danikancil), 129 cbc (DanSchmitt), 119 crb (DaveLongMedia), 51 tr (davemhuntphotography), 71 c (Davesphotographs), 148 weedy sea dragon (David Haintz), 127 tc (DavidCallan), 189 ct (DavorLovincic), 130 bc (dawnn), 136 br (Decent-Exposure-Photography), 185 c (defun), 104 tl (derejeb), 159 cr (DerrenMeadwell), 193 cl (DeVil79), 70 br (Dgwildlife), 143 c (DieterMeyrl), 194 cbr (Dmitrii Melgunov (Ritam), 170 Atlantic blue crab (DPFishCo), 171 sea star (dpruter), 206 l (drakuliren), 70 t (DrMonochrome), 10 ant, 85 bl (DrPAS), 44 cl (dssimages), 20 c (duncan1890), 167 bcr (eco2drew), 26 tl (EcoPic), 59 bullfrog (EcoPic), 73 cl (EcoPic), 171 flatworm (EdwardSnow), 154 br (ElizabethHoffmann), 80 booby (elmvilla), 93 tl (elmvilla), 54 tr (EMPPhotography), 191 cl (englishriver), 11 eastern wormsnake, 116 eastern worm snakes, 135 eastern red-spotted newt (epantha), 92 bc (eROMAZe), 23 tr (EstuaryPig), 179 clb (eye-blink), 144 bl (FabioMaffei), 11 smooth-sided toad, 11 bushbaby, 16 bushbaby, 50 c, 134 Awarape dyeing poison dart frog, 134 Troschel's tree frog, 135 smooth-sided toad (Farinoza), 118 t (Favor of God), 167 t (FionaAyerst), 208 (FlamingPumpkin), 38 c (Foto4440), 11 European common toad (Foster), 177 green iguana (Gaschwald), 143 bcr (gatito33), 59 tl (Gatsi), 109 br (gemredding), 27 c (georgeclerk), 163 c (ginosphotos), back cover parrot, 10 jellyfish, 10 spider, 10 black millipede, 11 mossy frog, 11 false tomato frog, 11 axolotl, 11 spectacled caiman, 11 coral snake, 11 parrot, 11 chaffinch, 11 sea lion, 11 aardvark, 11 koala, 11 bear, 16 bear, 16 echidna, 16 sea lion, 17 shrew, 17 aardvark, 17 koala, 17 mandrill, 17 pine marten, 18 l, 21 tl, 21 bl, 21 bc, 27 tl, 27 br, 29 r, 33 cb, 34 b, 40 br, 41 cr, 45 r, 49 br, 52 cougar, 53 tc, 53 tr, 53 bl, 71 t, 73 cr, 76 chaffinch, 77 starling, 77 parrot, 79 l&c ostrich chicks, 79 r ostrich chick, 79 tr, 81 tr, 84 tr, 89 condor standing, 96 tl, 97 tl, 97 c, 98 bl, 100 cr, 111 br, 116 American alligator, 116 corn snake, 116 spectacled caiman, 117 panther chameleon, 117 Saharan horned viper, 117 Hermann's tortoise, 119 b, 121 c, 125 bc, 130 c, 134 black poison arrow frog, 134 mossy frog, 134 false tomato frog, 134 golden poison arrow frog, 134 axolotl, 136 cr, 143 cr, 144 tc, 149 Kole Tang, 165 cb, 170 black millipede, 170 leaf insect, 170 Macleay's spectre, 181 crtr, 191 blb, 192 tl, 201 (GlobalP), 120 bl (GordonImages), 50 cl (GP232), 101 cr (gqxue), 34 tr (grafxart8888), 165 bl (grandriver), 140 tr (Hailshadow), 149 yellow-banded sweetlips (hansgertbroeder), 87 tl (Harry Collins), 159 t (haveseen), 195 bcl (HAYKIRDI), 125 tr (heckepics), 175 ctl (HeitiPaves), 87 goshawk (Henk Bogaard), 181 ctl (Henrik_L), 91 tr (Hermsdorf), 69 cr (Himagine), 189 cl (hlansdown), 130 br (hocus-focus), 38 cl (Howard Chen), 80 bl, 88 cl (hstiver), 188 c, 191 tl (Ian_Redding), 89 kestrel (Ian_Sherriffs), 148 giant frogfish,173 tcl, 175 bl (ifish), 104 bl (Ilza), 10 rabbitfish, 148-149 main (ImageGap), 141 tl (inhauscreative), 84 bcl (invisiblewl), 116 box turtle, 129 ctr (irin717), 191 blt (itsmejust), 113 bl (Ivan_Kozhevnikov), 84 bcr (jaboticaba), 17 wildebeest, 43 bc cr (JackF), 17 bat, 141 tc (JAH), 49 tc (JamenPercy), 41 tr (Jamie_Hall), 185 tr (Janos, 26 br (javarman3), 10 yellow pipefish, 149 yellow pipefish (JaysonPhotography), 9 b (Jean-Yves caleca), 41 cl (jeanro), 175 cb (Jenhung Huang), 74-75 (JeremyRichards), 33 br (jez_bennett), 49 cr (Jillian Cooper), 165 cbr (Jman78), 121 tl (joakimbkk), 43 white (jodiemusic), 148 canary rockfish, 149 fringehead blenny (joebelanger), 174 crbl (johnandersonphoto), 170 tarantula, 189 tr, 189 bcb (johnaudrey), 79 tc, 111 tc (JohnCarnemolla), 61 c (JohnPitcher), 79 c (JTBOB888), 59 bc (juerpa), 22 tr (Juhku), 109 cr (JunotPhotography), 185 tl (_jure), 116 frilled-neck lizard (Kaan Sezer), 72 cl (Katrina Patuli), 43 black, 45 cl, 78 cl, 78 r (KeithSzafranski), 70 cl (kellyvandellen), 62-63, 91 bl (KenCanning), 129 cbl (Kevin Wells), 129 ctr, 137 tr (kikkerdirk), 190 bc (kirisa99), 159 bl (Kirk Wester), 150-151 bg (Kvini), 121 bc (kwiktor), 103 bc (kyletperry), 36 cl (Lazareva), 171 sea nettle jellyfish (LeeYiuTung), 61 br (lemga), 50 bl (Leonardo Prest Mercon Ro), 190 cr (Leonid Eremeychuk), back cover orangutan (leonp69), 30 bl (leonp69), 85 tr (Leopardinatree), 52 in cave (lightasafeather), 95 tl, 95 cl (Liliboas), 148 leopard torpedo ray (liilithlita), 57 tl (Lingbeek), 26 bl (lnzyx), 71 bl (longtaildog), 149 gold-spotted rabbitfish (Lophius), 150 cr (LPETTET), 145 tr (lrosebrugh), 81 cl (mantaphoto), 140 br (Mantonature), 10 rose chaffer, 10 jewel beetle, 170 jewel beetle, 171 dung beetle, 193 bc (marcouliana), 33 ct (Marek Stefunko), 41 bl (mari_art), 53 c (MarieHolding), 136 bl, 154 bc, 189 br (Mark Kostich), 185 tcl (marrio31), 135 red-headed poison dart frog (mashabuba). 65 cl (master2), 194 cr (Mathisa_s), 144 br (MATJAZ SLANIC), 152 bl (Matt_Potenski), 80 grebe, 93 bl, 96 br, 108 br, 181 cbtr (mauribo), 189 cbr (maxontravel), 9 tr (MDoubrava), 48 tl, 48 tr (MediaProduction), 10 coral (mehmettorlak), 11 European tree frog, 135 European tree frog (mgfoto), 11 shoebill, 76 shoebill (Michael Fitzsimmons), 72 tc (michael meijer), 60 tr, 60 cl (Michael Zeigler), 85 bc, 125 bl, 194 ctl (michaklootwijk), 143 br, 172 tl (micro_photo), 86 c (Miguel Angel Berbegal Vazquez), 113 tl (mikedabell), 50 br, 89 br, 92 tr, 93 br, 110 crt, 119 clb, 134 palamate newt (MikeLane45), 101 t (MikeNorkum), 61 bl (mikeuk), 43 pack (milehightraveler), 11 python, 116 royal python, 193 ct (MirekKijewski), 161 tc (Mirko_Rosenau), 89 gyrfalcon (Missing35mm), 66 bl (Mlenny), 35 br, 37 t (mlharing), 60 cr (MogensTrolle), 120 cl (MollyN2), 18 tr (MoMorad), 49 cr (moose henderson), 40 tr (MortenLau), 11 owl, 76 owlet (MriyaWildlife), 96 bc (mthaler), 36 cr (Musat), 193 tlb (Musat), 110 crb (mwennerwald), 118 cl (NajaShots), 11 gharial, 59 br, 116 gharial, 124 bl (NaniP), 113 crt (Nataba), 67 boar and piglets (Nataliia_Melnychuk), 173 tl (naturediver), 11 dolphin, 16 dolphin (neirfy), 65 t (nicholas_ dale), 151 cl (Nigel Marsh), 109 c bg (Nikada), 52 in tree (nikand3), 109 bc (nikpal), 11 ring-tailed lemur (nizha2), 26 tr (nizha2), 10 water flea, 60 c, 125 tc, 149 Siberian sturgeon, 170 water flea (NNehring), 17 manatee (npassmann), 102 br (nplion), 135 Asian painted frog (npps48), 198 r (obewon), 116 green lizard (Oks_Mit), 170 Giant African land snail (OlegShvydiuk), 178 bl (OlegShvydiuk), 86 br (pablo_rodriguez_ merkel), 11 bee eater, 77 bee eater (panda3800), 35 European rabbit (paparazzit), 37 cr (Paralaxis), 110 cr (Pascal_p10), 48 in bin (passion4nature), 109 bl, 40 l, 89 tr (Patrick_Gijsbers), 171 pillbug (paulrommer), 38 bl (PaulWolf), 101 bl (pchoui), 37 br (PeakMystique), 150 cl (PEDRE), 179 bcb (peilien), 117 tokay gecko (PetlinDmitry), 117 alligator eggs (phasinphoto), 119 ct (phasinphoto), 92 l (PhilipCacka), 71 tl (photographer3431), 188 t (photography-wildlife-de), 72 c (Photokanok), 76 penguin (photomaru), 67 zebras in grass (Photoservice), 54 b (Pierre Aden), 73 necking (pliesasriiiles), 80 albatross, 104 cbr (pilipenkoD), 50 diving gannet (piola666), 103 tl (Piotr Krzeslak), 158 cr, 166 tl, 179 br (Placebo365), 77 wreathed hornbill (Plamuekwhan), 10 Atlantic herring, 148 Atlantic herring (pomarinus), 44 bc (powerofforever), 67 tr (prapassong), 91 tl (predrag1), 23 l (PrinPrince), 93 cr (pum_eva), 153 tl (quentinjlang), 10 quentinjlang, 104 cbr (RainervonBrandis), 178 tr, 181 bcl (randimal), 59 northern gannet (RelaxFoto.de), back cover lizard, 11 spotted turtle, 11 armadillo lizard, 17 grisson, 116 armadillo lizard, 117 spotted turtle, 121 bl, 137 cl, 141 tr, 190 bl, 33 cr, 163 cl, 179 clt (RibeirodosSantos), 100 tr (RichardSeeley), 11 green turtle, 117 green turtle (richcarey), 66 cr (RichLegg), 21 cl (RollingEarth), 71 cl (RomanBabakin), 96 tr (Ruben Ramos), 43 bl, 69 br, 77 dove, 97 tl, 117 Nile crocodile (rusm), 184 br (S_Lew), 61 tc (Sahelan), 143 tl (SashaFoxWalters), 179 tc (schmez), 175 ctr (skjdigital), 60 br (SeaNymphJess), 10 rottifer, 170 rotifer (Sergii_Trofymchuk), 80 male courting (shalamov), 37 cl (ShaneGross), 10 hydra, 170 hydra, 171 sponge (Sinhyu), 53 br (SKapl), 64 cl (skilpad), 192 cr (skydie), 20 tr (smuay), 158 bc (Snekk), 159 br (solarworksart),

23 c (SoumenNath), 190 cl (spxChrome), 57 br (Staincliffe), 35 beaver cutting tree, 48 in tree, 112 bc, 170 blue swallowtail (stanley45), 170 spider (stephanie phillips), 89 bl (Steve Adams), 137 tl (SteveAllenPhoto), 111 cr (SteveByland), 116 Pacific rattlesnake (stevelenzphoto), 195 t (StevenEllingson), 86 tr (Stuartb), 129 bl (Subaqueosshutterbug), 81 bl (Sunil mavidi), 103 bl (SweetyMommy), 11 bullfrog, 134 American bullfrog, 203 l (tacojim), 71 tr (tatisol), 11 horned viper, 116 horned viper, 135 common spadefoot toad, 135 European green toad (taviphoto), 35 beaver dam (Teacherdad48), 97 tc (TerryJ), 117 Texas coral snake (texcroc), 22 tl, 22 cl (thawats), 128, 154 tr, 173 trt (THEGIFT777), 170 octopus (TheSP4N1SH), 52 b (through-my-lens), 4 bl, 10 sea urchin, 66 cr, 185 cr (TomekD76), 204 l, 207 (tonaquatic), 64 tc (topten22photo), 21 br (Tramper2), 178 tl (treetstreet), 30 c, 52 tr (Trevorplatt), 125 cl (tswinner), 27 tr, 28 tr (tunart), 11 sunda pangolin, 16 pangolin (ugniz), 119 tc (ugurhan), 148 bullethead parrotfish (ultramarinfoto), 44 br, 64 br (USO), 23 cl, 40 cb (Utopia_88), 37 r (Uwe-Bergwitz), 9 tcl (VargaJones), 173 br (Velvetfish), 145 tc (VEX Collective), 54 cr (VII-photo), 39 cl (Vipersniper), 148 common carp (Visivasnc), 33 tl (VisualCommunications), 171 earthworm (VitalisG), 97 br (vkp-australia), 166 ctl (Vlada_Z), 130 blb (Vladimir_Krupenkin), 154 tl (vladoskan), 43 brown (Waitandshoot), 110 l (webguzs), 181 c (Westbury), 52 tc (Whirler), 10 jewel cichlid, 148 jewel cichlid (wiljoj), 21 cr (Willem Van Zyl), 193 cb (wischakorn), 14-15 (WLDavies), 52 cheetah (WLDavies), 41 tl, 44 cr, 50 tr, 50 cr, 73 tl, 124 br, 166 tr (wrangel), 36 tl (wwing), 66 br (xeni4ka), 181 bl (xtrekx), 148 flowerhorn cichlid (Yupaluk Phangpun), 10 medicinal leech, 10 leech, 175 ctcl (Yutthasart Yanakornsiri), back cover turtle (Zeamonkey), 10 praying mantis, 171 praying mantis (Ziva_K), 148 copperband butterfly fish (Zocha_K), 41 c (ZU_09); Library of Congress: 91 cl, 91 c; Matt Doggett Photography/www.mattdoggett.com: 82-83; NOAA: 174 crt (Emma Hickerson), 174 cl; Oceanwideimages.com/Rudie Kuiter: 163 t; Science Source: 59 icefish (British Antarctic Survey), 145 cr (Colin Keates/Dorling Kindersley/Natural History Museum, London), 101 br (Craig K. Lorenz), 140 tl (Daniel Heuclin/Biosphoto), 145 tl (Dante Fenolio), 163 cr (Dr. Paul A. Zahl), 173 bc (Jeff Rotman), 184 bl (L. Newman & A. Flowers), 174 tl (M. I. Walker), 172 cl (Marek Mis), 162 (NOAA Okeanos Explorer Program), 59 bl (NOAA/Nature Source), 195 br (Science Stock Photography), 143 cl (Stuart Wilson), 142 (Ted Kinsman); Shutterstock: 112 bl (2630ben), 56 tr (Aaron Amat), 28 l (Abeselom Zerit), 76-77 owl, 88 tl (Adam Fichna), 95 r (Adam Stockland), 166 cbl, 166 cbr (aDam Wildlife), 129 bc (alarico), 80 colony (Alberto Loyo), 141 bl, 141 br (Aleksey Stemmer), 72 cr (Alexander Cher), 183 tc (Allexxandar), 70 bl (Ana Gram), 42 (andamanec), 21 c (Andre Coetzer), back cover dolphin, 36 b (Andrea Izzotti), 192 tc (Andrea Mangoni), 181 bcr (Andreas Ruhz), 118 bl (Andrew Burgess), 111 tr (Andrew M. Allport), 38-39 top (Andrew Sutton), 122-123 (Andy Deitsch), 127 tl (Angelo Giampiccolo), 149 longhorn cowfish (asawinimages), 95 tr, 96 bl (Attila JANDI), 29 cb (bimserd), 98 br (bluedog studio), 111 br (Bonnie Taylor Barry), 33 bl (Bouke Atema), 112 r (Brian E Kushner), 88 bc (Bridgena Barnard), 154 bcl (BW Folsom), 192 bl (Cathy Keifer), 126 (ccarbill), 183 blb (Chelsea Cameron), 148 powder blue tang (chonlasub woravichan), 141 cr (Chris Ison), 37 b (Colette3), 193 brb (Cornel Constantin), 84 tl (cyo bo), 195 bcr (D. Kucharski K. Kucharska), 140 bl, 140 bc (Dan Olsen), 105 tr (Darryl Hernandez), 61 tl (David Osborn), 76 storm petrel (David Osborn), 151 bl (Dirk M. de Boer), 151 br (Dirk van der Heide), 179 cr (Divelvanov), 188 br (Dmitry Fch), 191 cb (EcoPrint), 29 c (Edwin Butter), 93 c (Ekaterina V. Borisova), 195 cr (Elizabeth Grieb), 81 cr (Enrique Aguirre), 57 bl, 60 bl, 67 boar, 73 cr, 76 vulture, 91 br, 161 ct, 170 grasshopper (Eric Isselee), 167 bcl (Evlakhov Valeriy), 102 tr (Fabio Maffei), 131 c main (Faiz Zaki), 112 tl (feathercollector), 110 tr (Fernando Calmon), back cover chameleon, 120 br (fivespots), 11 robin, 76 robin (FotoRequest), 77 turkey vulture (FotoRequest), 113 ctl (Four Oaks), 56 tl (francesco de marco), 153 tr (frantisekhojdysz), 92 br (Gelpi), 87 bl (Gerald Mark Griffin), 148 blacktip reef shark (Gino Santa Maria), 77 hummingbird, 95 l (Glass and Nature), 165 tr (Gorb Andrii), 28 ct (Grass-lifeisgood), 113 tr (Greentellect Studio), 158 bl (Greg Amptmann), 86 bl (Hendrasu), 165 tl (Hennadii H), 152 tr (HQuality), 56 c (Ikhanka's Africa wildlife), 90 (Imran Ashraf), 202 b (Isis Medri), 88 r (Iv Nikolny), 132-133 (janusz.kol), 54 l (jeep2499), 87 br (Jesus Giraldo Gutierrez), 58 (Jiri Hrebicek), 104 c, 105 tl (JNB Photography), 100 tl (Joao Luiz Lima), 76 scarlet roller (Johan Swanepoel), 165 ctr (John A. Anderson), 100 br (John C Evans), 153 tc (Joost van Uffelen), 11 yellow caecilian, 135 yellow caecilian, 144 tl, 145 bl (kamnuan), 51 br, 79 br (Karel Bartik), 39 cr (KAVSS), 118 cr (Keith Michael Taylor), 13 cr (Kev Gregory), 184 cbl (kikujungboy), 193 brt (kingfisher), 183 tl (Kondratuk Aleksei), 7 (kungveryluck), 188 bl (Kyle Lippenberger), 93 cl (kyslynskahaal), 185 br (KYTan), 172 bl, 184 t (Lebendkulturen.de), 137 bl (LifetimeStock), back cover butterfly (Lotus_studio), 183 blt (Lueke), 153 cl (LuisMiguelEstevez), 113 crb (Luke Shelley), 119 cb (Marc Pletcher), 165 tl (Marcutti), 20 b, 28 br (mariait). 114-115 (Maridav), 105 brr (Mario Wong Pastor), 10 yellow tang, 148 yellow tang (Martin Bech), 143 bl (Martin Janca), 11 crane, 76 macaw, 76 snowy owl, 77 crane, 102 cr (Martin Mecnarowski), 153 tl (Martin Prochazkacz), 105 clb (Melinda Fawver), 131 tlr (Mercury Green), 127 blt (meunierd), 97 tr (MH STOCK), 167 br (Michael Bogner), 167 tr (Michael Warwick), 137 bc, 189 bctl (Milan Zygmunt), 30 tr (miniak), 189 bctr (Mirek Kijewski), 120 bc (Mirek Srb), 150 br (MORETHANALEGEND), 135 green paddy frog (Mr. Suttipon Yakham), back cover fish (Mr.Soonthorn Thonglor), 189 cbl (Muhammad Naaim), 191 ct (MyAerialStock), 80 albatross pair (MZPHOTO.CZ), 183 br (NaniP), 103 br (Natalia Kuzmina), 160 b (Natursports), 34 bl, 136 cl (Neil Bromhall), 153 cr (nicolasvoisin44), back cover beetle (Nixx Photography), 98 bc, 103 tr, 105 bl (Ondrej Prosicky), 189 bl (ottmaasikas), 203 r (ozgur kerem bulur), 125 c (Patrick K. Campbell), 181 tl (Paul Reeves Photography), 92 c (Paul Tessier), 113 clb (Paul Wittet), 12-13 background (Pedarilhos), 102 c (Pete Evans), 87 red kite in flight (Peter Schwarz), 104 cr (Petr Simon), 82-6 (Photonell_DD2017), 167 bcb (pixs4u), 129 br (Protasov AN), 143 bc (Rachel Portwood), 33 cl (Reddogs), 143 cl, 140 cl (reptiles4all), 10 titan triggerfish, 13 tr, 148 titan triggerfish, 178 br (Rich Carey), 173 bl (RLS Photo), back cover frog, 56 bl, 76 woodpecker, 134 Surinam horned frog, 135 greater siren, 205 (Rosa Jay), 150 bl, 161 tl (Rostislav Stefanek), 119 crt (Rudy Umans), 174 br (Ruslan Mamedov), 125 cr (Ryan M. Bolton), 178 c (S.Rohrlach), 85 cl (SanderMeertinsPhotography), 8 (Sarawut Kundej), 149 pygmy seahorse (scubaluna), 192 bct (Sebastian Janicki), 10 wobbegong, 148 wobbegong (Sergey Popov V), 29 bl, 30 br (Sergey Uryadnikov), 11 wren, 77 wren (serkan mutan), 105 br (sh.el.photo), 153 br (shooarts), 191 br (Simon Shim), 143 bcl (skapuka), 88 bl (Smiler99), 179 tr (Squidshooting), 34 cr (Stacey Ann Alberts), 161 tr (Stefan von Ameln), 108 cl (Sunti), 127 tr (Suriya99), 144 c (Susan Schmitz), 4-5 (tahirsphotography), 1 (taviphoto), back cover crab (thanapol thanalad), 51 br (Tomas Hulik), 160 c (topseller), 145 cl (tristan tan), 113 bc (UlyssePixel), 161 bl (underworld), 105 brl (Vaclav Sebek), 174 tr (val lawless), 86 cr, 103 c (Vishnevskiy Vasily), 181 hr (Vladimir Wrangel), 2-3, 11 ibis, 76 ibis (Volodymyr Burdiak), 195 c (WA van den Noort), 95 cr (Wang LiQiang), 131 ctr (Webitect), back cover nautilus, 151 tl (wildestanimal), 87 tr, 110 br (Wildlife World); Wellcome Collection: 175 cctcr (Pierre Boaistuau), 69 cl, 130 tl (Science Museum, London), 12 t, 67 painting, 72 t, 127 blb, 204 r; Wikipedia: 192 tr (Courtesy Bernard Dupont), 184 ctl (Courtesy Dr. Dieter Ebert), 172 tr (Courtesy Dr. Oliver Voigt), 11 trichoplax adhaerens (PLOS), 171 tardigrade, 184 ctr (PLOS), 9 tl, 171 European lancelet, 175 br.

The publisher would like to give particular thanks to the following people for their help: Katie Devlin, Ali Scrivens, John Goldsmid, Jael Fogle, Marybeth Kavanagh, Guiseppe Diomede, and Aerin Csigay.

Sectioned
nautulus
shell

ACKNOWLEDGMENTS